The Jewel Ornament of Liberation

The Wish-fulfilling Gem of the Noble Teachings

Je Gampopa's

THE JEWEL ORNAMENT OF LIBERATION

The Wish-fulfilling Gem of the Noble Teachings

Commentary by
KHENCHEN THRANGU RINPOCHE

MOTILAL BANARSIDASS PUBLISHERS
PRIVATE LIMITED • DELHI

First Indian Edition: Delhi, 2014
First Edition: USA, 2003

ISBN : 978-81-208-3698-3

MOTILAL BANARSIDASS
41 U.A. Bungalow Road, Jawahar Nagar, Delhi 110 007
8 Mahalaxmi Chamber, 22 Bhulabhai Desai Road, Mumbai 400 026
203 Royapettah High Road, Mylapore, Chennai 600 004
236, 9th Main III Block, Jayanagar, Bangalore 560 011
Sanas Plaza, 1302 Baji Rao Road, Pune 411 002
8 Camac Street, Kolkata 700 017
Ashok Rajpath, Patna 800 004
Chowk, Varanasi 221 001

Note

We have italicized the technical words the first time that they appear to alert the reader that their definition can be found in the Glossary of Terms

Illustrations

Cover: This thangka of Gampopa, Milarepa, Atisha and the three yogis from Kham was painted by Kardruk Lama for Zhyisil Chokyi Ghatsal.
Frontispiece: This thangka of Marpa, Milarepa and Gampopa is courtesy of Venerable Lama Shedrup from the treasures of Venerable Lama Doday Rinpoche.
Line art drawings throughout the text were selected by Venerable Lama Karma Shedrup as was the cover design.

Printed in India

by RP Jain at NAB Printing Unit,
A-44, Naraina Industrial Area, Phase I, New Delhi–110028
and published by JP Jain for Motilal Banarsidass Publishers (P) Ltd,
41 U.A. Bungalow Road, Jawahar Nagar, Delhi-110007

May this supreme, peerless teaching,
The precious treasure of the Victorious Ones,
Spread and extend throughout the world
Like the sun shining in the sky.

Acknowledgements

We would like to thank the many persons who helped make this book possible. First and foremost, Khabje Khenchen Thrangu Rinpoche, for his great wisdom and compassion in giving these teachings. We would like to thank Ken and Katia Holmes for translating this work and the rest of the Samye Ling staff for making the tapes of these talks available, and Gabrielle Hollmann for the immense job of transcribing and editing. Also we wish to thank Keith Hale for going through the manuscript and Clark Johnson for his ongoing and invaluable assistance in helping make this work available.

In addition we wish to thank Snow Lion Publications and Khenpo Konchog Gyaltsen Rinpoche for allowing us to copy and use excerpts from their translation of *The Jewel Ornament of Liberation.* The text summary is indebted to and grateful to teachings given by Khenpo Tsultrim Gyamtso Rinpoche. This work has also been greatly assisted by the earlier translation of the text by Ken and Katia Holmes *Gems of Dharma, Jewels of Freedom.*

Table of Contents

TOPIC 2: THE WORKING BASIS
Chapter 2
The Precious Human Life

TOPIC 3: THE CONDITION
Chapter 3
The Spiritual Friend

Chapter 7

The Instructions on Meditation on Loving-kindness & Compassion

THE REMEDY TO ATTACHMENT TO THE PLEASURE OF PEACE

Developing an Attitude Towards Bodhichitta

THE REMEDY TO NOT KNOWING THE METHOD OF PRACTICE FOR ACCOMPLISHING BUDDHAHOOD

Chapter 8
Refuge & Precepts

Chapter 9
Cultivation of Bodhichitta

Chapter 10

Training In Aspiration-bodhichitta

Chapter 11
Training In Action-bodhichitta

Chapter 12
The Perfection of Generosity

Chapter 13
The Perfection of Moral Ethics

Chapter 14
The Perfection of Patience

Chapter 15
The Perfection of Diligence

Chapter 16
The Perfection of Meditative Concentration

Chapter 17
The Perfection of Wisdom-awareness

Chapter 18
The Aspects of the Five Paths

Chapter 19
The Levels of the Path

TOPIC 5: THE RESULT

The Result is the Body of Perfect Buddhahood

Chapter 20

Perfect Buddhahood

TOPIC 6: THE ACTIVITIES

The Activities are Benefiting Sentient Beings Without Conceptual Thought.

Chapter 21

Activities of the Buddha

THE KARMAPA

Our lineage is that of the incomparable protector of living beings, Sonam Rinchen, the founder of the teachings of the incomparable Dakpo Kagyu and a noble being predicted by the Buddha. From the ocean-like oral instructions, which give loving advice to disciples who are suitable vessels, there are *The Precious Garland of the Supreme Path*, the heart of the core teachings, and the *Ornament of Precious Liberation*. Here are presented talks on the second text, given during almost four months by the unequaled spiritual friend, Khenchen Thrangu Rinpoche, to Dharma students in Scotland so that they might attain full awakening. These talks are especially wonderful in presenting the teachings so that they are easily understood and their meaning realized. I rejoice in the publication of this volume by Venerable Lama Shedrup Chokyi Senge and others who have helped. It is said that if one practices the profound Dharma given here, now and in the future, one will become truly joyful.

Karmapa Ogyen Trinley Dorje

February 21, 2003

Foreword

by

Ven. Lama Karma Shedrup Cho Gyi Senge Kartung

One of the shining jewels of the Kagyu lineage is the Dharma Lord Gampopa. As the manifestation of a Buddha his qualities are vast and inexpressible. He taught and propagated the teachings according to the needs and capacities of beings in inconceivable ways, bringing countless beings to enlightenment and establishing the complete teachings of the Buddha in Tibet. One of his main disciples, Dusum Khyenpa, the First Karmapa, continues this golden rosary lineage today as the Seventeenth Gyalwa Karmapa, Orgyen Trinley Dorje.

Among many great accomplishments Gampopa is particularly well known for merging into one river the Kadampa lineage with the Mahamudra lineage he received from his root teacher Milarepa. *The Jewel Ornament of Liberation*, although a text on the graded path and of the sutra tradition, represents the blending of these two traditions.

For many Kagyupa students the first book they were instructed to read was probably the *Jewel Ornament*. However, this is not just a text for beginners, but one of the primary Kagyu texts and of immense relevance and benefit to all practitioners regardless of what stage they are at. In addition to providing a step-by-step outline of the path to Buddhahood, the teachings on the innate Buddha nature can provide students with the confidence to enter the path, while those already on the path can find in its twenty-one chapters much to inspire and keep them moving along the unmistaken path of liberation.

Often texts such as this with their vast scope are in parts necessarily quite pithy. Therefore, to gain clear understanding it is traditional to receive thorough commentaries on these aspects. However, due to their great length detailed explanations are quite extensive and thus can be difficult to receive. Yet, here we have the great blessing of a complete commentary by the great contemporary Kagyu master Khenchen Thrangu Rinpoche in which he gives a detailed explanation of this text particularly for the benefit of Western students.

Much is spoken of pith teachings such as Mahamudra that lead to Buddhahood in one lifetime. However, such realization and accomplishment is dependent on unifying Mahamudra with bodhichitta, which is the heart topic of this text. As a lineage deriving its fruit from practice these teachings must be experienced directly and not merely dependent on an intellectual understanding.

Gampopa said that in the future, for whoever encounters this text, it will be like meeting him in person. Therefore, may all who read this profound text develop the mind of awakening and accomplish Buddhahood for the benefit of all sentient beings.

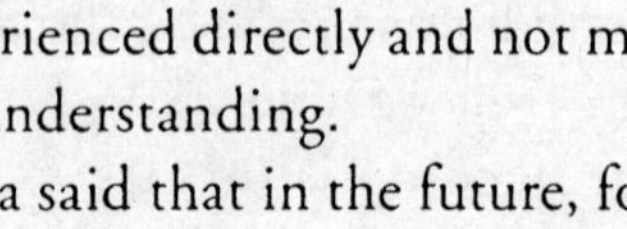

Lama Karma Shedrup
January 2003
Auckland, New Zealand

A Brief Biography of

Dharma Lord Gampopa *(1079 - 1153)*

Generally, the story of Gampopa's life and liberation is as deep as the ocean and as vast as space. Only a Buddha could relate it fully. The following is just a drop in his ocean-like life story.

Following a dream Milarepa had, the great translator Marpa Lotsawa prophesied:

A chick born to the vulture
Is a sign of the appearance of an unparalleled disciple.
The whole of space filling with birds
Is a sign of the flourishing of the Kagyupa lineage.

Thus was foretold the coming of Dharma Lord Gampopa, all his disciples and his lineage.

During the time of Buddha Shakyamuni, Gampopa had taken birth as the bodhisattva Candraprabhakumara. In response to his request the Buddha taught the teachings on the ultimate nature of mind in the *King of Samadhi Sutra*. The Buddha then asked his assembled disciples which of them would vow to take birth in the future to serve as guardian of this precious wisdom, the bodhisattva Candraprabhakumara vowed to do so. The Buddha thus foretold the birth of Gampopa as the Bhikshu Physician in Tibet in the *King of Samadhi* and the *White Lotus Sutra*.

To Gampopa's teacher Milarepa, Vajrayogini said he would gather many disciples like the sun, moon, and stars. Among them, Gampopa would be like the sun. Thus, Gampopa is the object of offerings and a refuge to all beings.

Gampopa was born in Nyal, in southern Tibet accompanied by many marvelous signs. Even as a child he was of gentle and compassionate nature, without a trace of anger, and quickly became expert at many arts and games. His father was a great scholar, practitioner and doctor. By the time Gampopa was sixteen he was an acknowledged scholar of the tantric teachings and a great physician. He became such a great healer and physician, benefiting so many beings, that it was as if the Medicine Buddha had reappeared.

He married when he was twenty-two and had a son and daughter. The law of impermanence somehow took both his son and daughter. Soon afterward, a serious disease tortured his wife, and she could not recover by any means. At the end, with attachment to him, she said, "There is no happiness in the householder life. After my death, Physician, practice dharma wholeheartedly." He replied, "Whether you die or live, I promise to practice the dharma."

This event gave rise to great renunciation in Gampopa, and at age twenty-five he took full ordination vows and received the name Sonam Rinchen (Precious Merit). He studied the Vinaya well and became the best of all the monks at keeping precepts. He had many teachers and received the bodhisattva vows and instructions, the practices of Chakrasamvara along with many other tantra teachings and empowerments. He eventually

Dharma Lord Gampopa

realized all phenomenal appearances to be as a rainbow and experienced the great non-conceptual thought where there is no differentiation between day and night. He could dwell in meditative absorption for many days and go without nourishment for five days at a time. He had little need for sleep but when he did various signs presaging liberation arose in his dreams.

Furthermore he studied monastic discipline as well as the perfection path and so forth. He studied the graded path of the Kadampa tradition in vast detail and became the light-beacon of that school.

During this time, there appeared to him in dreams and during ordinary experience a tall yogin of bluish color wearing a cotton cloth slung loosely over his shoulder and carrying a walking stick. This figure would put his hand on Gampopa's head, then blow on it and disappear. Following this Gampopa's meditation developed even better than before. When he mentioned this to another monk, the monk advised, "You are a bhikshu with very pure morality. The appearance of such a yogin is an obstacle created by Pekar (a Dharma protector). You had better meditate on Miyowa." Gampopa practiced as instructed but the visiting yogin came more often.

Meanwhile, Milarepa, the Lord of Yogins, who attained the state of Vajradhara in one lifetime, was giving teachings to his disciples at Red Rock Cave. The senior disciples said to him, "Now you are getting old. In case you depart to another Buddhafield and need a regent, please appoint whomever you trust and give them the complete teachings. Otherwise there will be no one who can lead disciples."

Milarepa said, "I am a yogin. There will be no regent for me. But there will be a disciple who can perform all my activities. Tonight I will see where he is. Come back early tomorrow morning."

The next morning, all his disciples gathered anxiously and Milarepa said, "Soon will come one named 'Physician' who became a monk in the Vinaya tradition. He will receive my complete teachings like filling one vase from another. This one can perform activities in all ten directions. Last night in my dream, he came with an empty crystal vase and I poured all the ambrosia from my silver vase into his."

He continued, "A son is born and the father is old. There will be a great being to advance the dharma like the sun rising and benefit countless beings."

At that time, Gampopa took a walk and came upon three beggars talking about the miraculous qualities of Milarepa. Upon hearing this, Gampopa spontaneously developed such great devotion for Milarepa that tears came to his eyes and for a long time he couldn't even walk.

Later he invited the three beggars to his room and made them a nice meal. He inquired as to the whereabouts of the great yogin they had been talking about. The beggars replied that they had not seen him but that he stays in the mountains of Drin and Nyenam. They said many people go there to see him but many do not find him. He manifests in many different forms, some see a crystal stupa, while others see him as Buddha Shakyamuni.

Gampopa set out to find Milarepa, traveling like a man possessed, sometimes fainting from exhaustion and weakness. Eventually he reached the feet of Milarepa, made offerings of a gold mandala, prostrated and requested Milarepa to accept him as his student. Milarepa then said, "I have no need for the gold you have offered me. Gold does not agree with this old man. If you want to practice the dharma properly, observe my conduct and my practice and do as I do." So Milarepa returned the gold to Gampopa for provisions for his meditation and then bestowed all the blessings of the Hearing Lineage, including the Six Yogas of Naropa. He then sent Gampopa to meditate in a desolate cave where many experiences quickly arose. On one occasion Gampopa received a vision of the Five Dhyani Buddhas, on another occasion he saw the entire universe turning like a wheel. Another time he saw myriad Chenrezig forms seated on moon discs, filling all of space. On another he saw the Hell Realm of Black Lines. Each time he recounted these experiences, Milarepa told him not to cling to what appeared, saying, "It's neither good nor bad. Go on with your meditation."

He continued to follow the practices Milarepa had taught and all his obstacles were dispelled and he progressed rapidly. Eventually Milarepa transmitted to Gampopa all the precious teachings, empowerments, and pith instructions he possessed and sent him to Central Tibet to develop his practice.

As Gampopa was departing Milarepa called him back, saying he had one last pith instruction. Gampopa was very happy and asked, "Should I make a mandala offering?" Milarepa said, "No, there is no need, but do not waste this instruction." Milarepa then raised the back of his clothes and showed his buttocks, which was full of calluses. "In all the pith instructions, there is none more profound than meditation practice. I meditated persistently until my buttocks became like this and I achieved great qualities. So you should also practice meditation with perseverance." This made a deep impression on Gampopa's mind. Then as the lama foretold, he went to Central Tibet.

After meditating in hermitages and wild mountains for many years, Gampopa realized the basic nature of the mind and the full meaning of his lama's words. Realizing the lama's great kindness he thereafter had no increase or decrease in realization, nor any acceptance, rejection, or doubt. Even his sleep became the experience of clear light.

Later Gampopa said, "It took me a long time to stabilize the mind, and I had to work hard, but for you it will be less difficult because you possess the instruction of the profound method path. This Kagyupa lineage has a blessing like no other. If they meditate diligently, many will reach the path. To dispel obstacles, experience the teachings and increase meditation practice, it is enough to follow the profound guru yoga, Mahamudra practice and Tummo."

As Milarepa prophesied local deities invited Gampopa to establish a monastery and teach at Dagpo, where vast numbers of disciples gathered to receive the Kagyu teachings he expounded. During this period, Gampopa frequently displayed supernormal powers, often manifesting as Buddha Shakyamuni and the bodhisattva Chenrezig. In addition many people reported seeing him simultaneously presiding over a feast in one place, performing a consecration in another, and teaching in yet another.

Once, Geshe Gyalwa Chungtsang Chen thought, "The precious lama does not permit the novice monks to do anything but meditation, so how can they acquire knowledge?" That night he dreamt that the entire mountain of Dagla Gampo was transformed into caves, in each of which was a precious stupa beautifully carved and radiating light. Some were fully finished and some were still being painted. Many people were doing prostrations before them, saying that they were the refuge of all beings in samsara, including the gods.

The next morning he went to Gampopa's room to tell him of the dream. Before he had time to recount it, Gampopa said, "Generally, those who rely on intellect hate me and have contempt for me, but my novice monks are exactly like the stupas in your dream. These beggar children are the refuge of all beings in the six realms of samsara, including the gods. I can encompass the needs of all, both high and low. Some say I cause the teachings to decline, but if you watch closely, those who benefit from the Buddha's teachings will be well known in the years to come."

Gampopa led all his disciples through the graded path, and to advanced practitioners he gave Mahamudra instructions and the Six Yogas of Naropa. Thus, he gave countless vast and profound teachings to many great disciples. This Dharma Lord, who was the embodiment of compassion, had excellent skill in leading disciples to the enlightenment that is free of all confusion and the causes of suffering.

Even though he himself had transcended the concepts of birth and death, he thought to demonstrate the impermanence of all phenomena, particularly the subject of birth and death, in order to warn those who are lazy. Close to death, Gampopa said, "When I enter the non-dual, all-pervading element, you shouldn't think, 'Now the lama does not exist.' My mind is inseparable from all the precious lamas and Buddhas of the three times, permeating all time and all places. Meditate, supplicate, and think of me, and my blessings will be there without yielding."

Further he said, "In the future, those who think, 'Alas, I haven't met him' should simply study and practice the texts that I composed: *The Precious Jewel Rosary of the Supreme Path*, *The Jewel Ornament of Liberation*, and others. There is no particle of difference; it is the same as meeting me. Those who are having a hard time understanding and practicing the dharma, think of me and supplicate with devotion. The blessings will arise naturally.

At the age of seventy-five, during the sixth lunar month, on the fifteenth day, wearing the three dharma robes and sitting in full lotus position with straight posture, his eyes gazing toward the sky, absorbed in the clear light free from all arising and cessation, the mode of abiding of all phenomena, Dharma Lord Gampopa passed away. At that time the sky was filled with countless rainbows, images of white stupas, and a rain of flowers, music and offerings to mark the passage of a fully enlightened being.

Thus, Gampopa, one of the greatest teachers, a manifestation of Buddha, purposefully appeared at the right time and in the right place to establish the complete form of Buddha's teachings. Even though Buddha's teachings had already been introduced to Tibet and flourished in some parts, he was the one who made the teachings come forth like the rising of the sun. Because of him, all the sutra and tantra teachings can be practiced by one person without contradiction.

Khenchen Thrangu Rinpoche

A Brief Biography of

Khenchen Thrangu Rinpoche (b. 1933)

The lineage of the Thrangu Rinpoche incarnations began in the fifteenth century when the Seventh Karmapa, Chodrak Gyatso visited the region of Thrangu in Tibet. At this time, His Holiness Karmapa established Thrangu Monastery and enthroned Sherap Gyaltsen as the First Thrangu Rinpoche, recognizing him as the re-established emanation of Shuwu Palgyi Senge, one of the twenty-five great siddha disciples of Guru Padmasambhava.

Khenchen Thrangu Rinpoche is the ninth incarnation of this lineage and was born in Kham, Tibet in 1933. When he was four, His Holiness the Sixteenth Gyalwa Karmapa and Palpung Situ Rinpoche recognized him as the incarnation of Thrangu Tulku by prophesying the names of his parents and the place of his birth.

Entering Thrangu monastery, from the ages of seven to sixteen he studied reading, writing, grammar, poetry, and astrology, memorised ritual texts, and completed two preliminary retreats. At sixteen under the direction of Khenpo Lodro Rabsel, he began the study of the three vehicles of Buddhism while staying in retreat.

At twenty-three he received full ordination from the Karmapa. When he was twenty-seven, Rinpoche left Tibet for India at the time of the Communist invasion. He was called to Rumtek, Sikkim, where the Karmapa had his seat in exile. At thirty-five, he took the geshe examination before 1500 monks at Buxador monastic refugee camp in Bengal, and was awarded the degree of Geshe Lharampa. On his return to Rumtek he was named Abbot of Rumtek Monastery and the Nalanda Institute for Higher Buddhist Studies at Rumtek. He has been the personal teacher of the four principal Karma Kagyu tulkus: Shamar Rinpoche, Situ Rinpoche, Jamgon Kongtrul Rinpoche and Gyaltsab Rinpoche.

Thrangu Rinpoche has travelled extensively throughout Europe, the Far East and the USA. He is the abbot of Gampo Abbey, Nova Scotia, and of Thrangu House, Oxford, in the UK. In 1984 he spent several months in Tibet where he ordained over 100 monks and nuns and visited several monasteries. He has also founded Thrangu Tashi Choling monastery in Boudhnath, a retreat centre and college at Namo Buddha east of the Kathmandu Valley, and has established a school in Boudhnath for the general education of lay children and young monks. He also built Tara Abbey in Kathmandu. In October of 1999 he consecrated the college at Sarnath which will accept students from the different traditions of Buddhism and will be open to Western students as ell.

Thrangu Rinpoche, a recognised master of Mahamudra meditation, has given teachings in over twenty-five countries and is especially known for taking complex teachings and making them accessible to Western students. More recently, because of his vast knowledge of the dharma, he was appointed by His Holiness the Dalai Lama to be the personal tutor for the recently escaped Seventeenth Karmapa.

Preface

Two thousand five hundred years ago the Buddha began delivering a remarkable set of teachings. He taught that instead of relying on a god or on materialistic pursuits, we could attain true and permanent happiness by simply examining and working with one's own mind. He then set out a series of teachings that fills over fifty volumes the size of the Christian Bible on exactly how to achieve this goal. Besides giving teachings on how to banish all the millions of obscurations we have accumulated he taught how to develop insight into reality shared only by enlightened individuals.

About 1,000 years ago one extraordinary individual, Gampopa achieved Buddhahood by working with his lama Milarepa and decided to set down this Buddhist path in a single book that he called *The Jewel Ornament of Liberation*. In this classic text of the Kagyu lineage of Tibetan Buddhism, he combined an explanation of the path of the accumulation of merit, which he learned from the famous pandita Atisha, with the development of realization using Mahamudra meditation, which he learned from his guru Milarepa. The result is one of the really classic texts in Buddhism.

The text itself is very terse and hard to follow as witnessed by Herbert Guenther's attempt to translate it into English in the 1950's. For this reason when Thrangu Rinpoche was asked to teach in the West, after having taught all the principal regents of the Kagyu lineage, he chose to give an almost four month teaching on this text to acquaint Westerners with the Path.

Clark Johnson, Ph. D.
Managing Editor
Namo Buddha Publications

Je Gampopa's

The Jewel Ornament of Liberation

The Wish-fulfilling Gem of the Noble Teachings

The Homage

I prostrate to the noble Manjushri in youthful form.
I pay homage to the Victorious Ones, their followers, the holy Dharma, and to the lamas who are their roots.
This noble teaching, which is like the wish-fulfilling jewel, will be written for the benefit of myself and others by depending on the kindness of Lord Mila.

Introduction to the Text

The basis of all of Gampopa's teachings was Milarepa's instructions on emptiness in the *Mahamudra*.[1] These instructions allow us to realize the true nature of the mind. These instructions provide us with the means to accomplish two things: the elimination of the thoughts that are disturbing our mind and the ability to develop the positive qualities that are naturally present in the mind. The faults that have to be eliminated are all the negative factors that are disturbing the mind such as ignorance, desire, anger, etc. Mahamudra practice can dissolve all these negative factors completely, naturally and automatically. And all the qualities that are intrinsic in the mind will develop naturally until they reach their fullness.

In *The Jewel Ornament of Liberation* Gampopa merged the stream of instructions of the *Kadampa* school with the Mahamudra instructions. The Kadampa teachings, from the philosophical viewpoint, are not the teachings with the highest view, but they put a great emphasis on proper conduct and practice. The Kadampa teachings came to Tibet after the destruction of the *dharma* by King Lang Dharma. First King Trisong Deutsen (718-785 AD) introduced Buddhism to Tibet. Then there was King Lang Dharma (863 906 AD) who persecuted the Buddhists and suppressed the dharma in Tibet creating great difficulties for the teaching of Buddhism. During this time a number of teachings were lost and practice degenerated. Although *Vajrayana* practice continued, it was slightly corrupted. Some people began understanding the dharma just in terms of the words, for example, they would say, "everything is empty" or "everything is the *Great Perfection* or Mahamudra." They did not understand this correctly because they just clung to the idea that everything is empty or Mahamudra and did not see that on the relative level[2] there is *karma* and *bodhichitta* and the various qualities that one must accumulate. To stop this misinterpretation of the dharma two great kings of Tibet, Yeshe Ur and Chang Chup Ur invited the great Indian *mahapandita* Atisha to come and give teachings in Tibet. They asked him to teach specifically on refuge, the resolution to reach *enlightenment*, and the *paramitas*. These are what became known as the Kadampa instructions. What Gampopa did in *The Jewel Ornament of Liberation* was to merge these Kadampa instructions with the Mahamudra instructions he received from Milarepa.

The Name of the Text

The short name of this book is "Tak Chin"[3] which means "the ornament of liberation." The longer name of this book is "Tak pa Rinpoche Chin" which means "the ornament of precious liberation." To explain this more: the goal of our dharma practice is *liberation*. It is the liberation from all our problems, all our troubles and all the suffering of conditioned existence in *samsara*. We meditate and practice to attain liberation, freedom from suffering. But suffering is just the result of a definite cause and the cause of this suffering is the negativity that disturbs our mind. So we have to eliminate this cause to be free of the effect, which is suffering.

This liberation is given the name "precious" or "rinpoche" in Tibetan, which is what is used for a precious stone or jewel. Here the word "rinpoche" is to be understood as a wish-fulfilling jewel. Liberation is a wish-fulfilling jewel because when we have achieved it we receive everything that we have ever wanted.

The way to achieve liberation is here with an ornament. This might seem strange at first because when we speak of ornaments we usually refer to something we put on to look beautiful. Here an ornament is understood in the sense of something that clarifies, like a mirror, which brings clarity. This teaching then is the ornament which will make us see what is this wish-fulfilling jewel of liberation, how we can achieve it, what are the benefits of achieving it and what a shame it is if we don't achieve it. That is why this book is called, "The ornament which makes it possible to see the wish-fulfilling jewel of great liberation."

The Homage

The homage says, "I prostrate to the noble Manjushri in youthful form." There is a tradition in Tibet to begin every Buddhist text with homage, to offer one's respect to the Buddhas and bodhisattvas. This phrase varies depending on which of the three portions of the teachings it belongs to, the *Vinaya*, the *Sutras*, or the *Abhidharma*. So we can tell which of these the text came from by simply reading the homage. When a text came from the Abhidharma, which is quite difficult and subtle to understand, the homage is to Manjushri because Manjushri represents *prajna*, the highest wisdom. So the *Jewel Ornament* belongs to the Abhidharma.

Manjushri's name in Tibetan is "Jam pal" with "jam" meaning "smooth." So Manjushri is completely smooth and therefore totally free of roughness or coarseness of negativity. The other part of Manjushri's name "pal" means "magnitude," "full-ness," or "splendor." It is the great splendor of possessing the best possible virtue. So "Jampal" means the splendid and smooth one. In the homage one prostrates to the "youthful" Manjushri who is referred to as a youth because he is not yet fully mature but also no longer a child. This means that Manjushri is referred to as a bodhisattva. In terms of spiritual development a bodhisattva is not a child, an ordinary person, but also is not yet a mature person, a fully developed Buddha.

Gampopa also includes homage to show his respect for the deities and to give students an example of humility. By paying homage to others Gampopa acknowledges the higher qualities of other beings, which shows he has enough purity of mind to acknowledge them without pride. This shows students how they should behave and how they should have faith and devotion towards those with higher qualities.

The Six Topics of the Book

The *Jewel Ornament* can be summarized into six main points that show us how to reach unsurpassable enlightenment. The first point is called "the primary cause." We want to accomplish enlightenment, *Buddhahood*, and the cause answers the question, "Can we accomplish this?" The answer is that everyone can reach enlightenment because everyone has this seed of enlightenment. So, whoever tries to accomplish enlightenment in the right way will eventually succeed. It is incorrect to believe that some people when they try will succeed and others won't.

The second point is that we need the "right basis" or right foundation to work from. This basis means the right kind of existence. For example, an animal has the seed of enlightenment, but an animal doesn't have the opportunity to accomplish enlightenment. An animal will have to wait until it is freed from the animal realm[4] before it can work towards enlightenment. One therefore needs the right kind of foundation to work towards enlightenment.

The third point is known as the contributory cause or "the condition." We may have the seed of enlightenment and the right basis of a human birth, but we still need the right kind of condition of a person who can encourage and motivate us towards working to accomplishing enlightenment. This condition is a spiritual friend or *lama* who can guide us.

We may wonder if having the right cause, the right basis and a spiritual friend is enough to accomplish enlightenment. No, this isn't enough. The spiritual friend can lead us, but cannot take all our negativity and simply wash it away. We need the "right means" or method to work towards enlightenment. The fourth point then is the right means, which are the instructions of the spiritual friend that are the tools we need to work with.

Once we have the right means, what can we accomplish? This is explained in the fifth point, which is the "right fruition" or result, which is Buddhahood.

What we can achieve on accomplishing Buddhahood is explained in the sixth point, which is the "right activity," spontaneous activity to benefit all beings. When we accomplish Buddhahood we achieve realization, but we also automatically engage in trying to help all other beings.

So that is a summary of the subject matter of this book.

Then each of these six basic points is further developed with an explanation of their meaning.

For the first point "cause" means the essence of Buddhahood or the essence of the sugatas. "Sugata" is a Sanskrit word which means "the one who has gone to happiness or bliss" or "dewa shepa" in Tibetan. The person described is the Buddha and this term describes what happens at Buddhahood: one leaves suffering and goes to happiness. This term (sugatagharba) is not only the name of the Buddha, but it also describes what happens at that point. The essence of the sugata, of the Buddha, is the pure wisdom of the Buddha that all beings possess and this is the cause of enlightenment, the seed of Buddhahood that is present in each and every being.

The second point is the "basis" and this is explained in terms of the precious human body or the jewel-like human body. The reason a human body is compared to a jewel is not because it resembles a jewel physically, but rather because it can function as a wish-fulfilling jewel insofar as it allows us to achieve our ultimate goal, so it is very beneficial.

The third point is the "condition" and this is explained in terms of a spiritual friend. These are those who can show us the path and lead us towards enlightenment.

The fourth point is the "method" and this is described in terms of the instructions of the spiritual friend.

The fifth point is the "fruition" and this is described as being the *kayas* of the Buddha.

The sixth point is the "activity" and this is explained in terms of the non-conceptual activity for the sake of all other beings. This means that when enlightenment is accomplished, we don't have to make any effort to benefit other beings because this activity will arise spontaneously, without any need for thought and without any need for effort.

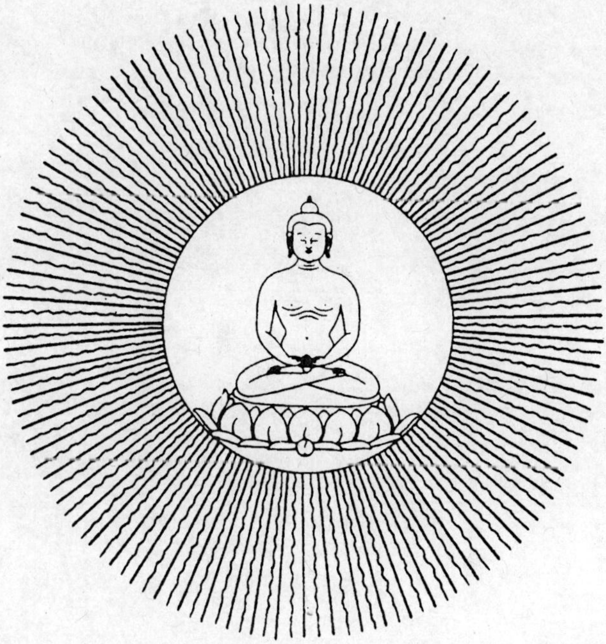

TOPIC 1: THE PRIMARY CAUSE

The Primary Cause is the Essence of the Buddha

Chapter 1
Buddha Nature

The first topic in *The Jewel Ornament of Liberation* is Buddha nature or Buddha-essence[5] that deals with the Buddha potential within all beings. The first point says, "The cause is the essence of the Buddhas." When we practice the dharma we need great effort and diligence to carry on with our practice. If we practice diligently we need not worry that we won't accomplish Buddhahood. For example, if we churn milk we will get butter. But if we take water, no matter how long we churn it we will never get any butter. In the same way, if we press sesame seeds, we will get sesame oil. But no matter how hard we press sand, we will never get any oil. This is all because we need to have the cause (or causal condition) before a result will appear. The reason we get butter from milk is that the potential for butter is present within the milk. Similarly, the sesame oil is potentially present in the sesame seed, so when we press it, we obtain sesame oil. However, water doesn't contain any potential for butter and similarly sand doesn't have the potential for sesame oil. So pressing water or sand will not produce butter or sesame oil. In the same way, to reach enlightenment, we make great efforts meditating. Once we do this we shouldn't have any doubts because everyone possesses the essence of enlightenment within their mind. With this essence we have the seed for enlightenment and so when we work on it in the right way we will accomplish enlightenment.

Evidence in the Scriptures

It was the Buddha himself who stated in both the sutras and *tantras* that everyone has the seed of enlightenment. In the second turning of the wheel of dharma[6] the Buddha explained that all phenomena are empty and this emptiness pervades everyone and everything. Since everything is empty, all thoughts, all negativity, can be relinquished because they have no inherent nature of their own, and therefore we can accomplish the final result, the final realization.

In the third turning of the wheel of dharma it was demonstrated that the nature of all things is not just emptiness, like voidness. This emptiness has the quality of clarity (Tib. *salwa*), which is the quality of very vivid intelligence that is part of the very nature of mind. This clarity and intelligence is present innately in all beings. What we have to do through Buddhist practice is to allow this original clarity to increase. Then all the other positive qualities of the mind will develop and manifest. This essence of Buddhahood, which is the clarity of the mind, is something we can develop with effort and the right practice in the same way that we can develop the qualities of knowledge with the process of education. So, we can accomplish Buddhahood because the seed is within us. In the Vajrayana teachings the true nature of the mind is spoken of as the Mahamudra. This is what we have to realize and recognize to become enlightened. The Vajrayana's position was described from the Buddha's teachings during the third turning of the wheel of dharma.

The sutras and the tantras say that all beings have this seed of enlightenment. But how do we know this essence of Buddhahood is in all beings? The *Jewel Ornament* provides us with two answers: evidence in scriptures and through logical reasoning. The first answer comes from the scriptures in statements from the Buddha and the bodhisattvas. There are four different texts mentioned in the *Jewel Ornament* discussing the presence of Buddha-essence in all beings. The first three sutras quoted are: the *King of Meditation Sutra* (Tib. *Tingne Dzingyi Gyalpo Do*),[7] the *Sutra of the Great Paranirvana* (Tib. *Do Nyanyenley Depa Chenpo*), and the *Small Paranirvana Sutra* (Tib. *Nyanyen De Chunggi Do*). These last two sutras were given by the Buddha just before he passed away and contain very profound instructions. These sutras clearly state that the Buddha-essence is in all beings. The fourth text, the *Ornament of Mahayana Sutra* (Tib. *Dode Gyen*), is one of the five works of the bodhisattva Maitreya. This is a *shastra*, which is a work written by someone commenting on the work of the Buddha, and it also states that the Buddha-essence is present in all beings.

Now there are individuals who have a great deal of faith in the Buddha and believe what the Buddha said and trust his word. These people simply accept that Buddha nature or Buddha-essence is in all beings because the Buddha said so. However, not everyone has immediate faith and trust in the scriptures. For these people it is not sufficient that something is stated in the scriptures; they need good reasons. In fact, the scriptures say that we shouldn't accept statements on faith, so they include valid reasons and logical proofs.

Three Reasons Why Beings Possess Buddha Nature

There are three reasons given why everyone possesses Buddha-essence. The first is that the body of the Buddha, the *dharmakaya*, pervades all beings, which means that in the future beings are capable of giving rise to Buddhahood. In other words, Buddhahood can manifest in all beings because they are completely pervaded by the dharmakaya already.

The second reason is that within the ultimate nature of every thing, the *dharmata*, there is no separation between a good and a bad nature. There isn't the bad nature of ordinary beings and the good nature of enlightened beings in the ultimate nature of phenomena. It is completely undifferentiated. Because the bodhisattvas of the past accomplished the state of realization, we also can accomplish the same if we practice properly.

The third reason that all beings possess the Buddha potential in them is that it is evident in different degrees [categorized into five types of potential]; but having the potential in them they can all accomplish Buddhahood.

These are the three reasons that demonstrate the presence of Buddha-essence in all beings and why Buddhism believes the seed of enlightenment is present in everyone. Buddhism does not believe that someone can gain enlightenment from the outside. For example, enlightenment cannot be granted to you as a favor from a god or anyone else. Enlightenment must come from within because it is already there within your mind. So, by developing that potential in the right way, we will make it manifest. Enlightenment must come from us and will manifest only through our own efforts. No one can make us accomplish enlightenment and no one can prevent us from accomplishing enlightenment. If we have the right desire to accomplish enlightenment and apply the right effort, then it is certain that we will accomplish enlightenment. We also have the choice not to reach enlightenment, so the choice is completely ours.

The Shakyamuni Buddha was an exceptional person with all the highest qualities. Physically he had the thirty-two wondrous marks and the most outstanding qualities of speech which enabled him to teach the three turnings of the wheel of dharma, and mentally he also had the most perfect qualities. All these outstanding qualities of the Buddha we also can have. We don't need to think, "I could never reach that point," because we have the essence of all of the Buddha's qualities within us.

Sometimes when we examine the examples of great practitioners such as Marpa or Milarepa, we may become discouraged and think, "Well it's all very well for them. They had the energy, the diligence and the courage to practice the way they did, but that's not for me." We might think, "They had 100% of the causal conditions for Buddhahood, while I have only 50% of these conditions." But we shouldn't feel discouraged like that because the causal conditions they had are exactly the same for us and everyone else. This seed is there without any difference between beings.

To summarize, there are three reasons why everyone possesses the enlightened essence. The first reason is that the dharmakaya pervades everyone and therefore Buddha-essence is in everyone. The second is that the ultimate nature of everyone is the same without any distinction of good or bad. Third, even though the potential is the same in everyone, at different points in time in a person's spiritual development there will be differences. For example, a being can be born in the human realm while another being a dog in the animal realm. Both have the Buddha potential within them, so in the ultimate sense there is no difference whatsoever in the potential. But in the relative sense, in terms of the situation and different circumstances and the amount of effort people put into practice – the human being will have more opportunity to practice than animals – this potential will manifest in different ways.

So, here it is not said that the potential is the same in all respects. It is the same as far as the ultimate nature goes, but superficially, in terms of the various situations of beings, there are of course differences.

Five Categories of Potential

All beings can be categorized into five different groups based on this potential: The first group has signs of the "cut-off" potential. The second group has an "uncertain" potential. The third group is the *shravakas* whose potential will reveal a certain kind of quality. The fourth group is the *pratyekabuddhas* whose potential will have specific qualities. The fifth group is those with the *Mahayana* potential. These categories are not however static, because one can change from one category to another. If someone has, for example, the cut-off potential, he or she can change this and develop one of the states with more potential. Conversely, someone with all the signs of great potential such as a pratyekabuddha could do certain actions and they would end up with a cut-off potential.

I. The Cut off Potential. The first way in which one can possess the Buddha potential is called "the cut off potential." This prevents one from practicing the dharma and therefore prevents one from accomplishing enlightenment. Six specific signs that are very important to know signal this potential. If we find these six signs in ourselves we should eliminate them so that we won't have this limited potential.

The first sign is not having any wariness or dissatisfaction with the suffering of conditioned existence. For instance, when these individuals face suffering they don't really feel the urge to do something about it; they just endure what happens. This, of course, is of no benefit because they just go on like this. The sound attitude in the face of such difficulties and sufferings is to be motivated to make an effort to eliminate suffering, to get out of this difficult situation. So, if one does not have dissatisfaction with suffering one will passively remain in that state and not seek liberation. That is why one has to eliminate this mistake.

The second characteristic of this potential is that people do not have any "confidence," to be understood here as aspiration or motivation. When they begin to know that there is a state of happiness they do not feel motivated to achieve it. They may just think it is nice and then forget about it. So it is important to try to eliminate the defect of not having any aspiration to achieve a better state and try to develop the aspiration that does.

The third and fourth signs of the cut-off potential go together because they describe a similar feeling which is experienced in two different ways: one with regard to oneself, the other with regard to others. We generally try to act in the best positive way in regard to others and we strive so our actions, thoughts, and words are beneficial and not harmful to others. But sometimes we don't succeed and our actions, words and thoughts become quite negative. When this happens we need two qualities that are lacking in those with the cut-off potential. The third quality is thinking, "What I'm doing now is not right. I can't act like this." This is a sense of self-respect which makes you feel within yourself that something is not right, that you can't act in such a way and need to do things better. This sense of self-respect is directed towards yourself. The other facet, the fourth quality, is directed towards others. It is realizing that if you act in such a negative way others will realize this and you don't want them thinking badly about you; so this quality is a sense of shame. So the third sign of self-respect is in relation to oneself and the fourth sign of shame is in respect to others.

The fifth sign of the cut-off potential is the absence of compassion. When we speak of compassion we usually refer to someone who is suffering. But more broadly compassion is towards a person who has the cause of suffering within them. This means that we can feel compassion towards a person who is not suffering at the time because the cause of suffering is there so suffering will arise sooner or later. This compassion arises from knowing from our own experience how powerful it is to undergo this suffering and then to realize it is just as unbearable for others as it is for us. So we develop the wish to get out of suffering. Some people do not have this compassion even though they see people suffering because they don't realize that other people's suffering is the same as their own suffering. So these people don't feel the need to help others to get out of suffering. Without compassion they will not be able to practice altruism.

The sixth sign is the absence of repentance or regret. Normally, we try to act as positively as we can, but we do make mistakes that cause suffering for both others and us. It is important to feel regret about the harmful things we have done. Regret in itself is not positive because what has been done has been done. But it is important for the future because if we regret what we have done we will make sure it won't happen again. If we don't have a sense of regret then we will feel that it is all right to do the same harmful thing again. If there is an absence of regret it is a sign one's potential is of the cut-off type.

When one's potential is cut-off it means one still has the potential or power of accomplishing Buddhahood, but temporarily this power is repressed because of the six negative characteristics. So one's potential can't reach fruition; therefore it is like it has been cut-off.

II. The Uncertain Potential. The second type of potential is called the "uncertain potential" and it is called this because we don't know if this potential will turn out good or bad; things can go either way depending on the circumstances. If we meet the right kind of people and learn the right kind of things it could go well. But if we meet the wrong kind of people and learn the wrong kind of things then things can turn out very bad. So this potential depends on the people one associates with, what one reads, what education one receives and trains in. Here, speaking in terms of the Mahayana path, it is important to avoid going to the lower motivation of the *Hinayana* path. We must strive to develop and follow the greater motivation of the Mahayana.

Different Motivations

The next three types of potentials refer to the shravakas, pratyekabuddhas and those of the Mahayana. The difference between these three types is the scope of their motivation, how open or great it is, and the way they think; what their aim in practice is. The highest or vastest motivation is the great or Mahayana motivation that treats all beings without any bias. A person with this motivation wants to help not just the people they love or like, but wants to help all beings including non-human beings because they realize that they are all the same in trying to find happiness. This is the most open and pure motivation.

The opposite of this is the "impure motivation" in which one is only searching for one's own happiness and satisfaction without any consideration for the happiness for others. In fact, only being intent upon one's own happiness and satisfaction often implies creating suffering for others in order to fulfill one's own goals. The motivation of shravakas and pratyekabuddhas is not this impure motivation, but it is a fairly narrow motivation that leads one to search only for the happiness and liberation of oneself; one's own benefit is the main thing. So this motivation is narrower than the Mahayana motivation that focuses on all beings.[8]

III. The Shravaka Potential. There are three characteristics that describe this third potential of shravakas. The first is that they have a great fear of samsara. The second is they have aspiration for *nirvana*. The third is they have very little compassion. In general it is good to be afraid of samsara because this leads to the motivation of wanting to gain freedom from samsara. This brings about the second characteristic, of yearning for nirvana, which is the permanent liberation from samsara. However, the fear of samsara and the aspiration for nirvana can only lead up to a point but not to the ultimate liberation[9] because of a lack of courage and determination. In the Mahayana it is essential to have courage and not to feel depressed or discouraged at the prospect of the amount of work involved in liberating all other beings from samsara. This is what the shravakas don't have, the courage to overcome this difficulty. The shravaka motivation is one of trying to escape samsara out of fear; one runs away from samsara and rushes towards nirvana. So this fear and wish are faults and come from a lack of compassion. A Mahayana practitioner has no fear. Shravakas are aware of their own suffering, but not that of others. So individuals having this lesser motivation will follow the path of the shravaka and get the results of this path. So, if one is on the Mahayana path and finds these three characteristics in oneself, one should try to abandon them.

IV. The Pratyekabuddha Potential. The fourth type of potential are the pratyekabuddhas who have a far greater accumulation of virtue than the shravakas, but are below those of the bodhisattvas and Buddhas because they don't have sufficient courage and openness to act for the sake of other beings. The pratyekabuddhas have practiced and created a great accumulation of virtue during many lifetimes, but their motivation has been only to achieve nirvana and liberation for themselves. While they were doing this practice they had a teacher helping them. But when they are nearly ready to realize their last birth, the one they are going to realize nirvana in, they are able to find the right path by themselves without any more support from a teacher. Usually they take rebirth where there is no Buddha and where no teachings of the Buddha survive or are available. They will then achieve realization on their own, through the power of what they have previously accumulated. They will feel no attraction to worldly activities and don't feel any need to help others. They go and live in very remote and solitary places feeling they must realize the truth about everything. They go, for example, to cemeteries to understand the end result of life in samsara. They meditate on the corpses and reflect that all of this only causes suffering to oneself and one's family and friends. They think that the nature of phenomena is suffering and wonder how they can eliminate the suffering. They will work through "the twelve links of *interdependent origination*"[10] learning that to stop old age and death, one must stop birth. They also learn that to stop birth, one must stop desire, and so on, working through all this and finally they gain realization.

The pratyekabuddhas have six characteristics, with the first three being identical to the shravakas: they fear samsara, they believe in nirvana, and have little compassion. In addition to these three they have a fourth characteristic of a secret teacher. This means there is no teacher obviously there for them. Fifth, they have very strong pride because they are convinced that they can achieve realization themselves. The sixth is that they have a strong fondness for solitude; they like to stay in solitude because they have a very strong disgust for samsaric life.

The Purpose of these Instructions

The purpose for giving teachings on the different kinds of Buddha potential is that if we want to follow the Mahayana path we can avoid the signs of the other groups. We can therefore eliminate the characteristics of the cut-off, the uncertain, the shravaka and the pratyekabuddhas when they come up. We must remember that these characteristics are not permanent and can be changed from one to another. It is like cooking good food; we must experiment with various ingredients to see what makes it taste good. If we cook something and it tastes good, then we will want to find out why it tastes so good. If it tastes bad, we might think that it has too much salt or was cooked too long, etc., and the next time we will use less salt and cook it with the right amount. In the same way, we are taught these various signs and characteristics so that we can eliminate them and therefore be able to follow the real Mahayana path.

V. The Mahayana Potential. The fifth type is the Mahayana potential, which is taught so that we know how to acquire the right kind of potential and how to develop it correctly. In the *Jewel Ornament* the Mahayana is described in six points: classification, definition, synonyms, the reason why it is superior to other potentials, the characteristics, and the signs.

A. Classification. The first point describes the two aspects of the Mahayana potential. The first aspect: this potential is naturally present in all beings without any distinction. If this potential were not present there would be no way of accomplishing the final fruition of Buddhahood. This means that everyone has the power and ability to accomplish Buddhahood, provided that all that is obscuring the potential is removed and all that has to be realized is realized.

The second aspect is the potential that is in the process of being developed. This refers to the people who are actually working on developing this potential, who are on the path.

B. Definition. The second point concerns the nature of the Mahayana potential. This has two aspects. First, the naturally present potential that has the ability to bring forth all the qualities of the Buddha. This ability has always been there since beginningless time, which means it wasn't made by anybody and it didn't come from anywhere; it is part of the nature of mind. That's the first aspect of the Mahayana potential.

The second aspect, the nature of the potential being developed, is slightly different because it requires effort unlike the inherent potential which is spontaneously present. This potential can also produce all the qualities of Buddhahood but it is due to one's former practice of virtue; the proper practice of virtue will bring all the qualities of Buddhahood.

We can now understand the difference: in the first aspect it is present because it is the nature of the mind, in the second aspect we need to work on the potential that is the nature of the mind. To clarify this I will give an example: the innate potential can be compared to a seed placed in a leather bag. The potential being developed is compared to a seed placed in the ground because in the ground it can begin to develop, while in a bag it cannot.

C. Synonyms. The third point of Mahayana potential gives synonyms to describe it. It can be called "potential" in the sense that it is capable of giving rise to all the Buddha qualities, or it can be called "a seed" in the sense that it can later bring forth a fruit, namely Buddhahood. Another word is "nature" in the sense that the gradual development of this nature will finally manifest as the nature of the Buddha, or it can be called "essence" or "a pure nature" in the sense that the nature of the Buddha is completely unfabricated and natural.

D. The Reason Why it is Superior. The fourth point of the Mahayana potential tells us that this is the very best; it is superior to all the other potentials. It is clearly superior to the cut-off and uncertain potentials, which won't even allow us to enter the path. Also it is better than the shravaka and the pratyekabuddhas, who do follow a proper path, but not the best path. This can be shown in different ways. In terms of the degree of purification that they achieve, the shravakas and the pratyekabuddhas can only eliminate their *emotional obscurations* but not their *cognitive obscurations.*[11] This is also true in terms of what they will realize: the Mahayana path is superior in terms of realization because the shravakas and the pratyekabuddhas can only realize the non-existence of a personal self, but they won't realize that all phenomena are devoid of any nature of their own.[12] In the Mahayana what is realized is complete enlightenment.

E. Characteristics. The fifth point describes the different forms of the Mahayana potential, which can be two: awakened and unawakened. When the Mahayana potential is awakened it means that the person who has awakened that potential will show all the signs that they have entered the right path and are correctly following this path. The unawakened potential means that, although one possesses the potential that is always innately present, there will be no signs to show clearly that it is there.

How does one awaken the Mahayana potential that is innately there? By eliminating unfavorable conditions that prevent it from awakening and by cultivating favorable conditions that will help awaken it.

The Four Unfavorable Conditions

There are four unfavorable conditions that prevent awakening. The first one is to be born in realms that prevent one from practicing the dharma. The second unfavorable condition is to have no natural inclination to practice virtue, which would have come from a predisposition inherited from a previous life. In our mind we have subconscious conditions that are made from our former practice of virtue. If we don't have that, then we won't have any inclination to practice virtue. The third unfavorable condition is to follow a wrong path, to act in a very negative way. The fourth unfavorable condition is to have a lot of obscurations, namely to have ignorance, anger, jealousy and so on.

If one has these four unfavorable conditions the Mahayana potential will not awaken. That is why it is necessary to eliminate the unfavorable conditions and the way to do this is to use the two favorable conditions.

The Two Favorable Conditions

The first favorable condition is an external condition and the second is an internal condition. The first favorable condition is to seek the help of a teacher, a lama or *guru*. From receiving instructions we can practice properly. The second favorable condition is an inner condition, which is to develop the correct attitude; we must have the right attitude to really aspire to the dharma, to have trust in it and want to practice the dharma properly. With these two favorable conditions we can overcome the four unfavorable conditions and the Mahayana potential, which is dormant within, can awaken.

F. Signs. The sixth point of the Mahayana potential is the signs of the awakened Mahayana potential. These signs are indications of the presence of the awakened potential. It is the same as seeing smoke and inferring the presence of fire or seeing waterfowl and inferring the presence of water. The signs are the absence of hypocrisy and deceit and the presence of great loving-kindness and compassion. If these two signs are absent we can conclude that the potential is not awakened.

Summary

To summarize, all beings possess the essence of the Buddha and have the potential to accomplish Buddhahood. This is why if they practice they can accomplish Buddhahood. There are three reasons why everyone has this Buddha-essence in their mind. The first reason is that the dharmakaya pervades everything. Therefore emptiness permeates absolutely everyone and everything, so everyone has this empty essence, the essence of Buddhahood. Because emptiness permeates everything we can eliminate all illusory appearances and manifest Buddhahood.

The second reason is that the essence, or the essential nature of everything, is completely undifferentiated. For example, we should not think the Buddha would have a good nature and ordinary beings have a less positive nature so we cannot accomplish Buddhahood. There is, in fact, not the slightest difference between the nature of a Buddha and our own nature. Therefore, since the Buddha accomplished enlightenment we also can accomplish enlightenment.

The third reason for the presence of Buddha-essence within all beings is that they all possess the potential to accomplish enlightenment. I have explained how his potential can be present in five different ways (cut-off, uncertain, shravaka, pratyekabuddha and Mahayana) but this is not really the main point, rather just the details. The main point is the way the potential is present within bodhisattvas, the Mahayana potential. The actual potential is the same and all we must do is change our motivation, change our attitude. Then we can accomplish the result, which will necessarily come about through the power of the potential within us. The most important aspect is the potential innately present within all beings; this is what makes it possible for everyone to become a Buddha.

To give an example to illustrate the point of the difference it makes to have the potential within or not: If I see Prince Charles and begin to think that he has a very nice life, that he is very happy and very rich, then I start wishing to become like him. But this is a useless wish because it could not happen. I don't have what it takes to become like Prince Charles. Similarly, if we didn't have what it takes to become a Buddha it would be a useless wish. But, since we have the potential, the possibility within us, it is possible to achieve the result.

So, the main point is the Mahayana potential. The five conditions, except the Mahayana potential, represent unfavorable conditions that prevent one from practicing properly. They are all temporary handicaps. The Mahayana potential represents the close and direct cause for accomplishing Buddhahood, and the shravakas and pratyekabuddhas represent a more remote cause for accomplishing Buddhahood.

However, it is important to bear in mind that even the cut-off potential doesn't imply that for those there is no liberation, that such persons are cut off from the chance of Buddhahood forever. It only means that the prospect of accomplishing Buddhahood is very remote. In the end, however, they too will accomplish Buddhahood because the basis, the Buddha potential, is present within them.

This is what we have been given to understand in the teachings of the Buddha potential, which is what makes it possible for everyone to accomplish Buddhahood.

That concludes the explanation of the first chapter,
on the primary cause, from
The Jewel Ornament of Liberation.

TOPIC 2: THE WORKING BASIS

As a Working Basis, the Precious Human Life is Excellent.

Chapter 2
The Precious Human Life

The second topic in the *Jewel Ornament* is the basis from which we can work towards enlightenment. This, along with the first topic, is taught to remedy one of the greatest obstacles on the path, namely laziness. There are many different types of laziness, but one type takes the form of discouragement, of putting oneself down without any good reason. It is the feeling that others can achieve spiritual realization, but I cannot. Thinking there is no need for me to try because I will get nowhere. This discouragement prevents us from practicing, but it is unfounded because we all have this Buddha-essence and we have a human birth endowed with all the necessary qualities, which are the best circumstances for accomplishing Buddhahood. So there is no real reason to feel discouraged because we have all the best conditions for accomplishing enlightenment.

So here we learn what it means to have the right basis or foundation to accomplish enlightenment: this foundation is the precious human body.

After reading the first chapter on Buddha potential we may wonder why we haven't accomplished enlightenment many lifetimes ago. What has gone wrong that we aren't all Buddhas already if we have this potential? The answer is that up until now we probably haven't found ourselves in a human life with all the right conditions to achieve realization. But presently we have all the right conditions so we don't have this problem now. Therefore, we should make use of this special opportunity in the best possible way, by practicing diligently in order to realize the ultimate fruit of practice. This is the reason why the teaching on the working basis is given.

Gampopa introduces this topic with a summary in five points. There are two points that refer to the physical aspect of the precious human birth and three points that refer to the mental aspects.

Two Points of the Physical Aspect

The two physical qualities are explained in terms of the eight freedoms and the ten endowments. The eight freedoms are to be free from conditions that make it impossible to practice on the path, such as lower states of existence. The endowments are the particularly good conditions for practice that come from both others and us.

The word "freedom" or opportunities is to be taken as the absence of unfavorable conditions. In general, when we want to do anything we need two things: to be free of unfavorable conditions and to have the favorable conditions to do it. An example might be that if we have to do a job, but we find that we do not have the opportunity or possibility to do it, we do not have the time or chance. So "freedom" is like an opportunity. Opportunity in this context means the absence of anything that would prevent us from practicing the dharma so that we have the opportunity to practice. The ten assets are the favorable conditions to practice the dharma. When we want to practice the dharma we feel we need all the right conditions and if we look at our life right now we will find all the conditions are there. Some come from us and some come from others.

I. The Eight Freedoms. The eight states that are associated with the eight freedoms include three states which have so much suffering that one cannot practice dharma at all. These are the states of the hell realms, the hungry ghost (or *craving spirits*) and the animal realm. Then there is the realm where there is abundant happiness, but this happiness creates so much attachment that one doesn't want to practice: this is the realm of the long life gods[13].

So this realm is also unfavorable for practicing the dharma. Those are four unfavorable non-human states.

Then there are four states that involve those born in the human realm. The fifth are people who are "barbarians," who live among savages in remote places and do not have any experience with dharma; they have no chance to even hear about spiritual practice. The sixth are persons with wrong views who have no interest to find out about truth or in finding the right way. The seventh is living in a world where no Buddha had appeared or taught the dharma teachings.[14] The eighth may have none of the above seven conditions but may be mentally handicapped such as being dumb, insane or whatever, then they won't be able to practice.[15] Since we are free from these eight conditions we therefore have the eight freedoms to practice the dharma.[16]

II. The Ten Endowments. In addition to the eight freedoms one needs the ten endowments or the presence of all the right conditions. Five of the ten endowments that allow for dharma practice come from us and five come from others.

A. Five Endowments from Oneself. Of the five favorable conditions that come from us, the first is having a human birth. If for example you are born in a world where a Buddha has taught but are born an animal then you are unable to practice. You need the human body to be able to hear the teachings, to contemplate them, and to meditate on them.

The second endowment is being born in a place where the proper teachings are being practiced. We could be born in a place without dharma such as a very remote country. For example, in primitive areas the people may have religious practices, but these may be related to negative things such as killing as in animal sacrifices. So, a person born in those situations would find themselves in complete contradiction to the dharma.

The third endowment is to have all your faculties complete. If you have a mental or physical handicap, so that your faculties do not function properly, that will make it harder to practice.

The fourth endowment is to be free from wrong livelihoods, mistaken ways of life or activities. For example, some people are fishermen or hunters and engage in acts which rule out the possibility of living a life according to the dharma.

The fifth endowment is to be interested in the truth and to have faith in the truth as explained in the dharma. Accomplishing enlightenment relies completely on ourselves; we are the ones who accomplish enlightenment, nobody can accomplish enlightenment for us or take us there,; it is up to us. However, nothing can take place until we take the first step, we have to begin to move in that direction. If we are not interested in the dharma, in the truth explained in the Buddha's teachings, then we will not have any hope of achieving liberation.

B. Five Endowments from Others. The five endowments that come from others begin with the sixth, which is that the Buddha must have come into the world that we are living in. For us, the Buddha Shakyamuni came into our world and gave teachings so that they are available to us.

The seventh endowment is that the Buddha must actually give teachings. Obviously, if the Buddha had not taught there would be no dharma practice.

The eighth endowment is that the teachings must be present during our lifetime. Dharma is impermanent just like everything else. Sometimes it is strong and sometimes it wanes and disappears. So the teachings have to be preserved. Even if there has been a great period in which the teachings were strong and flourished, if that happened a long time ago it would be no use to us now.

The ninth endowment is that we must have the opportunity to follow the path. In addition to the teachings of the Buddha being present we must have the opportunity to follow the path and to practice.

The tenth endowment is that we must have someone to guide us in practice. Even if the teachings are available and we have the possibility to practice, if nobody helps and guides us through their kindness we will not be able to practice properly, even if the teachings are available.

Examples Showing Preciousness

The human life, which has the eight freedoms and the ten endowments, is called the "precious human life." This precious human existence can be compared to a jewel, but in fact, it is much more valuable than a jewel. If we possess a jewel it can only bring us a little satisfaction. Consider a large diamond or nugget of gold, of course it may be special to us, but it won't be able to do very much for us. If we keep it, we can use it to buy anything and if we sell it, we will have lost it and we might even feel regret for having sold it. But when we consider the precious human life, it is far better than any jewel because with it we can cut the root of suffering once and for all and can plant the seed for future happiness, which will gradually increase more and more. So, once we have a precious human life it would be foolish to ignore it and not take advantage of it.

In the teachings there are three examples of how we must use our precious human life. First, it is compared to a boat that allows us to cross a river. The only reason to use a boat is to get to the other shore and unless we use a boat we won't get there. In the same way, we need to cross the great river of pain and suffering. To go across we must use this precious human life as a boat to go to the other side.

A second example is of a horse that allows us to go somewhere quickly and effortlessly. If we ride the horse of our precious human life we will escape samsara and all its suffering.

The third example is of a servant we can order to do work, and what we want to be done will be done. In the same way, we have to put our precious human life to work as a servant and if we make it work it will create future happiness for us and eliminate all suffering.

Three Points of the Mental Aspect

We have seen all the necessary qualities concerned with the physical aspect of the precious human life. Now, if we look at the three qualities that are concerned with the mental aspect, we see that they relate to our attitude and concern faith.

III. Trusting Faith. The first quality of faith is conviction, or trust in or a belief in the path that leads to liberation. If there isn't this confidence in the path, we will never actually begin to practice. So this basic confidence in the path as the right way is a prerequisite for any practice and the reason why confidence and trust are explained as the first aspect of faith.

IV. Longing Faith. The second aspect of faith is aspiration or interest. If we are not inspired or don't feel that we want to achieve what we are working for, then of course we will never achieve the goal. We need this basic feeling of interest, longing and aspiration. A classic example of this shows how the absence of interest can lead one to miss a chance. In Lhasa, in Tibet, there is a very famous statue called the Jowo Rinpoche. People come from all over Tibet to see and pay homage to this statue because it is extremely special. However, there are people living in Lhasa who have not visited this statue because they feel they needn't bother; they are not interested because they are so close and it is there all the time. This shows that if there is not enough interest or aspiration we cannot actually practice.

V. Clear Faith. The third aspect of faith that is required is clear faith. I have explained the necessity of the second quality of interest and longing for what we are aiming for, but in order to have this clear faith we must first have an appreciation for the object of consideration. Without appreciating something there seems no necessity to achieve it. So clear faith means we can appreciate the path and we are aware of the qualities of the goal.

This describes the three aspects of faith that are the necessary mental qualities for a completely precious human life. If we have these we can then enter the path of dharma and practice it properly.

Impediments to Faith

So, with faith we can practice dharma, however our faith must be very firm and stable because if our faith is changing then most likely we won't be able to complete the practice.

There are four ways in which the stability of our faith can be shaken and diminish. It could be shaken by desire, anger, fear, or stupidity. Our faith can change, degrade and even disappear due to these four factors. An example of it being shaken by desire is if someone came up to us and said, "If you give up your faith in dharma, I will give you anything you want, wealth, fame, power. If at that point you accept this offer, you have completely wasted your opportunity, your precious human life has become useless and your faith has been destroyed by desire.

An example of anger impeding or destroying your faith is when you become overpowered by your anger by someone you dislike and you feel you must hurt or eliminate that person. Once you are in this frame of mind there is no more space for faith and practice, so your faith has been shaken by anger.

An example of fear altering your practice is that someone may say to you that if you don't give up the dharma you will be put in jail or killed.[17] Even at this point you shouldn't be afraid because you know the dharma is the root of all forms of happiness. In such a moment you should feel great confidence and faith and not give up the dharma out of fear.

The fourth cause for loosing faith is one's ignorance or stupidity. This might happen if someone convinces you that whatever you are doing is a complete mistake or a waste of time. If you hear this and feel that maybe there is a point to that and feel that what you've believed in is a mistake, this means that your faith has been destroyed by your own stupidity.

These are four causes that can cause you to lose faith. The real faith is one that is stable and unchanging and is beyond any change that could come about by the above four factors.

That concludes the explanation on the second chapter,
on the working basis, from
The Jewel Ornament of Liberation.

TOPIC 3: THE CONDITION

The Condition is the Spiritual Friend

Chapter 3
The Spiritual Friend

We have the cause to achieve the state of a Buddha, which is the Buddha potential within us, and the basis from which to work for enlightenment, which is the precious human birth with all the necessary qualities. When we are taught this it isn't so we will feel good and enthusiastic about practice. It is telling us what is true so that we don't waste this potential and opportunity we now have. If we use our present situation properly then it will be extremely beneficial, not only for ourselves but also for all other beings, for all our parents from former lives.

Now we have the cause and the basis, but we also need a favorable condition[18] to help us achieve the right practice, namely a spiritual friend.[19] If we were left on our own it would be very difficult to practice correctly, so we need a spiritual friend to influence and guide us

The Tibetan word for "spiritual friend" is "ge she"[20] which literally means "friend of goodness." This is a friend who can lead us to the side of goodness, who can guide us on the path of virtue. There is a double meaning in the first syllable of the word "ge"; one meaning is "happiness" or "everything that is pleasant," and the second is "goodness" in the moral sense of everything that is virtuous. The second syllable "she" means an acquaintance, relative or friend. So a spiritual friend can lead us on the path that will eliminate suffering and reveal more and more happiness and also on the path of more and more goodness.

Since beginningless time we have developed very bad habits and have been used to doing things that are harmful to others. Most of the time we do very few things that are positive and benefit others. We haven't developed doing very many things that are in harmony with the ethics of dharma. Rather, we have done a great many things that were in contradiction to the dharma. This habit of negative behavior makes it very easy for us to act in a negative way. We don't have to learn how to do things in the wrong way, it comes spontaneously, instructively from the habits of numerous past lives. It is also difficult to do things properly because we haven't developed much habit for virtue. We can see this quite readily in animals. Animals are very ignorant and no one needs to teach them how to feel desire, anger, or stupidity because they have it instinctively. Animals will spontaneously kill, steal and harm others because it is part of their habits. There are few animals that act spontaneously in a positive way, properly and correctly, because most animals have not developed those kind of positive habits before. This is also true of human beings. Think back at what it was like when you were a child. When we were children our parents tried to teach us manners using all sorts of means, using rewards and punishments. They tried all sorts of ways to entice us to act wholesomely and properly, but still it was very hard for us to act properly and we had a natural tendency to act in a negative way.

The very bad habits we have developed in samsara have left a very deep and strong imprint in our subconscious so that it is always easier to do what is wrong than what is right. That is why we can't think, "I can manage on my own" when we are working towards enlightenment. In fact, we will need guidance because there are these very old habits of acting negatively.

There are five topics in this chapter on a spiritual friend. First is the reason why we need a spiritual friend. Second are the different types of spiritual friends; they can manifest as ordinary beings, bodhisattvas and so on. Third the specific characteristics of each type of spiritual friend. Fourth, how we should relate to and rely on a spiritual friend. Fifth, the benefits that come from relying on a spiritual friend.

I. Reason: Why We Need a Spiritual Friend. There are three different reasons why we have to rely on a spiritual friend. The first reason comes from the scriptures of the Buddha, the second reason is based on logical reasoning and the third reason is based on examples.

A. Scripture. It is said in the *Condensed Perfection of Wisdom Sutra* (Tib. *Shechen Dupe Do*), "The noble disciple who has respect for the lama should always attend the wise lama because one receives good qualities from him."

This text is saying that a good disciple needs to have the assistance of a good teacher and a good teacher must have all the necessary qualities and realization. If you rely on a good lama who has all the qualities then it will be of great benefit. It will provide the opportunity to develop and increase one's own qualities through this relationship. That is the reason coming from the Buddha's own words.

B. Logic. The second reason can be established by way of logical reasoning. What we are seeking is the state of omniscience of Buddhahood; freedom from conditioned existence. It is like traveling to a completely unfamiliar foreign country. So we need the help of someone who is experienced in that kind of traveling. In terms of practice, we must gather the accumulations and we must purify our obscurations. For this we need the assistance of a spiritual friend because we don't know how to go about this by ourselves. So we need someone to explain to us what to do.

C. Examples. The third reason we need a spiritual friend is given by way of three examples. The first is that of a guide. If we wish to go somewhere where we have never been before – the road may go through various places such as a thick forest, there may be many turns and crossroads, or the path may have many wild animals – we would need a guide, someone who has been there before. They can tell us, this is the right road or that road is too dangerous, etc. Whereas if we travel on our own there is always the risk of never getting to our destination, ending up somewhere else, or of having taken a route which is much longer. We might also take the most difficult road to the destination.

However, if we are traveling with an experienced guide, we will arrive where we want to arrive, we will be able to take the shortest route, and we will have taken the easiest route without wasting any steps. We are on the path to Buddhahood and have no experience on this path so we need a Mahayana spiritual guide to show us the way. Otherwise we will encounter the three risks of taking a mistaken path, of taking a longer route (like following the Hinayana), or of taking the most difficult path (like that of the pratyekabuddhas). However, if a spiritual friend guides us, we will reach the great city of enlightenment without any difficulty and with certainty.

The second example is that we need the help of an escort if we are going to a very dangerous place. If we have to go to a place infested with robbers, thieves, wild animals, dangerous vipers, etc., we shouldn't go alone because we will always be at risk and fear for our life and we would be in danger of being robbed of all our possessions. So, if we don't wish to encounter all these risks and dangers, someone who is very strong, very brave, and is armed with the proper weapons should accompany us. If we travel with such an escort we will not have to fear for our life or possessions. Similarly, when we travel on the path to perfect enlightenment[21] we need to gather the accumulations of virtue and insight. For this we need the help of our spiritual friend to be an escort and to protect us from the inner and outer robbers. "Inner robbers" means that while we are trying to act properly and gather virtue there will be negative thoughts coming up in our minds all the time. These thoughts of anger, desire, and jealousy will act as robbers and thieves who destroy our willingness to act properly. We need the help of our spiritual friend to teach us how to prevent being overpowered by these thoughts. The "outer robbers" are such persons we don't like who can cause great anger and aggression that will arise in our mind and this will become an obstacle to our practice. This obstacle could also come from a friend to whom we are too closely attached. All these feelings of anger or attachment will rob us of our proper and virtuous conduct; they will prevent us from acting positively. We therefore need our spiritual friend to act as our escort and to protect us from our own thoughts that can destroy the virtue we are trying to accumulate in order to reach enlightenment.

The third example is crossing a river with a boat. If we need to get across a large torrential river, we need an experienced boatman to help or most likely we will end up sinking in the middle or being carried away by the current. In the same way, we are now in samsara and need to cross this great river to get to the other shore, which is liberation and omniscience. When we take the boat of dharma without a spiritual friend we always run the risk of drowning in samsara or being carried away by the current of samsara. But if we take the boat of dharma, which is steered by a spiritual friend, then we will definitely reach the shore of nirvana.

II. Classification: The Types of Spiritual Friends. There are four types of spiritual friends: the spiritual friend as an ordinary being, as a bodhisattva on the levels (Skt. *bhumis*), as a *nirmanakaya* Buddha, and as a *sambhogakaya* Buddha.[22] Which spiritual friend is best for us depends on the degree of our own development. The more progress we make, the higher type of spiritual friend we can relate to. At the very beginning of our journey we are hopelessly lost in the suffering of samsara and there is no hope for us to meet with the nirmanakaya or sambhogakaya Buddha. So at this point, the one who can help us is the spiritual friend as an ordinary person. In that sense it is said that the spiritual person as an ordinary person[23] is really the most excellent because he or she is the one we meet at the very beginning and leads us out of our suffering.

III. The Characteristics of a Spiritual Friend. The characteristics of a spiritual friend are explained in great detail in various texts including *The Jewel Ornament of Liberation*. However, all these points are summarized in the *Guide to the Bodhisattva Way of Life* (Tib. *Jangchub Sempai Chodpai La Jukpa*) by Shantideva as being two main qualities: the quality of knowledge and the quality of reliability. The spiritual friend must have the knowledge to guide us on the path. But the spiritual friend must also be reliable, which means that this friend can only advise us in a practice he or she has already practiced and realized.[24] If you have someone who is a leper and this person tells you, "I know a really good way of getting rid of leprosy" you would never believe them because they wouldn't be sick with leprosy if they knew the cure. Therefore, in order to impart any knowledge to someone else, one must have the direct experience of it. So a good Mahayana teacher will have the experience of the Mahayana teachings that he or she can pass on to someone else. Not only must they have the knowledge, but they must also be reliable in that they can teach what they themselves have experienced.

IV. How to Relate to a Spiritual Friend. There are three ways to relate to a lama: through respect, through veneration, and through strenuous practice.

A. Respect. First, we should have great respect for our spiritual friend. When we are in the presence of a spiritual friend we should feel respect and reverence mentally and in our behavior. We come to them with a mind that is open and appreciative. We do this not because the spiritual friend is a king or somebody like that but because the spiritual friend will provide us with well-being and happiness in all our future lives. It depends on our spiritual friend what happens to us now, in the future, and ultimately. So, when we come to the lama we shouldn't come in a casual way as we do with others. Our physical behavior should be one of respect, and the way that we speak to them should be respectful. And in our mind we should have a very reverent attitude. So we don't behave towards a spiritual friend in the same way we would with an ordinary person.[25]

B. Veneration. The second way to relate to a spiritual friend is through veneration, which is very close to the first point of respect. This means we consider our spiritual friend or lama as someone very special because they can help us in the best possible way. When the lama tells us something we should really pay attention to him, heed and practice his advice. If we go against the lama's advice it won't make any difference to the lama but it will harm us because we are not using his or her beneficial advice. So whenever we receive advice from the lama we should take heed, just as Naropa did every thing he was told to do by his teacher Tilopa.[26]

C. Practice. The third way to relate to the lama is by practicing their teachings. In the sutras it says we should consider ourselves as a person who is sick and is trying to get rid of that disease and suffering. But if we don't know how to heal ourselves we must consult a doctor. The doctor will first make a diagnosis of the illness, then decide if it is curable or not, and if it is curable the doctor will prescribe the correct medicine. If we take the medicine and follow the doctor's advice we will then be gradually cured. In the same way, we are completely immersed in the suffering of samsara and we should consider the dharma as medicine that can free us from this ocean of suffering. The lama is like the doctor who can give us the medicine, and taking the medicine is actually practicing the teachings. If we practice properly, step by step, we will gradually develop more understanding and experience and so in the end we will be healed of all our pain. So it is said that this is how we should think about our spiritual friend and the practice of the teachings.

V. The Benefits of Relying on a Spiritual Friend. The Buddha said that those bodhisattvas who rely on a spiritual friend will not fall into the three *lower realms* because they will not have gathered any of the causal conditions to be reborn in these lower states. They will not associate with harmful and negative friends because they are with the right kind of influence, namely a spiritual friend who leads them on the path of goodness so that they won't go astray from the Mahayana path. Since they won't veer off this Mahayana path they will transcend the state of an ordinary person fairly rapidly and finally accomplish Buddhahood swiftly. These are the benefits that come from relying on a spiritual friend.

That concludes the explanation of the third chapter,
on the spiritual friend, from
The Jewel Ornament of Liberation.

TOPIC 4: THE METHOD

The Method is the Teachings of a Spiritual Friend

Introduction to Topic 4

Of the six main topics in *The Jewel Ornament of Liberation* we have now covered the first three. In the first topic we saw all beings have the potential for accomplishing enlightenment; they have the Buddha-essence. In the second topic we saw that the basis for accomplishing this enlightenment is the precious human life. In the third topic we saw the conditions for this was the spiritual friend who will guide us. Once we have a spiritual friend to guide us, we have to learn the means to accomplish enlightenment. This is the fourth topic, which is the means or method, the way of accomplishing enlightenment that is done through receiving the instructions of the spiritual friend.

We may wonder if we can accomplish enlightenment at all and whether we can really practice the teachings that lead us to that. The answer is, of course we can because we possess the essence of enlightenment within us. And we have the precious human life with all the necessary qualities to accomplish this and the necessary condition, the spiritual friend. So, we can indeed eliminate all the suffering of samsara and reach the state of unconditioned happiness, enlightenment.

To make this a reality we have to practice. However, we first need to know how to practice. We need the method of how to practice which we receive from our spiritual friend. We must find out how we can eliminate the suffering of samsara and how we can accomplish ultimate happiness. The way to learn this is to receive advice and guidance from our spiritual friend. If we can apply this advice and practice sincerely and diligently then we can accomplish Buddhahood.

We speak about accomplishing Buddhahood or "the state of a Buddha" but what this really means is "the state beyond suffering," which is the meaning of the word nirvana.

Presently we are in samsara so we will have to endure all sorts of physical and mental suffering. We do not want pain, difficulties and suffering, but this happens to us. So, we must find a way to eliminate this pain and suffering. In fact, eliminating suffering is the goal of all mankind; it is the goal of all beings to go beyond suffering and to find happiness. Furthermore, it is the goal of all beings to achieve this. We are all trying to transcend suffering, so one could say that eliminating pain and suffering is not only the goal of spiritual paths but also the goal of each and every endeavor. We are all trying to achieve this.

So, how can we achieve this? First we have to understand that suffering takes place in our mind. There are different thoughts occurring in our mind all the time and most of these are negative. These negative thoughts generate suffering; they create all of our suffering. If we can manage to eliminate them then we will be able to transcend suffering. But if we cannot eliminate them we will continue to experience suffering.

Four Obstacles to Accomplishing Buddhahood

We all want freedom from suffering but we still haven't managed to accomplish this. We haven't managed to leave suffering behind and find lasting happiness. We should contemplate why we haven't managed this. Is it because it is impossible, or is it because it is too difficult to accomplish? No, it is possible to eliminate suffering; it isn't that difficult. But the problem is that until now we haven't used the right means or method to eliminate suffering, and we have made either one or all of the following four mistakes: Being attached to this life's activities, being attached to the pleasures of samsara, being attached to peace, and not understanding the methods by which Buddhahood is accomplished.

The first mistake is that one does not try to work towards Buddhahood or freedom from suffering in samsara because one is too involved with the pleasures of this life. One is very attached to what one enjoys in this life and doesn't think about anything else. So the first mistake is too much attachment to this life.

The second mistake is that even though existence in the world entails both suffering and happiness, some people think it is just happiness. They don't see suffering; they look away, ignore or forget about it. In general they cling to existence, which prevents them from trying to go beyond suffering and trying to accomplish Buddhahood.

The third mistake is that some people will try to achieve a state of peace and enjoy the happiness and goodness of that but will not try and go further by completely transcending the suffering of samsara. They will not search for Buddhahood.

With the fourth mistake there isn't too much clinging to the pleasures of this life and existence in general but there is complete ignorance concerning how to find freedom from samsara and how to accomplish the true happiness of Buddhahood.

So those are the four reasons why we haven't accomplished Buddhahood and still remain in samsara with all its inherent suffering.

The Four Remedies

The first teaching we need to receive from our spiritual friend is the teaching on the truth of impermanence. I explained how some people are involved with the concerns of this life and others with existence in general, thinking that this is true happiness. If the experiences of life were to last forever, if they were eternal and unchanging there would be nothing wrong with wanting to hold onto them. There would be no reason to wish to abandon them. But unfortunately it isn't like that. We cannot deny that there is happiness in this life. However, we always think that this happiness will last, that it is permanent. This is a mistake. We have to realize that this kind of happiness doesn't last. Our life and all its experiences are by their very nature impermanent. Once we realize this we will then reduce our clinging to this life. So we have to accept the truth of impermanence.

The second teachings we need to receive from our spiritual friend are those on the viciousness of samsara and on the principles of karma; they are the remedy for clinging to the happiness of existence in general. If existence were only happiness there would be no reason to give it up. But what we have to realize is that although existence can often be happiness, because it doesn't last it is actually suffering. The very essence of what seems to be happiness is suffering. And because the law of karma, cause and effect, regulates our life it is constantly changing. Therefore we need to learn the truth about things, the way things really are.

The third teachings we need from our spiritual friend are those for the meditation on loving-kindness and compassion.

Fourthly we need teachings on the cultivation of bodhichitta.

So those are four main instructions we need from a spiritual friend and the four sections that this topic of the *Jewel Ornament* are divided into.

Chapter 4
The Instructions on Impermanence
The Remedy for Attachment to This Life

We learn about and meditate on impermanence in order to remedy the first obstacle to accomplishing Buddhahood, which is attachment to the concerns of this life. Although impermanence is the nature of all things, many people find this subject very unpleasant and depressing to think about. While this may be so it is worthwhile going through unpleasant topics first in order to receive a great benefit in the long term. If we shun anything that is unpleasant and only indulge in that which is pleasant, then in the future we will have to go through even more difficulties. For example, suppose I were sitting on a seat that I think is very nice but all the time there is a poisonous snake under the seat, which I am not aware of. I am talking to people and feeling relaxed and comfortable without any problems. Suddenly the snake creeps out and bites my leg which then causes me a lot of trouble and suffering. But if somebody had pointed out to me that there was a snake under the seat, I might have been very shocked, but I would have had the chance to escape. So the small fear I experience upon hearing about the snake is worthwhile. In the same way, when we hear about the impermanence of all things, including our life in samsara, it may not make us feel happy but the unpleasant feeling is worthwhile because it will provide us with the impetus to escape from all the suffering of samsara. This will enable us to follow the right path that will lead to a state free of fear, free of pain, and free of panic. So, it is worth taking the unpleasant feeling upon oneself for a short while in order to escape suffering and unhappiness forever. Therefore, although meditation on impermanence isn't the most pleasant thing in the world, it is very valuable.

The *Jewel Ornament* teaches in three parts how we should deal with this subject. The first part explains the different aspects of impermanence, which covers everything both gross and subtle. The second part explains the method of meditation on impermanence, how we should meditate on impermanence. Once we discover that all things are impermanent we ask if we can do anything to change this. We can't, all we can do is to know this. The way to know this is to contemplate impermanence. Then we can abandon our attachment and involvement with the idea of permanence. Then we are able to eliminate all the suffering involved with clinging to what is in fact impermanent. The third part explains all the benefits of this meditation, how becoming free from clinging and the involvement with the concerns of this life will be of great benefit to us.

I. The Classification of Impermanence. We have an idea that some things are impermanent but we may not know that everything without exception is impermanent. Not believing this we are inclined to cling to things and become very involved with them, which is a mistake. This error is a delusion because we are taking something that is impermanent as being permanent, thinking it will be there forever. This idea of things lasting is a delusion.

What happens is that we have this belief that things last and when they change we are quite shocked because we liked them a great deal and were so involved with them. So when we see the change it is a painful experience for us. However, knowing that all things are impermanent we will not cling so strongly to them and therefore clinging will not be a source of suffering. So we have to learn that everything in the universe is impermanent, the whole environment is impermanent and most importantly that all beings within the environment are impermanent.

All external objects are impermanent. This is true of our world, which is the impermanence of the environment. We may think the world has always been here, will continue to be here and will always remain the same. But if we think about the hundreds, thousands or millions of years that have passed, then we know how many changes have occured. For instance, scientists tell us that a million years ago the earth looked completely different, then, in the future after many thousand of years it will look completely different from what it does now.

In some of the Buddha's teachings he predicted that this planet would in the end be consumed by fire and dispersed by water. It will completely disintegrate. So we should realize that even this planet is impermanent and that there is no benefit in clinging to it.

The impermanence of external objects is true not only on a large scale as with this planet, but also on a small scale for much more subtle things. The gross impermanence of the world as I described is not something we can directly experience, but subtle impermanence which is always occurring we can directly experience.[27] We can experience the changing of the seasons from one to the next and see how the ground is different, the sky changes and the differences from summer to winter and so on. On a smaller scale are the changes from day to night which we see every day. In this way, we can see that everything around us is changing all the time, nothing remains the same and is permanent.

So those are the ways we must consider the impermanence of the gross and subtle aspects of the environment. The impermanence of beings is dealt with in the method for meditating on impermanence.

II. The Method for Meditating on Impermanence. The second part of meditating on impermanence is mostly to become aware of the impermanence of our life, the fact that we will die sooner than we think. This mediation isn't intended to scare us or cause us fear and distress thinking we are going to die any minute. The point is to make us realize how fortunate we are to have the very best opportunity in this life.

As explained, this life is even more precious than the most valuable jewel because this is the kind of life that can take us beyond suffering. If we have something precious then we must use it for what it is worth so that it accomplishes its purpose. If we use this life's opportunity properly we can accomplish Buddhahood for both others and ourselves. So, we should consider this time as precious, not ordinary and not a situation that we can afford to waste and render meaningless. One year is very important and we can't afford to waste it. One month is very valuable, one day is very valuable, even one hour is very valuable and shouldn't be wasted. We should think that every hour is an hour of gold or an hour of diamonds, that it is a very precious hour. Thinking this way we must use every moment fully to accomplish our own purpose as well as that of others. So, we should realize that this time of our life will pass very quickly and end. This is why we need to meditate on impermanence and the coming of death.

If someone is in a very unfortunate situation they will be very happy to experience time pass quickly. In that case they would rejoice at impermanence. For example, if someone were thrown in prison for three years and the first month had already passed they would feel very happy knowing only eleven more months of the first year were left. When the first year was over they would be happy thinking this has passed and only two more years remain. They would be happy to see time fly. But we shouldn't think in those terms because whatever time we have is very precious. We can't afford to waste it but must use it meaningfully.

When we meditate on impermanence we should realize how much time we usually waste. We waste time in many different ways. For instance, think of all the time we waste trying to earn a living and trying to accumulate possessions. Think of all the hours, days, months and years that go into that. Think about what benefit that effort brings. Will it benefit us forever? When we die we will have to leave everything behind, none of our possessions can accompany us. Think of all the time we spend trying to have a nice house for ourselves; we spend years of our precious time doing this. But if we think about it then we will discover what a waste of our precious time it is. When the house is finished, maybe we can enjoy it for twenty years, thirty or possibly sixty years but this won't last for hundreds or thousands of years. The amount of enjoyment we will have is very small in comparison to the amount of effort. It is hardly worth wasting so much precious time on this.

Another way in which we waste time is being involved with thoughts of our enemies, like the time we waste thinking about someone we hate and how we wish them harm. We could spend months or years scheming how to harm or kill them. This is a waste of time because that enemy won't be there forever. Maybe they will live only another thirty or forty years anyway. In the end they too will die; they are not eternal. So what is the point of wasting time contemplating how to harm or kill someone who is going to die anyway?

We also waste our time trying to make life pleasant for people we like such as our family, friends and so on. This is also a mistake because it takes so much time and effort, which in the end won't be of much benefit anyway. We may think we are helping these people but true help means helping in such a way that they need not undergo the suffering of change and to permanently free them from suffering and death. It is better to practice meditation than to spend all our time trying to make things nice for our family and friends. Of course it is good to think about helping others and to make them happy – this is in fact part of a bodhisattva's commitment, it is a bodhisattva's responsibility to help other beings – but the method is wrong, spending so much time and effort on useless priorities. So, instead of wasting so much precious time on little things, we should instead use the time and energy to work towards ultimate happiness, which will really benefit our loved ones and ourselves.

If we look at the people we are connected with, our enemies and friends, our family and those we care about, most of the problems they have will be caused by the inner states of their mind. For instance, they may suffer because of desire, anger or ignorance. As this suffering comes from the mind, the way to eliminate this kind of suffering is only through dharma. If we try and help through worldly means it will not be successful.

Worldly help is only temporary and has a limited effect. Of course it will help to a certain extent, but it won't solve their problems for good.

For example, if we say to someone that we will provide them and their family with everything they need for one month, that is very good, but what will happen after one month? Even if we help them for a year, then after one year they will have the same problem. Similarly it is good to help people financially if they need it, but when that money is spent they will encounter the same problem. What is being said here is that the extent to which we can help with worldly means is very limited, not that it isn't helpful at all. So, on a worldly level we can't do much, it is our dharma practice that can help on a larger scale. At the moment we may not be able to do much, but if we practice dharma properly then we will come to a point where we can help in a true sense, when we can really do something to help others.

Another thing needs to be distinguished, which is the motivation for helping others. If we help others with a good motivation, with the genuine and wholesome wish to help, then this is something good and should be done. What I am referring to here is as long as we focus only upon helping those near to us, there is a strong amount of selfishness involved because we are very attached to them. This is why it is better to diminish that kind of help because it hinders us from practicing the dharma. We become so attached to those close to us that we feel we want to do things with and for them all the time.

The great bodhisattva Shantideva said, "One day we are going to have to die and then we will leave everything behind, our enemies, our friends, our house, our possessions, our land, even our body. But now we ignore this and always invest so much energy in things we will have to leave behind anyway. All our efforts are in vain. There is no need to waste so much time on clinging and hatred because in the end all of that has to go. Instead, we should use our precious time in order to reach ultimate happiness. We will have to leave everything behind when we go, therefore it is absolutely pointless to cling to anything."

The teacher Lobpon Thayon said, "Wherever you look, people and animals are born. They will have to die eventually because all living beings are impermanent. But maybe there is the thought in the back of your mind that there is eternity. If you look around you will never find someone who hasn't died. Will you ever find such a living being? Maybe you think that just because you don't see such a being that it doesn't mean that there isn't someone who has managed to escape death. But have you ever heard of such a being? No. Even though you haven't witnessed or heard about someone who hasn't died, still you continue to hold onto the thought in your mind that maybe there is some form of eternal life somewhere. You continue hoping and therefore you spend so much time and effort acting as though nothing in life changes."

We handle things in our lives as though they were permanent and eternal. We try to solidify things and invest so much money and effort in doing this. If someone wanted to build a house to last a thousand years they would need to invest a great deal of money and effort. But of course, it would be pointless, because that person would not live a thousand years. So, not being able to fully enjoy such a house all the effort and time would be in vain. Therefore, avoiding such pointless aims we should direct our attention to transcending suffering, problems and fears of impermanence. This is how to make our life meaningful and how to use it properly.

III. The Benefits that Arise from Meditating on Impermanence. There are many benefits both in the short term and in the long term from meditating on impermanence. In the short term it helps us directly in life by showing us how we should use our life, what our goal should be and how to spend our time. It will show us the priorities we should have in life and how to use our time and energy well. We will know that there is no point in wasting our time and effort on worldly pursuits but instead strive towards the higher goal of eliminating suffering.

We know that suffering is something experienced in our mind. It is experienced because of all the problems arising from desire, anger, jealousy, ignorance and the like. We know that we must use this life in order to break the continuity of samsara and to accomplish Buddhahood. This is the first benefit of the realization of impermanence.

Another benefit is that this awareness of impermanence will inspire us to practice. It is said that understanding impermanence is like the friend who helps develop diligence; it will make you much more diligent in your practice.

Finally, it is said that through understanding impermanence we will ultimately need not fear because the realization of impermanence and change will inspire us to practice and to achieve ultimate and lasting happiness.

The *Jewel Ornament* is a complete outline of all the various stages of the path. It describes the full journey one engages in from the point of having entered the path of dharma up to the moment when one accomplishes Buddhahood. We now know we have the seed of Buddhahood within us, which is the cause that makes it possible to enter the path, how we need to receive instructions from a spiritual friend and how we encounter obstacles that have to be removed so that we can practice well.

The first kind of obstacle that we can encounter is attachment to the pleasures of this life, to what we like about life. We might become very involved with wearing nice clothes, with money, with possessions, with our friends, with fame, honor and all kinds of things. Strong attachment to such things will prevent us from practicing dharma. So, we have to learn how to overcome such obstacles. The method to do this is not by trying to suppress them with force or violence but by realizing the true nature of things. The dharma instructions therefore teach us that all these things we are so involved with, all the objects of attachment, are conditioned. They are not permanent and won't be at our disposal forever. Therefore there isn't any point in being attached to them or trying to guard them because they won't be of much benefit anyway. Only the dharma is of great benefit. This is the reason why impermanence is taught.

This concludes the explanation of the fourth chapter,
on impermanence, from
The Jewel Ornament of Liberation.

Chapter 5
The Meditation on the Suffering of Samsara
THE FIRST REMEDY TO ATTACHMENT TO SAMSARA'S PLEASURES

In order to remedy the second obstacle to Buddhahood, which is attachment to samsaric joys, we learn and meditate on the defects of samsaric existence and the principles of karma.

Once a person has heard the teachings on impermanence they may think, "Although this life is impermanent, so what, let's not make a big deal about it. I cannot take all the things I have acquired with me when I die, they will be left behind. But, there will be another life and maybe then I can get better set-up. Maybe I can be reborn as a god or a human being with a very pleasant life." Those thoughts are an obstacle to dharma, in which case there is clinging to existence as a whole, thinking that samsara is something pleasant and desirable. As long as somebody has this kind of attachment they cannot practice the dharma and work towards Buddhahood.

Because we all want happiness, and if samsara exclusively entailed only happiness, then there would be absolutely no harm in wanting to stay in samsara. It would be fine to remain in this state and enjoy its pleasures. There would be no point in going through all the hardships of practicing the dharma to be free from samsara. But actually, no happiness can be found in samsara; its very nature is suffering, and only all sorts of suffering can be found in samsara.

When faced with suffering, pain or difficulties we react by trying to free ourselves from them and try to find all sorts of ways to overcome the situation. Often we endure a lot to do this. Sometimes we are successful and for a while the difficulties and pain are reduced. But always something arises. Difficulties, pain and suffering are not accidents that happen only once in a while; it is the very nature of samsara that suffering is bound to come. This is why we have to try and gain liberation from samsara, this is the only way to transcend suffering.

In general, when most people encounter any sort of suffering or difficulties they tend to take it personally, thinking they are having all these problems and it only happens to them. They may cry, feel depressed and sorry for themselves or even contemplate suicide. What they don't understand is that what is happening to them is not a personal ordeal but something that everybody experiences. It happens to everyone in samsara.

Because suffering is always around the corner there is no real happiness in samsara. Everyone tries to eliminate suffering in some way or another. Some people who are poor may think this is the cause of their misery and unhappiness so they try and become rich in order to be happy. Even if that person does manage to become rich they will find that they still have lots of problems and difficulties because suffering will still come. Someone else may think that they are unhappy because they are not famous or powerful. But even if they achieve that they will still experience suffering. Other people think they are unhappy due to being stuck in this life and think it would be better to be dead. But committing suicide is no solution to eliminating suffering and would in fact only result in suffering accompanying them more forcefully.[28] So, no matter what we do in samsara, whether it be committing suicide, becoming rich or achieving fame, we cannot eliminate suffering because it is the intrinsic nature of samsara. As long as we are in samsara, suffering will be with us.

So, what is the way out, how can we manage to become free from suffering? The only way to eliminate suffering is to understand that suffering is part and parcel of the very nature of samsara, and the only way to transcend suffering is to completely leave samsara behind. This can only be accomplished by practicing dharma.

Let's take an example to understand this more clearly. We know that suffering is automatically present for those in samsara because this is its very nature. Imagine someone holding a piece of burning coal in their hand. Because the very nature of fire is to burn, if the person continues to hold it they will get burnt and that will be very painful. If that person thinks, "It hurts, what can I do? Should I take some medicine?" This will lead them to try all sorts of remedies. But this will not eliminate the pain because the coal is still burning in their hand. The only thing to do is to get rid of the burning coal. In the same way, we are in samsara where we experience all sorts of difficulties and sufferings. These all come from the same cause, from the nature of samsara. We suffer in all sorts of ways, both mentally and physically. Sometimes it seems that there are definite causes for our suffering and we may conclude that it is due to a friend, an enemy or such. We find all sorts of excuses but actually it is always the very same cause, which is that of samsara. The only way to eliminate the suffering is to work on the path of dharma and eliminate our own negativity.

There is a story of King Gesar of Ling, which makes sense in this context. King Gesar's mother fell into one of the hell realms and was locked up in an iron house. The King had some supernatural powers and managed to go to the hell realm and was pulling his mother out of the iron house when suddenly, due to her great attachment she thought, "Oh I don't want to leave this nice house behind. If I leave someone will take it and I will lose it." The point is that as soon as we form the idea of something belonging to us, whether it is good or bad, we develop attachment for it. We don't really consider whether it is really good or bad or pleasant or unpleasant, we have the idea, "It is mine" and we don't want to let go of it. We have to realize that our attachment to samsara will only lead to unhappiness and suffering and so we need to learn to let go of our attachment.

Three Types of Suffering

In the *Jewel Ornament* Gampopa explains that all the suffering of samsara has three forms. First is what as known as the all-pervasive form of suffering, which is the suffering inherent in the very process of existence. The second form of suffering is the suffering of change. The third is the actual pain of suffering.

The point is that sometimes in conditioned existence things are quite good and sometimes things are quite bad. But on the whole, the nature of our existence is unhappiness because we can never find the type of happiness that is not subject to change, in other words true happiness that never ceases. This is the reason why we must try and accomplish liberation by entering the path of dharma and practicing properly and the reason why Gampopa explains here all the details of suffering.

Now, the nature of samsara is suffering and if we consider this more closely we see that we experience things on three levels. One kind of feeling is that we can have very pleasant experiences and feel that things are really great. Another kind of feeling is intense pain and suffering. Third is the feeling of indifference.

In the face of these three different feelings we will react differently. When something pleasant happens we want it to continue and thus have great attachment to it. When something unpleasant happens we want to get rid of it and thus have aversion. When something neutral happens we feel indifference; we have neither a pleasant nor unpleasant feeling toward it. All beings, humans and animals alike, experience these three types of feelings. What we need to learn is to not feel attachment or aversion to any of these three types of feelings.

I. All-pervasive Suffering. The feeling of indifference is related to the all-pervasive suffering. The Buddha described this suffering as being the universal type of suffering which is inherent in the very process of samsara. This means that from the very moment something begins to be part of worldly existence, as soon as it is composite,[29] then immediately it is subject to change. It is impossible for it not to change. It is bound to diminish, to become exhausted and to end. Whatever takes place in samsara, conditioned existence, is never permanent and stable; it is always something that changes. Although this suffering does not bring a particular feeling with it, which is why it is called indifferent, there is the constant threat of change running through conditioned life. This is what is described as the innate suffering of the process of existence.[30]

II. The Suffering of Change. The second type of suffering is that of change. To define this the Buddha explained that the suffering of change is related to what happens when there is a great deal of happiness; the basis of it is something that brings great happiness like wealth or power. Sooner or later this happiness is bound to change. The Buddha is not taking a gloomy view of things and saying everything is suffering while there is happiness. He does not say that things entail suffering if they don't. What he means is that the happiness that we do find will inevitably change; it is part of the nature of the happiness of samsara that it will degrade and change. The Buddha is pointing out this truth for us. Of course the moment we experience happiness the feeling is one of joy. But what happens then is that we feel attachment to this experience of joy and become involved. This attachment to momentary happiness causes us to bear the suffering of wanting more. We then want bigger and better things. This frustration of wanting more leads us to do everything in our power to acquire and achieve more. So in the end we never have the opportunity to enjoy anything we have. Wanting more keeps us more frustrated and unhappy. So, due to this attachment to the momentary joy we will never find lasting happiness because we do not feel the need.

Let's take an example to illustrate this. If someone has $100 they may think that they have worked for that and it is fine, now they think they should try and get $200. Then they work hard and perhaps manage to get $200. For a short time they are satisfied and then want more, they want $1000, then $10000 and so on. They will be constantly chasing after more. Actually, it is irrelevant whether they are successful or not in acquiring the money, in either case they will suffer. If they can't achieve their goal they will be frustrated and unhappy and even if they achieve it they will be frustrated and unhappy because they will either continue wanting more or whatever they achieve will diminish. In any case they will suffer in the process. If we constantly strive for more happiness then we will waste our entire life pursuing pleasure and happiness. This is why Gampopa teaches that suffering is the intrinsic nature of happiness in samsara.

Let's look at another example of the suffering of change. If someone has an ordinary white cup from which they drink tea daily, then the process of enjoying tea from this ordinary cup doesn't involve pain. But if the cup were made of gold or some precious material and one day it broke and then they had to drink tea from an ordinary white cup they would be quite upset. They would think they had a beautiful cup, which they liked, and now have to drink from this lousy cup. We can see that person's pain comes from the fact that they enjoyed the nice cup and now suffer from the loss of that pleasure. If they had always had the ordinary cup it wouldn't make any difference. This is an example of the happiness of samsara, which begins with happiness but ends in the suffering of change.

There is nothing wrong about enjoying what is happy and pleasant; the experience of happiness is not wrong. What is wrong is being involved and attached to those things because that attachment will bring forth suffering. What we have to eliminate is attachment, which can be done by realizing that the nature of samsara is suffering.

III. The Suffering of Suffering. The third form of suffering is very obvious to all beings; it is the suffering of pain. All existence can be divided into six aspects of experience: Hells, craving spirits, animals, human beings, jealous demi-gods and gods. Although there are these six types of beings for us we can only see human beings and animals, we have no direct experience of the hell beings, craving spirits and gods. Some people argue that if these forms of life really existed then we should be able to see them, so they say that these are only symbolic ways of speaking and do not represent actual ways of existing. However, the Buddha did say that there are beings that live in the hells and also those who experience the life of gods and other forms of life. Simply to say that because we can't see something it doesn't exist is incorrect; we cannot make that inference. There are many things that we can prove exist and we accept without being able to see them.

For example, if I fell asleep and dreamt that a ferocious tiger or lion was about to attack me I would feel terribly frightened. However you would only see me sleeping and just think I am asleep. You couldn't see the terrible experience I was going through of being attacked or eaten by a lion. But for me the experience is real and I would have great fear. This is an example in terms of the six types of beings that different experiences are possible.[31] So other beings can be going through terrible experiences of pain and suffering which they experience but we cannot perceive. Therefore, just because we don't see it doesn't mean that beings are not going through great experiences of terror in their minds. So we shouldn't think that these six states described by the Buddha are only symbolic.

Gampopa gives very extensive descriptions of the various sufferings of the suffering of suffering. However, as this is something we can understand and know very easily – we know ourselves what suffering is – it isn't vital to go through all the details. The most important thing to know is that the nature of samsara is suffering. The Buddha, in the *Entering the Womb Sutra* (Tib. *Nyaljukgi Do*) said, "The whole of existence is on fire and within that fire all beings without exception are burnt by the flames of the inner and outer fire. The inner flames are the fire beings themselves kindle with their desire, aggression and stupidity." The fire of desire for example will create constant frustration, the fire of anger will create disturbance and the fire of stupidity will make the mind dull and unhappy. The outer fire is the flames of birth, old age, sickness, death, lamentation and so on. The Buddha continues in the sutra to say, "No one in existence is immune from those flames. The only way to become free is to become liberated."

We all know what suffering, problems and difficulties are; just think of our daily conversations in which this is often the topic of discussion. All sorts of problems arise which we tell each other about. The only way to eliminate these problems is to remove what creates the problems, as in the example of the burning coal in one's hand. Our hand will continue being burned as long as we hold onto the burning coal. Similarly, unless we eliminate samsara completely we cannot eliminate suffering. So we practice dharma in order to gain freedom from samsara. If we accomplish this, then all our problems, the big problems, little problems, long-lasting problems, short term problems, they all will be solved.

This concludes the explanation of the fifth chapter,
on the suffering of samsara, from
The Jewel Ornament of Liberation.

Chapter 6
Karma and Its Result
The Second Remedy to Attachment to Samsara's Pleasures

In examining the teachings of our spiritual friend, we have to seek something to remedy our attachment to this life, which is impermanence, the first remedy. Further, we need the second remedy which counters our involvement with the idea that samsara is something worthwhile and pleasurable. This remedy is given in the form of two types of meditation: The first, which we have now covered, is the meditation on all the different sufferings of samsara so that we understand what is wrong with samsara and why we have to give it up. The second aspect is the meditation on karma. Through understanding karma or causality, the relationship between cause and effect in our actions, we remedy our involvement with samsara.

We talk about our experiences in samsara, about our happiness, pleasures, pain and sufferings, but where do they come from, what are the causes for these experiences? The answer is that the cause for them is to be found in causality; the relationship between our actions and their results, which itself comes from the nature of our actions. Some people think that the whole idea of causality means that we have no choice at all, that everything is pre-determined and that things are already set from the start so that if we experience suffering it is the result of our previous karma and that there is no way to escape the suffering or to change it. In the same way, they think that if we have pleasant experiences and are happy it is the result of our former actions and nothing can be done about it. So these ideas of everything being pre-determined are not correct. In one way it is true that once you have done something you have planted a seed, which is the creating of a cause that will bring about a certain result. But the correct way to understand this is to know that from the start we have the choice of what seed we will plant, we have a free choice, and nothing is pre-determined.

Everyone wants happiness; that is our goal. But we have to realize that we create our own happiness, we have the power to produce it. All we need to do is to produce the causes of happiness, which are positive actions. This means we have a free choice to create all future happiness, both temporary and ultimate. This is entirely up to us. On the other hand there is suffering which we always try to avoid. Can we really do anything about suffering? Yes indeed. We have the free choice to avoid suffering. If we can eliminate the cause of suffering, the negative actions that create suffering, we will have eliminated suffering itself. So, everything is entirely up to us. We can create our own happiness and we can create our own misery.

Let us look at how other religions view the subject of karma. If we consider the view of anyone who is not a Buddhist, there are generally three different views. First, there is the view that nothing arises from former actions. Those with this view do not accept the principle of cause and effect and instead believe that a god creates everything. The god may be called by different names but the view is that a god makes everything and nothing depends upon actions. The second view is that of the nihilists. They say that the quality of our experiences, whether positive or negative, aren't the result of our previous actions but are merely due to our immediate effort, to our immediate way of living. The third view is that of those called "naked ascetics," who think that everything in the universe and in life is caused by previous actions, by karma. They say that everything is conditioned by karma and that nothing else can have any influence; there are no other factors other than karma.

Now let us look at the Buddhist position in contrast to the other views. The Buddha taught that not everything comes from karma, but also it is not correct to say that nothing comes from karma. The Buddha showed that some things come about as the result of our previous actions. But also there are things that come from immediate or accidental conditions, by chance, and this isn't from karma.

Let us look at those things that happen incidentally given there are certain conditions. For example, I have some string twisted around my hand, which if I pull will cause me pain. This pain will not be the result of my previous actions or karma, rather it is directly due to my twisting and pulling on the string. If I stop pulling on the string then the pain stops. This isn't the result of previous actions but of what I am doing now. Another example is our way of thinking and our attitude, which can arise spontaneously and isn't conditioned by former karma. For instance, sometimes we have negative feelings in our mind such as anger, desire and jealousy. These negative feelings are not the result of previous actions. They just arise in the mind instantaneously and are something that we can control, something that we can eliminate if we try. This is true of all thoughts we have, whether positive or negative. We have the choice to let them arise or not. So all of these thoughts arise from immediate conditions and not previous actions.

Now let us look at the things that happen due to our former actions. Without deeper investigation we can say that things come from karma, but actually this is a very subtle subject. We cannot see karma directly because the whole pattern of karma is very deep and difficult to understand. An example may clarify this. I was born in Tibet. I had no choice. I couldn't determine to be born in the West where there is wealth and industrial development. Being born in Tibet happened due to my former actions. Furthermore, I couldn't choose the time of my birth. I was born and lived during a time when there were many problems in Tibet due to the Chinese invasion and the communist dominance. Had I been born fifty years earlier things would have been different. There were no real problems then and the dharma was flourishing. Had I been born fifty years later there might have been no problems either because matters would have been more settled. But, I was born when I was and had to encounter these problems without the possibility of choice in deciding not to be born at that time or if I wanted to escape. My former actions caused my birth at the particular time and place in the particular country and that is why I had to experience the various problems from the communist invasion. In the same way, I couldn't determine to be born the son of a king; I had to be born according to my previous actions. Also, I couldn't reject my human birth and choose to become an animal because my body was determined by former actions. Looking at it from another perspective, no one can plan their birth because everything that is involved with birth (the form, the time and the place) are all determined by previous actions. So this is an example of how things are determined by former actions.

Let us look at the results that come from actions in former lives. If we have generated the causes it is true that we encounter the results. We cannot change things in this respect. So, our actions are very important for the future. Our future is in our own hands and we can determine the quality of our future experiences. If we practice the cause of happiness, if we practice virtue, then we are creating our own future happiness. And if we eliminate the cause of suffering by avoiding negative actions then we are freeing ourselves from future suffering. Also this can help free us from having to experience some of the painful results of negative actions that we have already generated. This means that if we can really atone for our past negative actions properly, such as through *Vajrasattva* meditation, this can purify them and so we can avoid the very painful results of those actions.[32]

This is why the Buddha taught the unmistaken way and gave the teachings on karma, in order to show how to escape suffering by eliminating the cause and how to experience happiness by creating its cause. He gave this teaching because he saw everyone wants to experience happiness and avoid suffering and we have to understand that we ourselves are responsible for this. If we trust these teachings we can use them and achieve the results we are looking for. We find the happiness we want and the elimination of suffering that we don't want.

The patterns of causality are presented in this book in six points: classification, primary characteristics, the action ripening for oneself, strict result, great ripening arising from small actions, and the inevitability of actions.

I. Classification. The first point describes the various sorts of karma, of actions and results. The first is known as the negative or non-virtuous karma. These are the types of actions that create all our problems. The second is known as the virtuous or meritorious karma, the type of actions that give rise to happiness and pleasure, what we are all seeking. The third type of karma is known as the karma of immobility, the type of actions connected with the practice of meditation. This is a state when the mind is totally absorbed within itself and is completely introverted.

Once we know these different aspects of karma it is then very easy to deduce what rule of actions we need. We need to practice the cause of happiness, virtuous actions, and we need to eliminate the cause of suffering, non-virtuous or negative actions.

II. The Primary Characteristics of Each Classification. The non-meritorious actions are divided into three types, those we do physically with our body, those we do verbally with our speech and those we do mentally with our minds. There are three non-meritorious actions done with the physical body: killing, stealing and sexual misconduct.

Some form of negative motivation usually accompanies these negative actions. Sometimes we are moved by desire, sometimes by anger and sometimes by ignorance. So we have a combination of a negative motivation and a negative action. This is something that would cause suffering to others. When we cause suffering to others we will later have to experience suffering ourselves, which would be the direct result of our negative actions. If we manage to avoid these non-meritorious actions done by way of our body, then we will eliminate suffering for others and consequently suffering for ourselves.

We shouldn't think that the workings of karma could only bring suffering in the next life and not in this life and therefore we can have a good time now. This is wrong because karma doesn't work like this at all. The effect of our negative actions can be experienced in this life. Let's take killing as an example. You may hate someone and think that if you kill them then you will be rid of them and that person will not bother or harm you anymore. What happens though is that after you have actually killed that person then their family and friends will turn against you. So instead of having eliminated an enemy you have made even more enemies than you had before. Alternately, if you try and cope with the strong anger you have towards the person you hate, it may be difficult to control that hatred, but slowly you will manage to overcome it. Whereas, if you actually kill the person, this life won't be better because not only do you now have many enemies but of course you have created very great causes to experience suffering in your next life. This is true not only for killing, but also true for the other negative physical actions.

So, we should always think twice before we act. We may think at first that it is all right to do things because they bring pleasure and there is no reason to give them up, but really we should think that it won't benefit us in this life and so will not be worth the trouble we are creating for ourselves now and in the future.

There are four non-meritorious actions of speech: to lie, to use divisive speech, to use harsh words and to engage in idle talk.

Let's take the example of lying. Without considering it carefully we may think it is clever, by just saying a few false words we can achieve our goals. If we say something untrue then the one who listens to us will think it is true and through lying we think we will have managed to achieve what we wanted. But if you look at it more closely it isn't clever at all. Sakya Pandita said that the one who tells a lie thinks that they are deceiving someone else but, in fact, they are not deceiving anybody but themselves because once the lie has been told then the other person will one day discover the truth and will then doubt everything that person ever says again. This means that once someone has told a lie, when discovered, whatever they say from that time onward, even if it is true, will be regarded as a lie because others have lost trust in that person.

What is said about lying, the end result being suffering, applies to the other three non-meritorious forms of speech – divisive speech, harsh words and useless chatter – as well. Any of these forms of unskillful speech will bring suffering. This is why we have to try and eliminate them and to practice virtuous speech, which will bring happiness.

There are three non-meritorious actions of mind: to covet, to have ill-will and to hold wrong views.

In Buddhism, the mental aspect is the most fundamental because the mind is the root of everything we do. It is said that if the intention is good, then everything will be good; if the intention is negative, then everything else will be negative. If somebody is doing something that looks negative but with a good intention, then it will go well and the result will be good. On the other hand, if somebody is doing something that looks positive but with a negative intention, then it will not go well and the result will be harmful. So, whatever we do that is motivated by the three non-meritorious mental attitudes of greed (which often takes the form of envy), ill will and wrong views[33] will necessarily be negative and have a painful result.

This is how the Buddha presented the rules of conduct, showing what we have to do and what we have to avoid. He showed that we should practice the ten meritorious actions[34] and avoid the ten non-meritorious actions. We shouldn't think that the dharma teachings tell us that we need to give up things that we like and choose a difficult life. For instance, we may think that by giving up negative actions we will experience pain and hardships. That is not the case. The Buddha only spoke about the truth. He taught us to give up negativity because it only brings grief. We are not taught to give up what brings happiness, rather we are taught to give up what brings suffering. If we do this then we will find peace and happiness and this is the reason why we are taught to do what is positive and to avoid what is negative.[35]

III. The Action Ripening for Oneself. The third section describes how karma is always experienced by its creator. A loose translation would be a boomerang that always returns to the person who throws it.

If we consider our actions and we ask, "Who will experience the results?" It is said that the earth will not experience the results, neither will stones or somebody else. The result will inevitably return to oneself, to the same body considered the self. If you have done something then the result will not be experienced by your children or by your neighbor, which is totally impossible. Whatever you do will necessarily come back to you; you and nobody else will have to experience the result. And there is no possible mistake; everything will return to you just because you were the one who did it.

IV. Strict Result. The fourth section deals with experiencing the effect accordingly and describes the correspondence between the quality of the action and the quality of the result. We are told that any virtuous actions will bring happiness as a result and that any non-virtuous actions will bring suffering as a result. Some people may think that this is the general rule, but there are exceptions. They may think that some virtuous actions are likely to bring suffering and that maybe some non-virtuous actions will bring happiness. In fact, there are no exceptions to the rule of correspondence. Whenever the intention and action are pure then anything that arises can only be happiness and never suffering. But whenever the intention and action are impure then anything that arises can only be suffering and nothing else. This is the inevitable correspondence between actions and results; the same quality in the action will be in the result.[36]

In the *Surata-Requested Sutra* (Tib. *Nepay Zhupai Do*) the Buddha said, "From the hot seed will be born hot fruits. From the sweet seed will be born sweet fruits. With these analogies, the wise understand the maturation of non-virtue is hot and the maturation of white deeds is sweet." This means that if you plant a seed that has the potential of being hot and spicy then the fruit that grows out of it will be hot and spicy, and if you plant a seed that has the potential of being sweet then the fruit that grows out of it will be sweet. In the same way, the quality of our actions determines the effect, just as the example of the seed. Negative actions give rise to suffering and positive actions give rise to happiness. There is no other way; there can be no mistake in the way in which an action is linked with its result.

V. Great Ripening Arises from Small Actions. The fifth section on karma tells us that even a very small cause can give rise to a very large result. This is something that we might not necessarily believe; we may think that if we do something small it will produce a small effect, but that isn't so. Take the action of killing, which takes place in an instant. That action can give rise to suffering extending over uncountable ages. Or if you consider a good action, which may not take very long or need a great deal of effort, however the result may give rise to happy experiences that go on for a very long time. Therefore, even small virtues may have a beneficial effect for many lives, and even a small negative action may generate suffering for many lives. This means that we shouldn't neglect even the smallest virtue and negative action. We should do our best to avoid the smallest negative action and do our best to practice the smallest virtue.

VI. The Inevitability of Actions. The sixth section of this topic deals with actions that are never lost; karma is never exhausted. Whatever we do will always bring a result. We can't expect actions to be lost somewhere and not to have any consequences.

There are two exceptions to this rule, namely consciously remedying something we have done in the past or creating an antidote to a previous action.[37] For instance, if a negative action is purified the result is destroyed. This isn't because the action itself is lost, rather we have consciously made an effort to erase the former negative action. The opposite is the case too. We may have done something positive but later regretted it. By regretting the former positive action it is erased and will not bear fruits. Apart from these two exceptions (of actually intervening with the process of former actions), all actions done will necessarily come to full maturity; they will necessarily generate consequences. It might take a very long time but nothing will ever be lost. The *Smaller [Type of] Close Contemplation* says: "Fire may become cold, the wind may be caught with a lasso, sun and moon may fall down on the earth, but the result of karma is infallible."

This concludes the explanation of the sixth chapter,
on karma and its result, from
The Jewel Ornament of Liberation.

Chapter 7
The Instructions on Meditation On Loving-kindness & Compassion
The Remedy to Attachment to the Pleasure of Peace

If we want to achieve ultimate and everlasting happiness we have to become a Buddha, and in order to become a Buddha we have to find the means to accomplish that. This involves getting rid of all the adverse conditions that hinder us from becoming a Buddha. If it is possible to remove the adverse conditions then it is possible to accomplish Buddhahood. In order to remove the adverse conditions it is important to clearly know what they are, which is why these have been discussed. The first adverse condition preventing us from working towards Buddhahood is being attached to the pleasures of this life. The second is being attached to the idea that existence on the whole is pleasant and happy. We now know that the remedy for the first is meditating on impermanence and for the second meditating on all the faults inherent to samsaric existence and on karma, the relationship between the cause and effect of all our actions. Now, the third adverse condition that stops us from working towards Buddhahood is being attached to the bliss of peace one tries to find for oneself. The remedy for this adverse condition is meditating on loving kindness and compassion.

The goal of peace is a very honorable goal; it is everyone's wish. Peace here means to become free from all the sufferings of conditioned existence, to achieve liberation. What is wrong is being attached to the bliss of that state of peace. Everyone is trying to work towards freedom from suffering and towards happiness and this happiness is only found when we achieve liberation. So, liberation in itself is not negative and wrong, it is not a mistake. The problem isn't liberation from happiness but having the wrong approach to liberation, which arises from a lack of courage and determination on the part of the person who seeks happiness and peace. This person is only trying to find liberation for him or herself. They don't realize that it is the universal concern of all living beings to seek happiness and freedom from suffering. They think liberation is only their personal wish, that only they want this. The right approach to peace and liberation is recognizing that everyone wishes to achieve this. So when we work towards this goal it should not only be for our personal welfare but in order to help all others. It is, in fact, our responsibility to help others achieve the same state of peace and liberation.

When someone lacks basic kindness and concern for other living beings and neglects others completely, only thinking of their own peace and happiness, then that is a very narrow attitude and signifies the absence of mental strength, courage and determination. Such an attitude isn't really the most worthy attitude. What is achieved with such an attitude is not the final result. Of course, there will be an achievement but not the ultimate achievement we all seek. This is the reason why *The Jewel Ornament of Liberation* teaches that we need to give up clinging to the happiness of peace, the state of quiescence.

If somebody wants to be able to really help other living beings, then they need the pure motivation of loving-kindness and compassion. Loving-kindness is the wish that other beings find happiness and compassion is the wish to help others find freedom from suffering. If someone has these two qualities in their mind then they will be able to be altruistic; their actions will not be selfish or self-centered but will always be turned towards others. With such qualities in mind we will try to help others be happy through loving-kindness and we will try to help them remove suffering through compassion. These are the two instructions that are given in the chapter on how to remedy attachment to the bliss of peace.

I. The Practice of Loving Kindness. The study and practice of immeasurable loving-kindness is summarized in six points: the classification, the object, the identifying characteristic, the method of practice, measure of the practice, and the benefits.

A. The Classification. There are three categories of loving-kindness: loving-kindness with *sentient beings* as its object, loving-kindness with phenomena as its object, and loving-kindness without any frame of reference.

The first of the three categories of loving-kindness is focusing on sentient beings. This means that we are considering sentient beings and the suffering they go through and we have the strong wish to help them accomplish the true happiness of Buddhahood.

The second category is loving-kindness concerning the nature of all things. This means that we realize that sentient beings suffer because they don't really understand the way things are. They don't know about karma and they don't know what things to engage in and what things to avoid. They do not know the cause of suffering which they create again and again and they do not know the cause of happiness and therefore do not create it. Because of their ignorance as to the way phenomena truly are they remain in suffering and do not find the happiness that they are actually seeking. This aspect of loving-kindness is finding the wish to help sentient beings understand what the causes of suffering and happiness are so that they can lead their lives accordingly and find their goal, which is true happiness.

The third category of loving-kindness is the most important and is called loving-kindness without any reference. It may sound contradictory that there is loving-kindness without an object and we may wonder how can there be that feeling without an object. In fact, there is no contradiction. For example, if we take someone who is asleep and dreaming, they might suddenly see a frightening wild animal or poisonous snake in their dream and experience great fear. If we consider what is really happening though, then there is no reason for their fear because they are actually sleeping in a warm and comfortable bed without being threatened by anything. If they have fear then it is due to the illusory projection arising from their mind that makes them see different dangers threatening them. If somebody was watching the person with the nightmare and had clairvoyance, then they would have love and compassion for that person experiencing the nightmare. They wouldn't feel love and compassion by thinking, "Oh, the poor person is going to be eaten up by a wild animal or bitten by a poisonous snake." Instead they would feel love and compassion because they would know that the dream is only a hallucination and that the fear is only due to that person's own mental projections. The clairvoyant would feel love and compassion for this reason only, not because they considered the threats real. In the same way, when the Buddhas and bodhisattvas see us suffering they do not think that our suffering is real, substantial and everlasting. They know it is illusory and will end. They know that we do not realize the illusory nature of our suffering and therefore that is the reason why we are entangled in samsara and suffer. They realize that we are frightened due to being in a state of illusion and therefore generate loving-kindness and compassion for us.

B. The Object: All Sentient Beings. Towards whom is loving-kindness directed? It is directed towards all living beings without any exception. Generally, we are quite capable of having loving feelings for some people such as our children, our partner, or for our friends. But we are usually unable to feel unbiased loving kindness and discriminate between those we love and those we dislike. True loving-kindness is impartial and the object of loving-kindness is all living beings without exception.

C. The Identifying Characteristic: The Mind Wishing that They Meet with Bliss. The third aspect is the form loving-kindness takes and that is the wish to help others find happiness.

D. Method of Practice: Reflecting on the Kindness of Beings Because Love Depends on Being Mindful of Kindness as its Root. The fourth point describes the technique of meditating on loving-kindness. In general, there are many different ways to meditate on loving-kindness but the one described here is based upon meditating on the kindness of our own mother. Once we have developed the feeling of loving-kindness for our mother then we can extend this feeling to more and more beings. This is really the best type of meditation on loving-kindness; it is very special. However, we should remember that nowadays this isn't something that people really like. It seems that in modern times parents aren't always regarded as they should be. In many cases people don't really care for and love their parents as they should. But this isn't how things should be. It is a mistake in our attitude not to feel love for our parents.

We should realize that the way we treat our parents has consequences upon our own life. If we cannot be kind and loving to our parents then we will experience negative results, but if we are kind and loving to them then we will experience happy results. There is a nice story to illustrate this point.

Once upon a time there was a man called Mr. Moon. He had a nice child, named Little Moon after his father. He was a very bright and clever boy. There was a nice old grandpa in this family who loved Little Moon immensely and Little Moon also loved his grandpa. They both got along really well and had lots of fun together.

One day the grandpa got blind and his son, Mr. Moon, got fed up, neglected his father and complained that his father is always in the house, in the way, and making life difficult. Mr. Moon decided to do something about this. He made a big basket, placed his father into the basket and left him in it in a cave at the back of the house.

Little Moon asked his father, "Where is grandpa today? I haven't seen him." He kept on asking the same question until Mr. Moon replied that he wasn't home.

"Where is he?" asked Little Moon.

"In the cave behind the house," answered Mr. Moon. "I had to tie him up in a basket and leave him there."

Little Moon was very shocked and replied, "Isn't it a nasty place for grandpa? It must be cold and dirty there."

Mr. Moon told his son, "It doesn't really matter because your grandad is too much trouble in the house. He will be all right out there."

Little Moon wasn't convinced at all and asked, "Daddy, where did you put the basket?"

Mr. Moon answered, "I don't know. I must have left it somewhere. Why did you ask?"

The child answered, "I want the basket because it will be useful for me some day. Later on when you go funny I am going to need that basket to carry you into the cave."

Of course, when Mr. Moon heard this he was very shocked and suddenly realized how nasty it was to be doomed to the dirty cave behind the house. He took his father out of the cave and brought him back into the house.

This story is an example showing that whatever we do to our parents will in some way eventually return to us. We should also realize that our loving-kindness should go beyond our parents. Once we are aware of how kind our parents have been to us then the feeling of love will naturally arise and we can develop it more and more.

Four Contemplations

The meditation itself begins with our mother. We have to become aware of our mother's kindness towards us. The way we become aware of this kindness is by four contemplations. The first is that it was our mother who gave us our body. The second is that she went through many hardships on our behalf. The third is that she looked after us and preserved our life. The fourth is that she taught us everything we need to know about life; she educated us.

First, the kindness of giving us a body: presently we have this very extraordinary human body that is so precious and has all the right opportunities and freedoms. We can practice the dharma with this body and it is the very best tool we could find in order to reach liberation. It is said that this human body is even more precious than a wish-fulfilling gem. We have all of this through our mother's kindness. Even if we are someone who does not follow the spiritual path, still this worldly body is better than other forms of existence. Comparing our condition with that of animals, they are more dependent on others for food and safety and they live in a state of stupidity and restrictions in many ways, whereas our human life is much better. We owe all this to our mother's kindness.

Second, our mother has gone through very many hardships and difficulties on our account. What was it like when we were born? Did we come into this world wearing nice clothes and jewels, carrying enough money and food with us? Of course we didn't. We came into this world naked and empty-handed. In fact, we mainly consisted of a mouth and stomach. Did we have any friends and acquaintances when we came into this world? No, we were completely alone. When we came into this world without any connections our mother didn't ask where we came from or about our background. She knew nothing about us, we were a complete stranger to her. She took this stranger and thought, "That is my boy" or "That is my girl." When this stranger was hungry she fed us, when thirsty she nourished us, and when cold she gave us clothes and so on. Our mother looked after us to make us feel happy and comfortable in all possible ways. As we grew up our mother made sure that we would not be destitute and tried to provide the right environment.

Was it easy for our mother to provide for us in all possible ways? We shouldn't think so because she was probably depriving herself in many moments so that she could make it nice for us. For instance, she may have deprived herself to make sure we always had nice and tasty food. Maybe she did the same with clothes and money and other things. She probably continually felt, "Maybe I shouldn't use this for myself, but I should keep it for my child." She probably made a lot of sacrifices to keep us happy and well.

The same applies to our possessions. If you think about how much she must have safeguarded for us. If somebody tried to take away something she owned she probably would have fought to save it for us. When it came to us she gave us everything she had. She even deprived herself of things so that she could give to us. This is how we should consider the kindness she had for us.

How could we ever tolerate that someone like this should be unhappy or suffer? We should really do everything we can to make someone like that happy. This is the way to meditate on loving-kindness, thinking of the sacrifices of our mother.

The third way to contemplate our mother's kindness is to be aware of what she did for us to preserve our life. When we were first born we couldn't look after ourselves at all. Our body was there, but we couldn't do anything for ourselves. We couldn't feed ourselves, we couldn't drink on our own, we couldn't stand on our legs, we couldn't make sure that we didn't fall into dangerous places and the like. We were in a worse situation than a worm, than the most miserable of worms, because a worm can move and walk on its own when born and can find its own food. When we were young it would have been very easy for us to lose this human body quickly. We could have crept straight into a fire or we could have fallen into a well. If we had broken our leg or gone blind we couldn't have done anything for ourselves. We were very much like a stupid person because we couldn't speak for ourselves. What our mother did was to take this stranger who was deaf and dumb and cradled us on her lap. She fed us, milked us and helped us in every possible way. All the time she made sure that we were safe and that no accidents like creeping into a fire, falling into a well or the like would befall us.

In fact, we can't really imagine all she did in order to preserve our lives. If we are what we are now and can live in the world, talk with people, do lots of things, all the more to practice the dharma, we owe all this to her kindness because she carefully saved our lives for us while we were totally unable to do anything for ourselves.

The fourth way to reflect on our mother's kindness is to think that she was the one who educated us; she showed us the world and how to live in it. When we were born we could not think properly; we had no experiences and no special skills. Even though we might have felt that our parents were friendly and helping we had no way of responding because we didn't even know how to formulate our thoughts and could only cry and scream all the time. Maybe we could kick around with our legs but that was all. At that point she taught us everything. When we didn't know how to walk she taught us, when we couldn't speak but could only grunt she taught us how to speak, so that little by little we became capable of expressing ourselves and doing things for ourselves. We owe all of this to the kindness of our parents. We should think about this and not be indifferent to such kindness. How could we help not loving our parents after all they have done for us? How could we bear not trying to do something for their happiness after all they did for us?

This is how we can meditate again and again in order to develop loving-kindness towards our parents. Yet, we shouldn't do it out of a sense of duty or obligation, thinking. "I have to meditate on loving-kindness," but we should do it because we realize that it is true and tremendous gratitude should naturally spring from our mind. That is the right way to feel because it is the way things are. If we can understand this then loving-kindness will be natural and will develop more and more.

We should also understand that the mother we have in this life has probably been our mother many times, life after life. Each time she has undergone the same hardships with us as she did in this life. We can even have a broader vision by thinking that all other beings have probably been our mother at one point or another. We have been spinning around in samsara for countless millions of years during which there was enough time for each and every living being to have been our parent over and over again. Every time each has had the same kindness for us as the mother we think of in this life.

When we think about all these living beings that went through so many difficulties for us, how could we forget about them? How could we be so ungrateful as to forget about all the goodness and kindness they showed us? If we become more aware of this then gradually we will be able to develop a loving attitude towards all living beings without making any limitations.

When we practice this meditation it applies to our present mother. It is true that there are many kinds of mothers and it is possible that some mothers aren't as kind to their children as others. Even if a mother is not particularly kind to a child, which is due to the fact that she didn't want the child in the first place, she will still have the two basic types of kindness of a mother, which is to give us a body and to put up with a lot of difficulties. No matter how bad a mother was, she will always have had these two kindnesses for her child and they provide a basis for meditation.

E. Measure of the Practice. Next the text explains the indications of loving-kindness we have within. The measure of having this quality is that the wish we have that others be happy is the same as the wish for ourselves to be happy; we do as much for other's happiness as we do for ourselves. The presence of this wish indicates the presence of loving-kindness. Loving-kindness is perfected when we no longer speak about or are concerned with our own happiness but only with that of others' happiness. We have to practice until we reach that level.

F. The Benefits. It is said that loving kindness is the source of all happiness for oneself and for others. As is stated in the *Precious Jewel Garland*: "One will be loved by the gods and human beings and will also be protected by them, will achieve mental peace and happiness, will not be harmed by poisons or weapons, will achieve his wishes without effort, and will be reborn in the Brahma world. Even one who is not liberated from samsara will obtain these eight benefits of loving-kindness."

There are two qualities to be developed, that of loving-kindness and compassion. We have seen that the practice of loving-kindness is based upon the wish that others be happy and find the causes of happiness. When loving-kindness is perfected in this way then the practice of compassion is not difficult. Compassion is the wish that they be free from suffering and its causes. Next is a detailed description of compassion.

II. Compassion. The study and practice of immeasurable compassion is completely summarized in six points: the classification, the object, the identifying characteristic, the method of practice, measure of the practice, and the benefits.

In general, compassion is an essential quality, so it is very important to develop compassion. We usually have compassion for ourselves, which is the wish to be free from suffering and to achieve happiness. But the meaning of compassion here is to apply this wish to others, to have empathy with them. This is how compassion should be: wishing to help others be free from suffering and to find happiness. Whether the beings are those we know or not, whether they are kind to us or not, our compassion should extend to all sentient beings without any exception. In previous lives we have been closely linked with all beings without exception. So all beings were kind and loving to us at some point. If we think of our closest friend, that closeness has previously been shared with others also. If we were to forget others and think, "What difference does it make to me if they suffer?" That attitude would be wrong because all other beings have helped and been kind to us before. That is why we need to develop compassion to all beings without exception.

A. The Classification. There are three types of compassion. The first is with reference to other beings, the second is compassion with reference to the nature of things, the way in which things are, and the third is compassion without a referential object.

The first compassion includes any sentient being in the state of suffering. So, all those who are undergoing any kind of suffering at the moment are the objects of compassion. This means that we think about beings in the hell realms, of the torture from heat and extreme cold they experience. We think about the craving spirits who are tormented by unbearable hunger and thirst all the time. We think about the animals that suffer due to their own stupidity. We think about human beings who suffer due to their excessive activities and constant frustrations. We think about all the sufferings that beings undergo; they are the objects of our compassion. We think that we want to help them become free from their sufferings.

The second type of compassion is focused on the nature of things. Presently some people may seem to be happy and even though they do not suffer they carry within them the cause for future suffering. They really do not know how to create their own future happiness and how to avoid their future suffering. Instead of finding the happiness they so strongly seek they will end up suffering and will have to undergo pain that they do not want. This is the second way to contemplate compassion, by focusing on the nature of things that remains unknown to beings, the reasons why they suffer.

The third type of compassion has no referential object. Just as in the case of loving-kindness, it might seem contradictory to speak about compassion without a referential object. It seems that unless we have a goal in our mind we cannot really speak about compassion and vice versa, for example, if we have compassion, then we are referring to someone special. So this might seem to be a contradiction, but, in fact, it isn't. If we look carefully, all beings are in the state of suffering in one way or another. But suffering is not real; suffering has no substance. And it is by the virtue of the fact that suffering has no substantiality that it can be eliminated, that it can be removed. If suffering were real and lasting there would be no way to overcome it. Furthermore, if it were real then compassion would be useless because there would be no way to get out of suffering. However, things are not like that. The nature of suffering is not real; the very essence of suffering is emptiness. This is why it can be eliminated. In that case compassion is justified: It is more than justified, it is necessary. This type of compassion is directed towards those who think that they are suffering although their suffering has no reality. This is the compassion of Buddhas and bodhisattvas who know that the nature of suffering is delusory but at the same time see that beings believe they are experiencing real suffering.

B. The Object: All Sentient Beings. The second of the six points speaks about the object of compassion. It is said that the object of compassion should be all sentient beings without any exception, without any bias and without discrimination. Why is this? Due to the way we experience life it seems to us that there are people we have a different relationship with. We are close to some people who we love and call "our family" and "our friends." We feel responsible for them and want them to be happy and free from suffering. Then there are others we are not close to, who we don't love and may even feel indifferent towards. We may even think that they are our enemies and think that their suffering is of no concern to us. We think that we have no responsibility to help them. Even more so, we might even feel happy by bringing more suffering upon someone we consider our enemy. However, there is no justification in our discrimination. If we look closely, the very idea of "friend" and "enemy" is something that has no substantial reality. There is a short story to illustrate this.

The Buddha had a disciple called "The Realized Katayana." One day Katayana went out to beg for alms and he happened to meet a family and experienced a scene in which he saw a father seated and eating a fish, a dog on the ground watching him, and a son on his lap who he was cuddling. He saw the dog try to nibble at the little meat left on the bone of the fish and the man then kicked the dog. Since Katayana was a realized being and clairvoyant he could see the relationship between these beings. He saw that the fish being eaten was the father of the man eating it in his previous life, the dog being kicked was the man's mother in a previous life, and the child being cuddled on the lap of his father was once his worst enemy. So Katayana witnessed this strange scene of a father eating his own father's body, kicking his own mother, and cuddling his enemy on his lap. Also, by way of these relationships, the dog, once the wife, was now eating what had once been her own previous husband's flesh. Katayana realized how everything in the world is so impermanent and unstable. He realized the instability of conditioned existence and expressed his experience in poetry.

What we need to understand from this story is that there is no need to think so strongly in terms of friends and enemies, because all such things aren't really valid. In fact, everything changes. In this life we might have a very intimate friend who we do not want to be separated from. But, we don't know what will happen. Maybe in a few months or years this person may turn into an enemy. Also there might be somebody who is our worst enemy right now, somebody we cannot even bear to see or think of. After some months or years they may very well become a close and dear friend. This clearly shows that the strong clinging to a friend and all efforts invested to strengthen that relationship are useless in the light of what may happen later, when that friend turns into an enemy or vice versa. All the time wasted on hating someone we considered an enemy and everything we do to make life difficult for them is useless in the light of what may happen later, when that enemy turns into a friend. So, it is a mistake to make strong differentiations between people, considering some as friends and others as enemies.

Really, the feeling of wanting to help others to be happy and free from suffering is a feeling we should have for everyone without any distinction.

C. The Identifying Characteristic: Wishing that They May be Free from Suffering and its Cause. The third point speaks about the aspects that compassion takes on. This aspect is the wish that other beings be free from suffering. But it goes even further than that; it is not just wishing others to be free from suffering but also free from the causes of suffering. It is good to wish beings be free from suffering, but if these beings continue producing the causes of suffering then later they will still have to encounter suffering and deal with it when it arises. That is why true compassion is the wish that others be free from suffering as well as the causes of suffering.

D. Method of Practice: Applying Compassion towards One's Root Mother in the Meditation. The fourth point speaks about the way to meditate upon compassion, which techniques we can use. Just like in the meditation on loving-kindness, this meditation is practiced in connection with our mother in this life. However, it is also possible to use any person very close to you. It could be an intimate friend, your child or someone very close. We imagine this person sitting in front of us and suddenly a gang of aggressive people we recognize as the enemies of the one we love rush in and start to beat up the person we love; they start to break their limbs, put them in boiling water or burn them. We immediately imagine what horrific pain this must cause and feel spontaneous compassion; we can't even put up with the idea of someone so dear to us suffering in such a horrible way.

We must realize that presently there are many beings in the hell realms who were once our mothers and fathers, our very dear friends, our children, the ones we loved, and that they are now undergoing the awful tortures of being cut to pieces, of being boiled or frozen alive. Now that they are undergoing all of these horrors, how can we possibly remain indifferent? How could we not want to immediately do something for them? How could we not want them to be free from such torture? This contemplation will make us feel that we want to do anything to free them from their terrible situation. This is what is known as meditation on compassion with respect to those suffering in the hells.

The second step of meditation still involves seeing the person we love in front of us; our mother, father, friend, whomever we choose. Then we imagine that this person looks starved and thirsty. As a result they have strong physical pain. We can also feel their fear and anguish. They are all alone and nobody is there to help them in any way. Of course, when we see this we have compassion, we want this terrible pain to stop. In the same way, once we feel this we realize that all those who were once so dear to us in previous lives may now be living as craving spirits. As such they have to go through all the torments of starving, thirst, frightened in their mind, sweating in heat or freezing from cold. We feel that there is nothing we wouldn't do to stop this situation for them, to free them from such terrible pain. This is known as compassion with respect to the suffering of the craving spirits.

The third step of meditation still involves seeing the person we love in front of us. This person has become dumb in both senses: they can't talk anymore or express anything and they can't think properly. Others come along and force this person we love to work very hard; they are going to use this person, beat and maybe even kill them. This person will be totally helpless. There is nothing this person can do because they are completely dependent and helpless. Of course, when we see this we have compassion and will realize that there are many, many beings who were once our very dear loved ones who are now born as animals and are forced to work for others; they are beaten up, they are abused, their limbs are broken, their flesh is cut and finally they are ruthlessly killed. How can we bear that all those beings who have been our dear loved ones go through such horrors? Would there be anything we wouldn't do to free them? This is meditation with respect to the sufferings of animals. It is the meditation of compassion to free beings from the sufferings of the animal world.

These first three aspects of meditation show how we can try to develop compassion with respect to beings who are in the three lower realms, where suffering is very intense, very acute and very obvious. If we think of the three higher realms where gods, demigods and humans live then we might think that there is no need to generate compassion for them because they are in a much better condition than those in the lower realms. But, in fact, it is still necessary to develop compassion towards them.

For example, suppose there are people we love very dearly and they go blind overnight and suddenly can't see anything anymore and nearby their home is an abyss that they do not know about. Because they can't see and don't have the faintest idea of the nearby abyss they don't care and aren't worried. Nobody is around to warn them and they remain in total ignorance of the danger. Of course, it is most likely that they will fall into the abyss because they don't know and can't see. We will be frozen with horror when we think of that situation. This thought will arouse great compassion in us and we will want to stop those people from running into so much danger. This example can be applied to the situation of the beings in the higher realms. Gods, demigods and human beings in the short term seem to have a good deal; they do not seem to have all the terrible suffering that one finds in the lower realms. But still, they are constantly producing the causes for future suffering because they do not know how to give up the causes of suffering. They haven't the faintest idea now that they are creating more suffering for the future and they have no connection with a spiritual friend who can guide them. They have nobody who can stop them from heading toward the lower realms. So, although it is certain that they will fall into the lower realms, there is nobody who points it out to them and who prevents them from falling.

When we realize this then we feel that there is nothing we wouldn't do to stop them from falling into the lower realms and that there is nothing we wouldn't do to help them get out of that terrible situation. This is meditation on compassion with respect to beings in the higher realms.

Those are four ways of meditating on compassion, of trying to develop compassion towards other sentient beings. The first way is to generate compassion that wishes to protect beings from the sufferings of heat and cold in the hells. The second way is to meditate in order to feel compassion that wishes to protect beings from the sufferings of hunger and thirst in the realm of the craving spirits. The third way is to develop compassion with a view to protect beings from the suffering of stupidity and enslavement in the realm of the animals. The fourth way is to develop compassion with respect to beings in the higher realms who are doomed due to their ignorance; we meditate to protect them from the ignorance which presents the danger of them falling into the great abyss of samsara. To protect them from this we develop this last aspect of compassion.

E. Measure of the Practice. The fifth point of the chapter on compassion shows the measure of perfection of compassion, at which point compassion is completely accomplished. This is when you genuinely feel a strong wish to protect all beings from suffering and to help them to be happy.

F. The Benefits. The sixth point of this chapter explains the benefits that come from having the quality of compassion. The *Expression of the Realization of Chenrezig* says, "If you had just one quality, it would be as if all the Buddhas' Dharma were in your palm. What quality is that? Great compassion." This means that if we were to hold one quality that represents all the other qualities of the Buddha in the palm of our hand, it would be compassion. As soon as there is compassion, then automatically all the other qualities of the Buddha would be present. This shows the ultimate benefit of possessing loving-kindness and compassion.

Eight Immediate Benefits

In addition there are more immediate benefits. If someone has a loving and compassionate mind it will immediately affect other beings; it will bring about eight kinds of benefits.

The first is that if we are loving and compassionate then everyone else will be kind and loving towards us. This is easy to understand because the reason why others may be nasty to us is because we ourselves are aggressive and jealous. This causes us to harm others. If we perceive others as enemies then of course they will perceive us as enemies too. They will also start disliking and hating us because we have generated the feeling of hatred to begin with. Eventually it will seem that they are doing everything to harm us. On the other hand, if we have a very loving mind then others will feel the same towards us. It is like a boomerang, whatever you do returns to you. So, if we are kind and loving towards a person we will surely receive loving-kindness in return. If we love one hundred people, then they will love us in return. If we are able to love ten thousand, one million or an infinite number of beings, then they will all be loving in return. They will respond to our love and give it back to us. That is why there is no way that others cannot help but love someone who has a loving and compassionate mind; they will want to help and benefit such a person in many ways.

The second good quality that comes from possessing loving-kindness and compassion is that everybody will try to help and protect us. This is easy to understand because if we are always intent upon harming others and feeling hatred towards others then those people will turn into our enemies.

People will not wish to help and protect us if we hate them. If we try to make it hard for them, of course they will respond in the same way. On the other hand, if we are loving towards someone, that person will become our friend. If we are in difficulty, pain, trouble and suffering, then automatically our friends will want to help us; they will do anything to help us become free from that suffering. So if we love other beings then they are our friends; they will try to protect us from suffering and difficulties.

The third positive result of compassion is that we will be happy and mentally at ease. If one wonders what the cause of various feelings of mental happiness and anguish are, the answer is it comes from the way we relate to other people. If we think that people are our enemies and they are causing us all sorts of trouble then we will constantly have worries and tribulations with them. We will think about their harsh treatment in the past, what a tough time they are giving us now, and what a terrible time they have in store for us in the future. Such thoughts trouble our mind and cause much unhappiness. If we love others and if we do not consider anyone our enemy then we aren't going to experience mental anguish because we aren't worried whether others are going to hurt us or not. When all others are like friends, our mind feels relaxed and at ease because there is no grinding anguish and pain in our mind.

The fourth positive result of compassion is that we would be happy and at ease in the body. What is true of the mind is also true of the body. If we have enemies, people we are fighting with, then we are bound to experience negative results, even physically. If there is nobody who harms us then we will not experience physical pain coming from enemies. So, even physically we would be better off if we were kind and loving.

The fifth and sixth benefits are freedom from fear of poison and weapons. If we are an angry and hateful person then this will bring many enemies. If we have many enemies then they are going to try to eliminate us by using poison or weapons and we will be in fear of what they will resort to in order to eliminate us. But if we are a loving person, if our relationships are kind and loving, then these people will automatically be our friends, so there is no danger or fear of poison and weapons. These dangers automatically disappear because these people will only relate to us as friends.

The seventh benefit is that all our efforts will be successful with only a minimum of effort; it will be very easy for us to succeed in anything we set out to do. The reason for this is that normally if we are hateful then we have no friends and when we have to do things we have to rely upon our own efforts. If we do something alone there is no guarantee that we will succeed and we will probably have to put a lot of effort into achieving our goal. But if we are a loving person, then from among the hundred or thousand people we love some will help us, at least one is ready to help us, making it easier for us. Any of our endeavors will easily and automatically succeed because there will always be one or many friends who help us.

The eighth benefit of possessing loving-kindness and compassion is that we will have a good body in our next life. This is because having a good form of life depends upon one's motivation and actions. If the quality of our motivation and actions is always pure – loving and kind – then the result will be very positive. In fact, the new life we take will be the very expression or the very embodiment of the loving quality of our mind and actions in our present life. This clearly shows what a waste it is to spend this precious life with negative or indifferent motivations. So, in order to get a very good form of life in our next birth we need to cultivate a very positive and pure intention.

This describes the eight kinds of short term results arising from possessing loving-kindness and compassion and concludes the topic on the meditation on loving kindness and compassion.

This concludes the explanation of the seventh chapter,
on loving-kindness and compassion, from
The Jewel Ornament of Liberation.

Developing an Attitude Towards Bodhichitta[38]

The Remedy to Not Knowing the Method of Practice for Accomplishing Buddhahood

The objective behind the pure attitude, the pure motivation of bodhichitta,[39] is to accomplish Buddhahood for the sake of all sentient beings. How can this be done? What means lead one to accomplish it? As explained already there must be the right means to accomplish Buddhahood. Normally there are obstacles in the form of unfavorable conditions that stand in the way of accomplishing Buddhahood. If we can eliminate these obstacles then we will definitely accomplish Buddhahood.

As already explained, the first obstacle is clinging to the pleasures of this life, the second is remaining involved with the pleasures of existence in general, thinking that conditioned existence is a happy and pleasant state, and the third obstacle is being involved with a selfish type of peace. In addition, there is a specific remedy for each obstacle that makes it possible to eliminate each specific obstacle. These are the teachings on impermanence, the defects of samsaric existence together with karma and its result, and meditation on loving-kindness and compassion.

Now we turn to the fourth type of obstacle that has to be removed. Assume that someone is not clinging to the pleasures of this life, is not captivated by the idea that existence is a happy state, and does not aspire for a selfish state of peace. Will this person accomplish Buddhahood? No. Because, even though there may not be the impediments of the first three hindrances, there is still the obstacle of not knowing how to accomplish Buddhahood. Obviously we cannot accomplish Buddhahood if we don't know how.

So, it is necessary to eliminate this last obstacle of not knowing how to accomplish Buddhahood. The obvious remedy is to learn the way, the means, to accomplish Buddhahood. The means are a complete outline of the path from the moment one first resolves to accomplish Buddhahood up to the time when Buddhahood has been accomplished. All the various stages of the path are based upon the pure motivation of bodhichitta.

Among all the means that one has to know in order to accomplish Buddhahood, the main point is the very pure motivation, the mentality of enlightenment, the wish to accomplish Buddhahood for the sake of all sentient beings, which is the precious bodhichitta. It will be described in this section, which is divided into twelve points: The foundation, the essence, classification, objectives, the cause, from whom one receives it, the procedure, the benefits, the harm (of violating it), the cause of losing it, the means of regaining it, and the training.

The first point describes the basis for developing a pure state of mind, the pure motivation, which we will now examine.

I. The Foundation for Developing an Attitude Towards Bodhichitta. In this section on the foundation for developing an attitude towards supreme enlightenment, the *Jewel Ornament* describes what we need in order to have the right motivation as three requirements. The first requirement is that we should possess the bodhisattva (Mahayana) potential. The second is that we should have taken refuge in the *Three Jewels*. The third is that we should keep either of the seven forms of the *pratimoksha* precepts, the vows of discipline that are part of what is known as "individual liberation." The fourth is to have developed the aspiration for enlightenment.

A. Having the Mahayana Potential. First, consider the aspect of the necessary foundation, which is possessing the Mahayana potential. The first chapter of this text explained that all beings possess the innate potential for reaching Buddhahood, of which there are two aspects, the innate potential and the potential that is being developed. All beings possess the innate potential, which means that by their very nature all beings have the possibility of turning their minds towards Buddhahood and of practicing to accomplish that state. The only difference between beings is that some will use that potential, they will work on it and develop it, while others are not going to do that straight away. The second aspect of the potential is when we are working on it, when we awaken that potential. Working and awakening it means to actually start thinking about reaching Buddhahood, to turning our mind towards enlightenment. This is something that depends entirely upon our own way of thinking.

When we speak about the potential that is not awakened or the potential that is awakened, the latter should not be seen to be out of reach or something of great profundity. The awakened potential just means that we don't have to rely on extraordinary causes and conditions to awaken it; it simply means that we start thinking in terms of wanting to achieve enlightenment and wanting to practice the dharma in order to achieve this. As soon as we start thinking in those terms our potential is awakened. The awakening of that potential is not to be sought in any other way than just by the thought, "I want to achieve Buddhahood."

For some people this kind of thought will not arise. They will not think, "I want to practice the dharma. I want to achieve Buddhahood." This means that those people are not using the innate potential that they have; they are not awakening it because they don't have the intention to achieve enlightenment, they don't have the basic motivation. That is why they will not start practicing and why they will not achieve the results of the practice. As soon as somebody has the wish to practice and enters the mainstream of Mahayana then nobody could ever stop their progress on the path.

Chapter 8
Refuge & Precepts

B. Taking Refuge in the Three Jewels. The second aspect of the foundation for developing the mentality of enlightenment is the refuge. You may have been practicing the dharma for quite a long time and have taken refuge in the Three Jewels a long time ago. However, this is the section in the *Jewel Ornament* when this is explained. Some might feel that taking refuge is very elementary because you have heard about it often and done it a long time ago, but it might be very meaningful to look at refuge once again. Refuge is something that we will need all the time until we accomplish Buddhahood. From the moment we take refuge until we become a Buddha, we will still remain exposed to the sufferings of existence and will still need protection; we will still need the protection of refuge.

When we speak about refuge it has two aspects; it is possible to see it in two different ways. There is what is known as "the cause refuge" and "the result refuge." Result refuge is the more important of the two.

While we are in conditioned existence we have all sorts of fears, problems, difficulties and sufferings. All other beings also experience this. When will all this stop? When will the time come when we need not be afraid of suffering? It will only come when we accomplish Buddhahood. But the accomplishment of Buddhahood depends upon ourselves; it is entirely up to us whether we accomplish Buddhahood or not. If we try it is impossible not to succeed and if we don't try then there is no possibility to succeed. Even if we practiced towards Buddhahood while all beings in the universe were armed against us, still they couldn't prevent us from accomplishing Buddhahood. On the other hand, if we do not practice and all beings in the universe tried to help us, we couldn't achieve it. It depends entirely upon us whether we become a Buddha or not.

Becoming a Buddha means transcending all suffering and all the fears one has of suffering. It means eliminating all the negative aspects and revealing or manifesting all the qualities of Buddhahood. Yet all of this is something that is taking place within our mind. This is the reason why we have to work on our own mind by eliminating all faults and negative aspects and work on our own mind to make all the qualities manifest and bring them to full fruition.

When we achieve the ultimate fruit it is the time when we achieve the transcendence of all forms of suffering; it is the time of real refuge as perfect protection, the ultimate form of refuge.

Result refuge speaks of refuge in the ultimate sense. Cause refuge is the refuge in the temporary sense; it is the refuge that we need to work on, refuge in the Buddha, the dharma and the *sangha*. The Buddha is the one who shows us the path, the dharma is the path itself; and the sangha are the friends and companions who help us on the path. Refuge is an entire chapter in this book and consists of nine points: classification, working basis, the object, the time, the motivation, the procedure, the function, the precepts, and the benefits.

1. The Classification. The first point describes the classification of refuge, which has two aspects. These two aspects are conditioned by our meditation and by the quality of our attitude. If we are taking refuge for our own benefit, with a self-centered motivation, then refuge is common.[40] If we are taking refuge for the benefit of all other beings that have been our parents in previous lives then refuge is special.

2. The Working Basis. The second point concerns the basis for refuge, which is what kind of individual is considered the basis of refuge. Again we find two aspects, the common working basis and the special working basis. The individual as a common base is someone who will take common refuge, who seeks refuge out of fear of the suffering of conditioned existence. The individual as a special base are those who take special refuge and who possess the Mahayana potential and wish to bring all beings to enlightenment; such individuals have a very high and pure motivation.

3. The Object. The third point in the chapter on refuge describes the object of refuge, the ones we take refuge in. Again, there is a twofold division into the common and the special object.

The common object of refuge is threefold: There is refuge in the Buddha who represents the very best realization and the very best possible purity arising from having eliminated all faults. There is refuge in the second object, which is the dharma, the scriptures of the words of the Buddha as well as the realization of the teachings. The third object of refuge is the sangha, the sangha of ordinary beings and the sangha of realized beings. These are the Three Jewels or Three Rare and Precious Ones who are the objects of common refuge.

The special object of refuge is also threefold: The first are objects abiding directly in front of us. The second is the object of direct realization, the object when really understood. The third is the ultimate object of refuge, suchness.

The first objects of refuge are objects that are present and near us. This will be the Buddha (images of the Buddha), the dharma (the Mahayana scriptures) and the sangha (the community of bodhisattvas).

We were not present 2,500 years ago when the Buddha Shakyamuni was present and teaching in the world and we could not see him with the thirty-two special marks and eighty special signs. One could think, "Well, I didn't have the good karma to see him. Maybe I had the wrong karma and missed the chance. Since I missed the chance there is nothing I can do and therefore I cannot practice." However this isn't true. It makes no difference whether you meet Buddha Shakyamuni or not because the main thing, as already mentioned, is that practicing the teachings depends on nobody but us, not even on the presence of the Buddha. It depends upon us alone whether we practice or not and whether we are able to generate the necessary qualities of faith, of respect and devotion, of courage and diligence, and of understanding.

If we can have faith and devotion in the Buddha then this is something that will immediately give us the sufficient determination to practice the path. Faith in the Buddha is explained here in terms of very deep appreciation for what Buddha stands for, to acknowledge his great qualities for what they are. Once we acknowledge this, once we appreciate these qualities, we will have profound respect and great reverence for the Buddha. But more than that, we will have the aspiration to achieve the same thing ourselves. And out of this aspiration we will want to practice as intensively and strongly as we can. This will give rise to diligence. And once we have diligence, automatically understanding will arise. So, in this case, the Buddha must be seen as the one who can generate in us the feeling of intensive faith, devotion and the aspiration to practice.

The present case we are discussing is that of the Buddha as a material representation; it can be a statue or painting. But in any case, we shouldn't think that this representation is merely a material object, like a piece of paper or cloth or clay. We shouldn't look down on it but realize that it is the symbolic representation of the Buddha and as such it is something that can help generate the faith and aspiration we need to really practice the path. In this sense it makes no difference whether we met the Buddha when he was alive or not because the pure and perfect mind of the Buddha is never far away from beings. If somebody has faith, there is no difference whether the Buddha is near or far, present or not, or only in the form of a representation. The essential point is to develop the right faith and aspiration. This concerns the Buddha as the object in front of us.

The dharma is represented in the form of books that teach the dharma. As mentioned, we didn't have the opportunity to hear the Buddha speak the teachings during his life but we have the teachings in writing; we have all the books that convey the dharma. And these books are not just ordinary books. They are the written words that can bring us to find the very best possible form of happiness; they convey the deepest meaning and therefore we must regard them with sincere respect. This is the dharma in the form of the object in front of us, represented by the scriptures.

The sangha in front of us refers to the sangha consisting of ordinary beings, which includes our dharma friends. We shouldn't look at the sangha as ordinary friends because these are the friends on the extraordinary path to enlightenment.

So, these three objects are the objects in front of us, the visible objects.

The second aspect of the object of refuge is the object of direct realization. It is the Buddha who possesses the nature of the three kayas, the one who is the dharmakaya, the sambhogakaya and the nirmanakaya. The dharma of direct realization is the very nature of peace, the nature of what is beyond suffering, and this is nirvana. The sangha of direct realization are the realized bodhisattvas who are on the bodhisattva levels. This is the object of refuge in the light of direct realization.

The third aspect of refuge is the ultimate object of refuge. This goes back to what was mentioned earlier. Ultimately, Buddhahood is the refuge; when one becomes a Buddha it is real refuge. So refuge in the ultimate sense is becoming Buddha oneself, referred to as real refuge.

This concludes the section on the object of refuge, the common and the special refuge.

*4. **The Time.*** The fourth point explains the duration of refuge. Concerning common refuge, we take refuge for this life only, until our death. Concerning the special refuge, we take refuge from now until we accomplish full and perfect enlightenment, until we accomplish Buddhahood.

5. ***The Motivation.*** The fifth point describes the mental attitude for taking refuge, of which there are two types. In common refuge, one takes refuge in order to be protected from samsara for oneself. In special refuge, one takes refuge in order to be able to protect all other living beings from suffering.

6. The Ceremony. The sixth point describes the procedure of taking refuge. As previously explained, the main difference between the two forms of refuge is simply a difference of motivation. As far as the ceremony is concerned, the main thing is to repeat after the teacher the formula of taking refuge; one repeats after him that one is taking refuge in the Three Jewels. But repeating the words of refuge after the teacher should not only be a formal matter; it shouldn't just be a repetition of words. When one promises to take refuge it should come from deep within and be done sincerely and purely.

7. The Function. The seventh point describes the function of refuge. In the short term, the function of taking refuge is to find protection from the three lower states of existence (the result of the common refuge). In ultimate terms, it is to find protection from all the suffering of conditioned existence in samsāra through accomplishing Buddhahood (the result of the special refuge).

8. The Training. The eighth point describes the training and practice that follow the ceremony of taking refuge. The practice and training are there to help us work towards Buddhahood. When someone has taken refuge their situation has changed. What has changed is the necessity to engage in certain things and to avoid others in order to bring refuge to life and to realize it. If we follow these practices it is a sign that something has changed.

There are nine practices to train in, which are divided into three groups of three: Three general trainings, three specific trainings and three common trainings. The first group pertains to all of the Three Jewels as a whole. The second set pertains to each of the Three Jewels specifically. The third pertains to the extension of the Three Jewels, to things connected with the Three Jewels.

a) The Three General Trainings. The first set of three practices we must train in apply to the Three Jewels together and in general. The first training is that we should always try to make offerings to the Three Jewels, to the Buddha, to the dharma and to the sangha. Making offerings means to give whatever part of our belongings, possessions or wealth we are ready to give away to the Buddha, to the dharma and to the sangha.

However, we shouldn't misunderstand the nature of offerings. We are not making offerings because the objects of refuge are poor or destitute or in order to please them so that they are nice to us. We shouldn't think that if we don't give them anything they will be very mad at us and throw us into the lower realms of suffering. We are not making offerings for that purpose. We make offerings because the offerings are an expression of great appreciation towards the Three Jewels. We need to develop a great sense of appreciation, confidence, joy and enthusiasm towards the Three Jewels. In fact, the degree of appreciation, enthusiasm and confidence we have in the Three Jewels will determine the extent to which our own qualities can develop and increase. Without adequate appreciation, enthusiasm and so on, our qualities will not develop very well. That is why we make offerings, to enhance our joy and enthusiasm for practice and our appreciation of the Three Jewels. If we have a very strong sense of appreciation then we will be able to offer our most precious belongings to the Three Jewels. That is the first training, to continuously strive to make offerings to the Three Jewels.

The second training is to never forsake the Triple Refuge, to never to give up the Three Jewels. We realize that the highest anticipated advantages come from the Three Jewels; there is nothing else that could ever benefit us as the Three Jewels will. That is why we should never give up refuge in the Three Jewels at any cost.

The third training is to always remember the Three Jewels; to always keep the Three Jewels in mind because it is most important for us.

b) The Three Specific Trainings. The second set of three practices we have to train in apply to one of the Three Jewels specifically. The first training has to do with the Buddha. Once someone has taken refuge in the Buddha it is said that he or she should not go for refuge in any worldly god. Upon hearing this some people may find that this is a very sectarian or biased view. Although it might seem to be like this, it isn't so. When it is taught that we should not seek another refuge other than the Buddha it doesn't imply that the Buddha would be jealous and would not protect us. It is taught with respect to the very essence of the Buddha.

How does the Buddha protect us? He gives us the refuge through teaching us the right path, by showing us the right way. If we follow that way we will achieve the ultimate result, which is protection from all suffering. But if we do not follow that path then we cannot expect to be on the right path and to achieve freedom from suffering. So, as long as we take refuge in the Buddha we are on the right path. If we go for refuge in other deities, gods or whatever, then it doesn't mean that the Buddha would be upset or jealous and would stop protecting us, rather automatically we would deprive ourselves of the benefits that come from following the right path, the path shown by the Buddha.

The second training has to do with the dharma. Once someone has taken refuge in the dharma they should give up harming other beings. This may sound like a very difficult thing to do but actually it isn't that hard because, as said before, everything depends upon the quality of our motivation; everything is a matter of the right way of thinking. We should understand that the very essence, the heart of the dharma is the path that frees all beings from suffering. If we harm beings it automatically goes against the very essence of the path of dharma, which is intended to free us from suffering, not bring more suffering. That is the reason why if we take refuge in the dharma then automatically this will imply not harming other beings.

The third training concerns the sangha. It is said that once someone has taken refuge in the sangha they should not associate closely with those who are not in the dharma. We shouldn't misinterpret this to mean not associating closely with others such that we cannot eat, talk or spend time with them. Instead, it means that we should not adopt their views and behave like they do. Basically, why do we take refuge in the sangha? We take refuge in the sangha because they are the ones who can accompany us on the path and help us to practice properly. If we stop having a close association with sangha members then we won't have refuge in the sangha who can help and support us. If we associate with others then we start taking on their ways. That is the reason why we take refuge in the sangha and associate closely with them, otherwise refuge in the sangha is pointless.

c) The Three Common Trainings. The third set of three practices to train in has to do with anything related with the Three Jewels. The first one has to do with what is related to the Buddha. When we take refuge in the Buddha it is out of a sense of great appreciation for what the Buddha stands for and out of respect for his great qualities. You may wonder why we have to consider the Buddha as being so special. If we think of all living beings in general, and ourselves in particular, the only one who can really help us – not only in the immediate future but also ultimately – is the Buddha. Because of his outstanding qualities the Buddha can show the path that leads to ultimate liberation, ultimate happiness. This is a very special quality that no other being has. So, we have great respect for the Buddha and appreciate his excellence because of his outstanding qualities.

Once we know this then we should consider that anything representing the Buddha is an object of respect because it symbolizes the Buddha. If we see anything, a statue, picture or any form of representation of the Buddha, be it small or large, be it of ordinary or precious material, be it broken or only a splinter, we should always treat it as something very special because it represents what can render true protection from suffering and what can lead to ultimate happiness. It represents what can take us out of suffering towards goodness and happiness. This is a quality that we never find in anything else. This isn't a quality we would ever find in the most precious stones like a ruby, lapis-lazuli, or emerald; they won't contain such qualities. But here, even the tiniest fragment of a representation of the Buddha represents for us all the blessings of the Buddha. As explained earlier, what we need is strong appreciation for the qualities of the Buddha as well as sincere respect and aspiration towards them. So, any representation of the Buddha, even a fraction of a representation, can help us to develop this sense of appreciation and aspiration and so as such it should be respected and treated as something very special.

The second training has to do with everything connected with the dharma. The books and texts of the Buddha's teachings explain the path and provide instructions that lead to ultimate liberation and ultimate happiness, Buddhahood. Therefore they are very precious and we should have great respect for even one syllable of these texts.

The third training has to do with everything connected with the sangha. We should consider that anybody who helps us on the path of dharma – even if only to a very tiny extent – is a very special person and someone we have to respect because they are the ones who help us travel on the path to Buddhahood.

This set of instructions reminds us to respect anything that is connected with the Buddha, dharma and sangha.

9. The Beneficial Effects. The ninth point of the chapter on refuge describes the benefits that come from refuge, of which there are eight: we enter the Buddhist path, refuge becomes the foundation for all the other precepts, refuge becomes a cause for purification of all the previous negative actions accumulated, we cannot be affected by obstacles caused by either humans or non-humans, accomplishing all our wishes, we achieve the great cause of merit, not falling into the lower realms, and we quickly accomplish perfect enlightenment.

We can summarize this into the immediate and ultimate benefits. The immediate benefits are that we are protected from the sufferings of the three lower states. The ultimate benefit is that through taking refuge in the Three Jewels we are protected from all the sufferings of samsara, insofar as this will help us accomplish Buddhahood.

These nine points show us everything we need to know about refuge.

C. The Pratimoksha Precepts. The third aspect of the foundation for developing the mentality of enlightenment is that one should keep any of the seven forms of the pratimoksha precepts.[41] These are the vows of discipline that are part of what is known as "individual liberation" and can be divided into those for lay and ordained people.

You may wonder why we need one of these vows in order to cultivate bodhichitta. The *Jewel Ornament* gives three reasons why they are needed as a foundation: analogy, scriptural authority, and reasoning.

1. Analogy. We would not invite a great king to reside in a place where there is filth and which is unclean. The place should be clean and decorated with many ornaments. Similarly, the king of bodhichitta cannot be invited to reside where our body, speech and mind are not free from non-virtue and are stained with the dirt of negative karma. Instead, bodhichitta should be invited to abide where our body, speech and mind are free of the dirt of defilements and are fully adorned with the moral ethics of abandonment.

2. Scriptural Authority. The *Lamp for the Path to Enlightenment* (Tib. *Jangchub Lamgyi Dronma*) says, "One who keeps one of the seven pratimoksha precepts has the fortune to receive the bodhisattva precepts. Otherwise not." Therefore, any of the seven pratimoksha precepts is said to be the foundation.

3. Reasoning. When we take the pratimoksha precepts we abandon causing harm to others and harboring harmful intentions. The bodhisattva's vow causes us to benefit others. Without avoiding harm, there is no method of benefiting others.

This concludes the explanation of the eighth chapter,
on taking refuge and precepts, from
The Jewel Ornament of Liberation.

Chapter 9
Cultivation of Bodhichitta

The subtle topic of *The Jewel Ornament of Liberation* is the pure motivation, the wish for enlightenment. We have begun to examine the section that explains everything about this motivation and all the different aspects that come from it. We saw that the first of the twelve points in this section described the necessary foundation for that motivation. That presented the opportunity to explain refuge. Now we will discuss the next point, which deals with the essence of bodhichitta.

II. The Essence. The second point of this topic describes the essence of the motivation to accomplish enlightenment, which is bodhichitta. We continuously say that this is very important, but what actually is the motivation? It can be described in two points. Firstly, it can be described as the wish to accomplish the good of other beings and secondly as the wish to accomplish Buddhahood. Both aspects together represent what we call "bodhichitta" or the wish to accomplish enlightenment.

The first aspect of bodhichitta is compassion. This is the wish to accomplish the good of other beings, altruism inspired by compassion. The second aspect, the wish to accomplish

Buddhahood, is understanding or intelligence, which means that we do not try to free beings in a limited way and do not go about it in a restricted manner that doesn't function properly. Rather, we go about it using the very best tools, the best means that can really free beings and bring them to Buddhahood. So, compassion and understanding are the two aspects of the mentality of enlightenment, bodhichitta.

Bodhichitta is compared with the philosopher's stone, which you have probably heard about. It is said that when the philosopher's stone touches any other substance it can change that substance into pure gold. Even if only a small fraction of the philosopher's stone touches a huge amount of ordinary iron it would change that iron into gold. In the same way, the pure motivation of bodhichitta is very small – it is only a motivation – but it is enough to transform all suffering and all the negative experiences of beings into great happiness, into the ultimate happiness of Buddhahood. So, this is what bodhichitta, the pure motivation is.

III. The Classification. The third point of this section describes the different aspects of bodhichitta. There are three classifications of consideration: by way of simile, by way of the different levels, and by way of their different characteristics.

A. Simile. Twenty-two similes are given in *The Jewel Ornament of Liberation* to show the different aspects that bodhichitta takes on in the process of an individual's development from an ordinary being to Buddhahood. Arya Maitreya in the *Ornament of Clear Realization* (Tib. *Nuntok Gyan*) expressed them as: earth, gold, the moon, fire, a treasure, a jewel mine, the ocean, a vajra, a mountain, medicine, the spiritual master, a wish-fulfilling jewel, the sun, a melody, a king, a treasury, a highway, conveyance, a well, an elegant sound, a river, and a cloud. These twenty-two examples range from sincere aspiration to realization of the dharmakaya. In addition, they will be related to the five paths.[42]

1. Earth: The Earnest Desire to Accomplish Buddhahood

The first example takes an individual who is new on the path and shows how we begin to use the motivation, the benefits this will have, how it can increase and become more efficient and bring results. At the very beginning – the moment we first develop this mentality – strong interest is of utter importance. We need a strong motivation and wish to accomplish Buddhahood in the beginning, the wish to become free from suffering, the wish to free all beings from suffering and the wish to practice the teachings in order to accomplish that goal. At the beginner's, level this motivation is accompanied by an extremely strong motivation, which is compared to the earth. The earth is an utter prerequisite for things to grow and develop; if there is no earth there can be no plants, trees, hills, rocks or rivers. Nothing can ever grow and develop in empty space. Likewise, in the beginning we need the strong aspiration that accompanies the pure motivation. This will act as the earth, as the ground from which everything else grows.

2. Gold: The General Intention to Accomplish Buddhahood

The second example is that of gold and exemplifies the time when we try to develop bodhichitta a little more. At this point what is needed is that the motivation of bodhichitta be accompanied by pure intention, a pure mental attitude. This means that besides the wish to bring all beings to enlightenment, or the motivation to work for enlightenment, there always has to be a pure intention. Pure intention means that it is pure all the time and will never have a negative influence on others; it will only have a positive effect. Also the pure intention can never change, the reason gold is used as an example. Gold never changes, whether it is burned, beaten or whatever, whereas brass is golden in color but turns black when burned, beaten and so on. In the same way, as the golden color of gold never changes, the purity of the intention should never flutter, no matter what happens, whether life is easy or hard on us. Our situation should never change our attitude because we realize that a negative attitude is useless; we always keep the pure intention.

3. The Moon: Possessing Altruistic Thought

The third example is that when bodhichitta is increasing more and more it is accompanied by the excellent intention. In the previous example bodhichitta was accompanied by the pure intention. When the pure intention culminates it is greater than before, it is excellent and superior. This excellent attitude goes hand in hand with the wish to accomplish enlightenment. It means that at this point we are wholeheartedly given over to the wish of liberating others from suffering, no matter what hardships we have to put up with. We are totally devoted to the task of helping others accomplish enlightenment, irrespective of the difficulties involved. At this level bodhichitta is compared with the waxing moon. While the moon is waxing from being a crescent until it is full on the fifteenth day,[43] it will grow larger from day to day. In the same way, once there is the superior attitude then what we do becomes greater, better and more pure from day to day.

The first three steps are related to the kind of attitude of our mind: the first with aspiration, the second with intention and the third with perfect and superior intention, and comprise the ordinary level of the path of accumulation.

4. Fire: Possessing Earnest Application

The fourth example is that of application, actual action. This factor of application must now accompany bodhichitta and this action can take on all kinds of forms. It can be study, reflection, meditation, whch will help bodhichitta become more powerful. Therefore, the fourth aspect is exemplified by fire; when bodhichitta is accompanied by actions it is like a fire. When a piece of wood is set on fire then the fire would normally blaze up by itself and burn the wood. In the same way, when bodhichitta is accompanied by practice, by application, it will naturally increase like the flames. At the same time it will consume and burn up all the negative factors of the mind, all the negative feelings of desire, hatred, jealousy, pride and so on. Anything which is negative in our mind, all forms of hypocrisy, deceit and the like, everything will be burned by the fire.

This comprises the path of junction.

5: A Treasure: Possessing the Perfection of Generosity

The fifth level is bodhichitta accompanied by the perfection or paramita of generosity. Generosity becomes a paramita when it is combined with bodhichitta. Generosity is "dhana" in Sanskrit and literally means "what can relieve from the cause of sufferings coming from deprivation." So, generosity relieves suffering and it also brings happiness to others in the immediate future. We will also experience the results in the short term as well as in the long term in the form of virtuous karma. In this sense the practice of generosity in combination with bodhichitta is compared to an endless treasure mine in the earth; it is one of those mines that contains so much treasure that it can never be exhausted. We can keep taking out more and more treasure while more and more is found.

In the same way, bodhichitta accompanied by generosity is like an infinite mine of gold or treasures.

6. A Jewel-mine: Possessing the Perfection of Moral Ethics

The sixth example for progress is bodhichitta accompanied by the paramita of moral ethics, which is the way to make bodhichitta increase more and more. In fact, there is an interaction between bodhichitta and the paramitas in that both support and enhance each other. Bodhichitta accompanied by moral ethics is compared with a source of jewels because it is the ground that can give rise to all sorts of different qualities. This paramita of moral ethics is "shila" in Sanskrit and means "coolness" freedom from the wounds of suffering, problems, and difficulties. Freedom from these disturbances brings on a feeling of coolness, ease and joy. So this example is that of a source of all kinds of jewels.

7. The Ocean: Possessing the Perfection of Patience

The seventh step in development is bodhichitta accompanied by the paramita of patience. As mentioned, both support and enhance each other. A great ocean exemplifies bodhichitta accompanied by patience. When the ocean is stirred it is only agitated on the surface while the depths remain unmoved. Lacking patience we flare up in anger and rage; in that case the mind is agitated and disturbed and thus our thoughts and actions are affected. Any virtue we may have generated is disturbed and affected also. Anger stirs up waves of disturbances, which wouldn't be the case if patience were present. The Sanskrit word for patience is "shanti," which means "not disturbed, or "not agitated" and is a state of mind which is not agitated or disturbed through anger. With patience we can deal with and face anger without being agitated.

8. A Vajra: Possessing the Perfection of Diligence

Now bodhichitta is practiced in connection with the fourth paramita, which is diligence. Bodhichitta will develop when accompanied by diligence. This practice is compared with a vajra, which is extremely strong and solid; it is indestructible. In the same way diligence is extremely strong; it provides great stability in the face of obstacles and adverse conditions. No matter what happens, no matter what difficulties and obstacles arise, diligence is not broken, we would be able to carry on without giving up. The Sanskrit name for diligence is "bilja" which means "joy," "enthusiasm." I would like to point out that there is the same etymology in the English word "diligence" which means to take delight. Diligence means that when we are acting we are not unhappy or under pressure, rather we do things spontaneously, out of joy and pleasure in what we are doing.

9. A Mountain: Possessing the Perfection of Meditative Concentration

The ninth example is that of a great mountain, which represents bodhichitta accompanied by the fifth paramita of meditative concentration. Nobody can shake, shift or move a very great mountain because it is very strong, stable and firm. If we practice meditative concentration, bodhichitta becomes stable, strong and unshakable. This means that we will not become distracted by involvements with worldly concerns; for example, the feeling of something being pleasant or nice will not influence our mind. Similarly, if we hear pleasant or unpleasant sounds or if we have various thoughts they will not shake or disturb the mind; there will be the quality of stability of mind. The Sanskrit word for meditative concentration is "dhyana" which indicates the meaning of "absence of movement" stability, firmness.

10. Medicine: Possessing the Perfection of Wisdom-awareness

The tenth point refers to the development and enhancement of bodhichitta accompanied by the practice of the paramita of wisdom-awareness (prajnaparamita, the perfection of wisdom). It is compared to medicine, which is something that is useful and beneficial, something that can remove suffering and bring about well-being. If you are sick, medicine will eliminate the disease, take away pain and bring back well-being and ease. In the same way, when bodhichitta is practiced in connection with prajnaparamita it will eliminate all faults, all negative aspects, and it will make all positive qualities develop more and more. The Sanskrit name is "prajna" the Tibetan is "she-rab" and both mean the very best knowledge and intelligence. There are many different kinds of knowledge and from among them some are good and beneficial while others are negative and harmful. For example, someone who is very skilled at making poison or weapons implies intelligence, but we wouldn't call this the best and deepest intelligence because it is harmful intelligence. Deep intelligence on the other hand is intelligence that brings peace, happiness and smoothness; it is knowledge that brings happiness to others and to oneself. Prajna, or "sherab" "deep knowledge" or "intelligence" is a good and positive form of knowledge.[44] Here it is compared with medicine because it is the remedy for the disease of our thoughts.

Up and until now we have looked at how bodhichitta is increased when it is accompanied by the practices of the six paramitas. The last, the prajnaparamita, can be divided into four aspects which show what happens when prajna becomes finer and finer so that it can be more and more efficient and beneficial for oneself and others.

11. The Spiritual Master: Possessing the Perfection of Skilful Means

The eleventh stage is when bodhichitta is practiced together with the paramita of skilful means. The paramita of skilful means signifies that if we have to do something on our own we will accomplish it easily without experiencing difficulties of any kind. If we are doing things to help others it will be easy for us and very efficient. It is compared to a friend turned towards goodness, a virtuous friend.

12. A Wish-fulfilling Jewel: Possessing the Perfection of Aspiration Prayer

Here bodhichitta is practiced together with the paramita of aspirations. This means that when our very pure intentions and wishes are directed towards something worthwhile, they become real at this point. This is compared with a wish-fulfilling jewel. If we have a wish-fulfilling jewel all we have to do is wish and request and everything comes naturally and automatically. In general, there are two kinds of wishes. There are wishes that cannot come true and wishes that will come true. Wishes that cannot come true are superficial wishes like hoping that the lid of my cup turns into gold. This wish will never come true, first of all because it is pointless and then because there is no condition to make this happen. On the other hand, if Akong Rinpoche thinks, "I am going to build a temple here," he is wishing but at the same time he is doing everything to make this wish come true; this is the kind of wish that can become true. In the present case, bodhichitta accompanied by the paramita of aspiration means that we are actually working towards our goal; we are practicing virtue in order to achieve the Buddhahood we want to accomplish so that we can help other sentient beings. This is the kind of wish that can be accomplished and it will be accomplished through the support of the paramita of aspiration.

13. The Sun: Possessing the Perfection of Strength

Bodhichitta accompanied by the paramita of strength is likened to the sun. When our understanding has become very great – when the development of prajna has reached its peak – then our strength and abilities become very great as well. This is compared with the sun. When the sun is in the sky all the different things on earth occur, plants and trees grow, and fruits ripen and develop. In the same way, when our understanding has become great and is combined with bodhichitta, then we will be able to ripen other beings; we can help them develop and come nearer to more and more happiness and goodness.

14. A Melody: Possessing the Perfection of Primordial Wisdom

The tenth paramita is primordial wisdom (jnana). When prajnaparamita has become fully and completely developed – when understanding has been brought to full completion – then it becomes what is known as the realized form of knowledge, of cognition, of wisdom, which in Sanskrit is "jnana." It is bright, lucid and stable cognition. The Sanskrit word just means, "to know" to know the nature of things, to know things as they are. It denotes a clear knowledge and cognition. The Tibetan word is "yeshe." "She" is the same word as in "she-rab" and means "knowledge" "recognition." However, when it was translated into Tibetan as "yeshe" another element was added in order to describe the meaning more clearly. The syllable "ye" was added, which literally means "beginning" or "origin." The word is explained in full as "the form of recognition which is there from the very beginning."[45] This connects to the seed of Buddhahood, the original intelligence of pure mind, which is in our mind from the very beginning. Here we are speaking of the time when original intelligence of the mind has been made manifest and when this takes the form of the paramita of realized intelligence, realized goodness. This is practiced in connection with bodhichitta.

Through the combination of these two great qualities there will be a tremendous benefit for oneself and others. That is why the example given here is that of a melody or beautiful song, because when anybody hears a nice song it immediately makes us feel happy. In the same way, here it means the union of the great qualities of primordial wisdom and bodhichitta, which brings great happiness to others and us.

We have now seen the development of bodhichitta in combination with the practice of the ten paramitas. These ten respectively comprise the ten levels,[46] beginning with Overwhelming Joy, and are the subjects for the path of insight and the path of cultivation. This is considered the cause. Now we will look at the result.

15. A King: Possessing Special Clairvoyance Accompanied by Great Wisdom

When bodhichitta is accompanied by the power of clairvoyance or intuitive knowledge then it is likened to a great king. A great king is somebody who is very powerful. In the same way, when someone has bodhichitta and clairvoyance or intuitive knowledge they can do a great deal to help others.

16. A Treasury: Possessing Merit and Perfect Wisdom

When bodhichitta is combined with virtue or merit and with insight or the realized form of knowledge it refers to the two accumulations: the accumulation of virtue being with a conceptual frame of reference and the accumulation of insight being without any conceptual reference. The accumulation of virtue relates to what we do with a pure motivation, a pure attitude. The accumulation of insight, of the realized form of knowledge or understanding, relates to the way things are in their true nature. When we have the bodhichitta accompanied by the two accumulations then it is compared to a great treasure, which would give rise to endless positive results.

17. A Highway: Possessing the Branches of Enlightenment

When bodhichitta practice is combined with all the factors conducive to enlightenment – all the qualities developed on the path to enlightenment – then this is compared to a great highway, the road everybody travels. It is the road that all the Buddhas have taken in the past, are taking in the present and will take in the future.

18. Conveyance: Possessing Compassion and Special Insight

Bodhichitta practice combined with compassion and deep insight is the eighteenth point. This is compassion towards all sentient beings and insight into the true nature of things. This is compared with a wild animal like a horse (literally) or a jet (a modern example). It is any vehicle that can carry you quickly from one place to the next without any difficulties. This means that somebody who has compassion and insight is not going to stray from the path and encounter difficulties; they will not stray into a selfish vision of nirvana or remain stuck in samsara due to the absence of insight. Because of the two qualities of compassion and insight they will go straight to Buddhahood quickly and without hardship.

19. A Well: Possessing the Power of Complete Recollection and Confidence

When bodhichitta practice is accompanied by the power of perfect memory and by what is called "intellectual courage that comes from great understanding" it is compared to a well or water-spring. If there is a spring, then water continuously flows.

No matter how much water you need and use, more water flows. In the same way, someone who has the power of perfect memory (who can recall everything they know) and who has the power of intellectual courage (which comes from sufficient understanding) they will be able to use everything they have been able to learn. The dharma will really remain in this person.

The previous five points described the short term result of the bodhisattva path.[47] The last three points are connected with bodhichitta at the level of Buddhahood, when one has accomplished the dharmakaya.

20. An Elegant Sound: Possessing the Grove of Dharma

Number twenty is compared to an echo. When Buddhahood has been accomplished, when the dharmakaya has been realized, then automatically the sound of dharma is heard – the Buddha's teachings take place, which is like hearing an elegant sound. All of this is done without any effort. There is never the thought, "Now I must say this, now this sound must be produced" and so on. Similarly with an echo, which is a sound that comes to the ears of whoever listens, without revealing the source. The nature of the echo is realized as a non-existent sound.

21. A River: Possessing the Path of One Direction

This is the example of the constant flow of a great river. Likewise, the activity of the Buddha is something that is always flowing. It spontaneously and continuously flows like a great river.

22. A Cloud: Possessing Dharmakaya

The last example is that of clouds in the sky. In the same way as clouds appear in the sky without any effort, similarly from the dharmakaya of the Buddha spontaneous activity arises to benefit all beings. This activity will pervade all beings like the rain from the clouds that falls on everyone without distinction.

That concludes the explanation of the development of bodhichitta on the various levels of progress in the form of examples.

B. Different Levels. The second classification of bodhichitta is in terms of the different levels that we go through until Buddhahood. In fact, this very much covers the same ground as explained in the twenty-two examples except it is in a much more concise form and explained in four stages: Bodhichitta accompanied by aspiration, bodhichitta accompanied by the pure noble intention, bodhichitta as the result of the first two, and bodhichitta at the time of Buddhahood, then called "bodhichitta free from all obscurations."[48]

C. Characteristics. The third way of examining the various aspects of bodhichitta is done in terms of their actual nature. We can see that there are two different classifications of bodhichitta, ultimate and relative bodhichitta.[49]

When we speak of bodhichitta, the mind of enlightenment, whether in the relative or ultimate form, the essence of this state of mind is the union of compassion and understanding or intelligence. The only thing that can be said about the relative and ultimate level is that it is not just a wish, rather it is the very cause for accomplishing enlightenment; it is not simply wanting enlightenment, but it is creating the cause for enlightenment.

Ultimate Bodhichitta

If we first examine the ultimate aspect of bodhichitta, the nature of that state of mind is prajna. It is said that it is the realization of emptiness, which also possesses compassion as its very essence. This means that when one realizes the true essence of all phenomena, without any interferences from phenomenal aspects – when the ultimate essence of things is clearly manifest – at that point nothing fades away and vanishes. It is the time when we are free from all impurities and when our qualities and realization are completely developed. At that point the understanding of emptiness automatically brings with it a great feeling of compassion; one cannot be present without the other; the more one realizes emptiness, the greater one's compassion.

We can take the classical example of the rope mistaken to be a snake in order to understand this. When there's a rope which is mistaken for a snake, then there is fear because we believe that there is a real snake and are therefore scared. But if someone who knows that the rope is only a rope comes along and says, "Well, it isn't a snake, it's only a rope. There is no reason to be afraid" then most people won't believe this and will continue being afraid of the rope, making a detour around the rope out of fear. Those who understand that the rope is only a rope and not a snake will feel great compassion for all those who think that there is a snake and are thus afraid. In the same way, when the Buddha realizes that everything is empty, compassion for all beings that do not have that understanding arises automatically. This is why the realization of emptiness is said to include compassion as its very essence.

Relative Bodhichitta

The ultimate aspect has to do with clear realization of what is ultimately true. The relative level of bodhichitta describes the willingness to accomplish Buddhahood for the sake of all other beings and is based upon and inspired by compassion that wants to help all beings accomplish enlightenment. This is the reason why we wish to become a Buddha, in order to help all beings reach that same state. The reason why these two aspects of bodhichitta are given the name "mind of enlightenment" or "mind intent upon enlightenment" is because both of them constitute the cause for accomplishing Buddhahood.

Acquiring Bodhichitta

How are the two aspects of the mind intent upon enlightenment acquired? The ultimate aspect of bodhichitta is acquired in a very subtle way. It is very subtle because we achieve it through understanding the ultimate nature of things. This means that we cannot have ultimate bodhichitta within us by taking a vow or by any form of external action; it is something that comes through meditation, through the understanding that comes in meditation. It is something that comes by means of the ultimate essence of everything becoming manifest for us.

The relative aspect of bodhichitta is different. It is not acquired through meditation. It is said that this aspect is the more obvious and the more external aspect that we receive through external symbols. This is something we will receive through our spiritual friend in the form of a commitment on our part; we will promise to make the commitment to try to develop that kind of state of mind within us. This is because at first we have no experience; we do not have the habit of that state of mind. It will require some effort in order to develop it and that is why we make a promise in front of our spiritual friend. Once we have committed ourselves we will try to work more to develop this state of mind and try to make it increase more and more.

So, once we have taken the commitment we will try to keep developing that state of mind and to prevent it from degrading; we will work on it diligently so that it increases more and more until we accomplish enlightenment ourselves. This is the second aspect called "bodhichitta that comes from formal or external symbols," the more obvious and external aspect.

IV. Objectives. The fourth point of this section tells us what the object of bodhichitta is. I have already spoken about this previously but since this point is discussed here in the *Jewel Ornament* I will go through it again.

The aim of bodhichitta is twofold: it is focused on both sentient beings and on enlightenment. It is aiming at enlightenment, but not only for oneself, because if we try to get enlightenment only for our own welfare our goal will be faulty insofar as it will be immersed in a self-centered aim. If there is too much egotism then the motivation isn't pure because where there is egotism there is the absence of caring for others. At the beginning this means indifference for what happens to others. It also means that if we think of ourselves as being the most important then in the end this will not only lead to indifference towards others but also to being ruthless towards others in order to achieve our own goals. We will then cause others to suffer. This is the danger of a self-centered motivation. Therefore, it is necessary to diminish the self-centered motivation as much as possible.

Whatever we focus on for personal gain must be reduced. Instead, we must try to emphasize the altruistic attitude of our motivation. There is no danger in emphasizing the altruistic attitude, whereas emphasizing a self-centered attitude leads to egotism and to neglecting others.

This motivation that is oriented towards the welfare and happiness of others is one that is basically altruistic, yet it is not restricted to just one or two beings; it embraces all sentient beings without any discrimination. It is the wish to help all beings without exception. The kind of help that we want to provide is neither limited nor temporary. The way to really help is to bring others to enlightenment and not to give an inferior form of happiness but the ultimate form, Buddhahood. So, the ultimate aim of this state of mind is twofold: it is directed towards trying to help all beings and it is directed towards enlightenment as the final goal.

V. The Cause. The fifth point speaks about the cause for the arising of the pure bodhichitta. So, we have to try to develop that state of mind. This is accomplished by trying to generate the four causes that give rise to that state of mind.[50]

The first cause is to be aware of the benefits of this state of mind. This means that if we want to generate the mind focused on enlightenment we first have to want to generate it. What will make us want to generate it is to be aware of just how beneficial it is for ourselves as well as all other beings. Once we know how beneficial it is we will, of course, want to cultivate it within ourselves. At that point, once we know how beneficial it is, it will arise effortlessly within us. That is the first cause.

The second cause is to have great faith and devotion for the state of Buddhahood. The state of Buddhahood is the result of the path that we want to follow, so we have to have strong appreciation for all the qualities of the Buddha, of the state we wish to work for. Once there is an appreciation for the qualities of that state we will want to work for it and wish to achieve it. That's the second cause.

The third cause is to consider the sufferings of beings. It is necessary to have compassion so that the mind intent upon enlightenment can arise. To have compassion we have to become aware of the sufferings of other beings, which is the third cause.

The fourth cause is to have the assistance of a spiritual friend who will explain everything we need to know about that state of mind, about its benefits, about what will be lacking without it and so on. This fourth cause would be the power of encouragement and support from our spiritual friend.[51]

VI. From Whom One Receives It. The sixth point tells us about the source from which we receive bodhichitta; of course we are speaking about relative bodhichitta here. It is said that this is something that arises through external symbols, in a symbolical way. This is something that we do in the presence of our lama and is done by way of a promise or commitment. How does this actually happen? There are several different ways, depending upon whether we are able to be with a lama to make the promise or not.

Let us look at the way the commitment is taken in the presence of a lama. The lama should have good qualities himself; he should be authentic and genuine. He should have bodhichitta himself and be able to take us on as a disciple and help us in our practice. If there is such a teacher for us then we take the bodhichitta vow from him. However, it is not compulsory to take the vow from a lama. When circumstances are not conducive and we do not find such a lama, or we have found him and it can be dangerous to see him – dangerous in relation to our practice or even our life – this doesn't mean that there is no way for us to take the vow. In that case we can do it in front of a representation of the Buddha and we take the commitment in the same manner as we would with a lama.

In the extreme case in which we do not even have a representation of the Buddha, then it is sufficient to imagine the Buddha in front of us and to then take the commitment as if the Buddha were really there with us. In fact, it doesn't really make any difference whether we see the Buddha or not or if we are with him physically or not. The pure mind of the Buddha is always perfectly aware of whatever is happening. So, if someone has faith and prays to the Buddha, then they will have the same benefits and will experience the same blessing in taking the commitment when imagining the Buddha as if taking the vow from the actual Buddha. These are the different ways in which the commitment can be taken.

VII. The Method (Ceremony). This point speaks about the ceremony we follow when taking the vow. If this is done with our lama, or a lama, then the procedure consists of three parts. The first part is necessary in order to gather enough positive virtue. So, first we do the "Seven-Branch Practice"[52] in order to gather enough goodness before taking the vow; that's the preparation. Then we make the promise, which is to take the vow and make the commitment. Finally, we rejoice in what we have just done and appreciate the goodness of this ceremony. That is the general procedure.

There are variations of the procedure that accord with the tradition followed. There are two main traditions; one is called "the tradition of the vast conduct" and one is called "the tradition of profound view."[53] Really, the details are different but the essential procedure is the same in both cases.

VIII. The Beneficial Effects. The eighth point of this chapter describes the benefits that come from possessing the positive state of mind of bodhichitta. There are two types: the countable, and the uncountable.

A. The Countable Benefits. There are ten benefits, which in fact cover two aspects. One aspect of the commitment of bodhichitta is the intention or aspiration-bodhichitta and the other aspect is the actual practice or action-bodhichitta. So there are eight benefits for the aspiration and two for the action, making ten in all.

1. *The Beneficial Effects of Cultivating Aspiration Bodhichitta*

a) Entering into the Mahayana

Once we have taken the commitment to accomplish Buddhahood for the sake of other beings we belong to the Mahayana, so the first benefit is to be a member of the Mahayana. The advantage of belonging to the Mahayana family is that from that moment onwards we don't do anything of the lower paths, the Hinayana or worldly paths. Instead, once we have taken the commitment, we have the intention to bring all beings to Buddhahood and whatever we do, whatever form of practice we engage in, will be very fruitful. If we practice meditation or if we are generous or if we keep the rules of conduct properly, all of this will become very great, much greater than if we do this for ourselves only. This is easy to understand: If someone does the same things without the altruistic motivation of bodhichitta the result will be limited and restricted because of the self-centered goal. As mentioned earlier, it may even become the cause for negative thoughts and negative actions; when only working for one's own benefit we find justification to harm others and to make others miserable. So, this can become the cause for more samsaric results and at its best it can be the cause for falling into a Hinayana attitude or a self-centered approach.

b) It Becomes the Basis for all the Bodhisattva Training

The second benefit is that this commitment provides the basis for all other aspects of training in the practice. If somebody doesn't have the commitment then whatever they do will be for themselves and will have a narrow perspective and a selfish goal. Even if the qualities like generosity, morality and patience are good they will always be tainted by slight impurity and the motivation will not be perfectly wholesome. Once the motivation is really wholesome then this provides the basis for all other aspects in our training.

c) All Evil Deeds will be Uprooted

The third benefit is that when there is bodhichitta it breaks and destroys all negative and unwholesome aspects. As already said, once there is the pure motivation we stop thinking in selfish terms.[54] The selfish attitude is the root of all negative states of mind; it is the root for anger, desire, jealousy and the like. While this negative attitude is alive all the branches and leaves will thrive and remain negative, whereas if we work on an altruistic motivation then the self-centered aspects will diminish so that the negative aspects of our thoughts and actions will diminish; everything arising out of anger, desire, jealously and the like will diminish.

Once someone acts out of an altruistic motivation it can only be beneficial for others and bring them happiness, whereas when somebody acts out of a selfish motivation it only brings more difficulties and sufferings. When someone tries to cultivate the pure mind of bodhichitta, called "the precious bodhichitta" or "the precious mind of enlightenment," then it will automatically diminish all egotistic ways of thinking and it will increase the altruistic state of mind. The result will be the elimination of all negative aspects of our behavior. That's the third benefit.

d) Unsurpassable Enlightenment Becomes Rooted

The fourth benefit is that bodhichitta is like the planting of the root of Buddhahood. Once there is the wholesome motivation then it will develop more and more. It is like a root: if we plant the root of a good plant then it will develop fully into a good plant; if we plant the root of a bad plant then it will develop into a bad plant. When we plant the root of the positive motivation then this plant will bring forth the branches and leaves of good qualities, of the paramitas and so on, and will eventually fully develop into Buddhahood. So, bodhichitta is the root of Buddhahood.

e) One Will Obtain Limitless Merits

The fifth benefit of bodhichitta is that it generates a tremendous amount of virtue. In the *Householder Palgyin-Requested Sutra* (Tib. *Chindak Pälgyin Gyi Zhupai Do*) the Buddha said, "The merits of bodhichitta – if they had a visible form which entirely filled all space, there would still be more." This means that if we tried to evaluate the amount of virtue that comes from bodhichitta and were to try to describe it in terms of a visible object, we would have to fill up the whole of space. But even the whole of space would not suffice because the merit is far greater than anything that can be measured in physical terms. This is due to the tremendous determination to help all beings.

Let us consider what happens on a small scale, like the help we give to someone who is in agony from being hungry. By feeding them we would be satisfying their hunger, filling their stomach and giving them physical and mental relief as well; we would protect that hungry soul from dying of starvation, which is something extremely beneficial. If we look at it closely though, it is only very limited help because it only lasts a day and reaches just one human being. If we consider what happens with bodhichitta, which is not directed towards only one person but towards all beings without exception, it is intended to remove not only the small suffering that starvation brings but all suffering. This is the kind of motivation that would keep us working and helping beings until all conditioned existence is emptied of suffering. It is a great and limitless motivation that leads to great and vast activity. As long as we have this pure motivation we continue acting positively. This is why it is impossible to say how much goodness and virtue can be generated by that state of mind because it would keep going on and on.

f) All the Buddhas will be Pleased

The sixth benefit is that once somebody has developed bodhichitta within, all the Buddhas would be very pleased. If we consider the way Buddhas feel about us – they are not concerned whether we make offerings or sing songs of praise to them and they won't feel happy or unhappy if we don't; their main concern is that beings may be protected and freed from suffering. If they see that only one person has generated the bodhichitta commitment to help other beings in their mind then they will be very happy because that's the true way to help other beings, to protect them from suffering.

g) One Becomes Useful to all Sentient Beings

The seventh benefit is that bodhichitta will truly and immensely help all beings. When we speak about bodhichitta it might seem small because we are only speaking about a way of thinking, a motivation that seems so little. But, in fact, it is very great because the power of this way of thinking can generate tremendous effects. Let us consider what happened with the Buddha of our present time, Buddha Shakyamuni who appeared 2,500 years ago. Consider everything that has happened since then, all the places and countries where dharma developed, the great number of people in those countries who themselves became realized, all the number of great teachers and bodhisattvas who arose in all those places. We see that what the Buddha did was to accomplish the ultimate fulfillment for himself as well as to bring about the conditions of perfect fulfillment for everyone else. It is really impossible to list everything that came about from that action of the Buddha 2,500 years ago. When we think about all the beings that achieved realization, all the teachers that emerged, all the people who understood something about the spiritual path and developed on that path, all of this came from one action of the Buddha, which was to teach, to turn the wheel of dharma. It would be impossible to describe all the goodness that arose from that one action. This one action of turning the wheel of dharma was conditioned by one thing, one very small thing. This was the moment when many, many lifetimes previously the Buddha first took the commitment to reach enlightenment for the sake of sentient beings. It only took one instant for Buddha to think in those terms and to generate that resolution in his mind, but that small instant was enough to generate a tremendous amount of benefit for so many beings over so many centuries. All those benefits are presently alive and will be felt until conditioned existence is exhausted. So this describes the tremendous benefits that can come for all beings from a small thing, which is the pure motivation.

h) One Quickly Accomplishes Perfect Enlightenment

The eighth benefit is that we will quickly accomplish Buddhahood. As is explained in the *Bodhisattva Levels* (Tib. *Jang Sa*), when bodhichitta has arisen one will not remain in the two extremes of samsara or nirvana but will quickly accomplish enlightenment.

Those are the eight benefits that come from the aspiration to accomplish enlightenment, which is one aspect of bodhichitta. The next two come from the implementation of that aspiration.

2. *Beneficial Effects from Cultivating Action-bodhichitta*

i) One's Own Benefit Arises Continuously

The first benefit refers to oneself, which means that the goodness of our actions and conduct will become like the uninterrupted flow of a great river. Normally, anything positive we do creates a good result while doing it but no result while not doing it. With bodhichitta it is different. When bodhichitta is present in the mind, once there is real practice for enlightenment, then whether we consciously think that we are doing something towards enlightenment or not – like at times when we are playing, sleeping or are distracted – at all times, whether we are aware of it or not, the power of our commitment is always there, it is always with us and it will be with us until we accomplish Buddhahood. The reason is that this commitment generates tremendous energy. The impetus of this first promise will carry us and will automatically be with us all the time; it will generate goodness and virtue automatically. That is why here it is compared to the uninterrupted flow of a great river because this motivation will always be with us, constantly. This will also be something that can bring great benefit and happiness to all other beings. The amount of goodness that springs from it will be as great as the whole of space.

j) Benefits for Others Arise in Various Ways

The second benefit is that with the pure motivation and practice the good of other beings will also be accomplished. Once we have the pure motivation (whether we are always conscious of it or not) it will always work in a way that is beneficial for others and this will go on until the whole of samsara is exhausted of pain and suffering.

These ten are regarded as the countable beneficial effects. The second category are the "uncountable beneficial effects," which means that all good qualities arise from this until one becomes a Buddha; they are too vast to calculate, so uncountable.

B. The Uncountable Benefits. This means that all good qualities arise from this time until we become a Buddha, so they are uncountable.

I have been discussing bodhichitta, the commitment to accomplish Buddhahood for the sake of all beings. This is the purest form of motivation and is very powerful. If we think about the moment someone first takes this commitment and makes this resolution nothing fantastic happens, it isn't a spectacular event. At first it seems very small and insignificant, but later on this small move will bring forth a great result. The positive activities and goodness that will come out of this small action will be immeasurable. The example already given is what happened to Buddha Shakyamuni, who turned the wheel of dharma more than 2,500 years ago. Everything was due to the power of his original and pure thought, the original wish to accomplish enlightenment for the sake of other beings. It is through this thought that the Buddha was able to teach and help beings.

How the Buddha Shakyamuni first made this commitment is explained in a sutra where he said, "A long time ago I was an extremely poor Brahmin and went to see the Buddha of that time, who was also called Shakyamuni. I had absolutely nothing to offer because I was very poor, so I offered a bowl of soup.

Having made the offering I first took the resolution to accomplish enlightenment for the sake of all other beings in front of that Buddha." Thinking of that, it wasn't really spectacular or impressive because the Buddha was destitute and poor and had nothing more to offer than a bowl of soup. His thought was a very simple one; it was the virtuous wish to accomplish enlightenment in order to be able to help other beings. It looks small and insignificant, but this pure intention of the Buddha was something that grew more and more and became very powerful so that it became inexhaustible power. It first allowed him to accomplish Buddhahood and then made it possible for him to help so many beings. This power will remain until the moment when all the teachings have disappeared from our world.

We can see how this first pure motivation the Buddha had when he first committed himself to enlightenment to help all beings is very small, but it does have tremendous power through the very purity of the intention and this is how in the end it can help millions and millions of beings. All of this came about only through the meritorious result of offering a bowl of soup and mostly through the power of the very pure intention. That is what this power is.

When we make the promise to work towards Buddhahood for the sake of other beings it may be a timid and small attempt on our part, but if our intention and motivation is really pure, then it will definitely grow into something very powerful. In contrast, if something is done out of a selfish motivation, then it never goes very far or develops to a great extent. We can see this even on a very ordinary level. If we are speaking to someone and our way of speaking and relating to that person comes from personal preoccupation and we don't really care about how the other person feels or thinks then what we say will not make much of a difference for that person. They will see that we aren't really concerned or interested in helping so our words are not going to have very much impact or be very meaningful. If, on the other hand, we speak to that person with the wish to help then that person will be attentive and feel that we are trying to help. They will feel that our words are helpful and not hypocritical and they will know that we don't just want them to feel good or happy but to improve their life. As a result this person will feel that they can use what we spoke about so that their life improves. The result of words inspired by altruism is a true benefit. Of course, we too will gain joy because we will see the change. Even though a commitment or new way of thinking may not be very strong, if it is done purely then it will grow into something very strong and powerful.

The Buddha left his life of royalty behind in order to teach the dharma, which wasn't something of little value but was something which would remain alive for thousands of years. You could ask, "Why could the teachings stay alive for so long and spread to so many countries? Where did this come from?" The Buddha didn't go around and try to conquer the world with weapons, enforcing his teachings upon others. All he had was a begging-bowl. How could his teachings spread so widely and remain for so long although he only had a begging-bowl and didn't impose himself upon others? The reason is that there was a great power at play, and this power was the power of the pure motivation, the power of the wish to accomplish enlightenment for the sake of all beings. He only thought about helping sentient beings, about helping us. There was no trace of a self-centered attitude. His thoughts weren't stained by selfishness. It is the very purity of such an intention that made all his work possible. If our wish to accomplish enlightenment for the sake of other beings isn't strong at first we shouldn't worry because in time it will grow into something very powerful.

This text has explained ten benefits of bodhichitta, eight related to the intention to reach enlightenment and two that have to do with the practice to reach enlightenment.

Once we know about the benefits of the pure state of mind, of the wish of bodhichitta, then we have to cultivate it and to really practice. But during practice one thing is important: we have to tend that precious state of mind, that precious motivation. We have to make sure that it remains intact. Although bodhichitta is very powerful and pure by nature, if we don't look after it, it will diminish. This brings us to the next point of this section, which describes the faults that arise from not keeping bodhichitta pure and intact.

IX. The Disadvantages of Losing Bodhichitta. Once we have a very precious jewel in our hands, which is bodhichitta, we should look after it very carefully and value it. If we fail, it will become inefficient and it won't be able to produce all the good results that it can. For example, even if we had a wish-fulfilling gem that could do anything for us, like protect us and everybody else from all suffering, but we did not care for it or use it properly then it will not function and will not stop us and others from falling into the lower realms. In the same way, if we don't value bodhichitta very much and we don't care for it properly then it won't be effective. This means that if we allow our pure motivation to diminish, then the power to really help beings will also diminish because we have lost the wish to trulty help.

Another fault from losing the power of the pure resolution to reach enlightenment is that we will have to put up with a very long delay to reach the levels of a bodhisattva and enlightenment. That is why we have to be very careful and to look after this jewel of bodhichitta very carefully. There is a little story that can help us understand this.

Once upon a time there was a man who had a very fine piece of sandalwood, the finest sandalwood you could find and very expensive. This man thought that maybe he should sell his piece of sandalwood and so set out to find someone to buy it. However, he couldn't find anybody and realized that nobody wanted to buy his precious object. As he was walking down the road he saw a coal merchant surrounded by many people buying the coal. He thought how this merchant was doing good business yet he couldn't even manage to sell his single piece of sandalwood. He thought if he turned his sandalwood into coal then he could sell it. So he took his precious sandalwood, burned it and let it turn into coal. Then he was able to sell it, but it was such a shame because the sandalwood was lost and he had wasted the preciousness of his treasure.

In the same way, we have this very precious jewel of bodhichitta which can bring the ultimate happiness to us and others, it can free us all from suffering, but we have to value it properly and keep it intact so that it can remain efficient.

These are the points that describe the faults of allowing bodhichitta to diminish. To sum up this topic: when bodhichitta loses its power it will not bring many results.

X. The Cause of Losing Bodhichitta. Now we will look at the cause for breaking the commitment of bodhichitta, the bodhisattva vow. There are many different ways to break it but it can be summarized in two points: to forsake beings or to give up helping them, and to start developing an attitude that opposes the bodhichitta way of thinking.

The first is to give up the idea of helping beings. As already said, the very heart of bodhichitta is compassion, the wish to accomplish enlightenment in order to help beings out of compassion. We would go against this motivation if we felt anger and consequently the wish to exclude someone from that wish. If we think, "Well, when the time comes to help that person I am definitely not going to" or "When the time comes for me to protect that person I am definitely not going to," we exclude or give up the idea of helping somebody. When we do that we automatically give up this pure motivation.

The second cause for losing bodhichitta is generating an attitude that goes against bodhichitta, like the thought, "Oh, bodhichitta is something that doesn't have much sense. I am not interested in trying to develop this and am not going to work in that direction anymore. I'm not going to bother." Of course, when we start thinking in those terms we have lost the pure motivation. In general, when we speak about breaking vows it is something we should be very careful about. We should try as much as possible not to break our vows.

The present vow, the bodhisattva vow, is of a mental nature. As such, it always involves different thoughts. Our mind is constantly loaded with so many different thoughts that it is very easy to break it because it all depends upon our attitude, our way of thinking. We shouldn't feel that since it is so easy to break it with mere negative thoughts that we can't keep it and so give it up altogether. This brings us to the next point, which teaches how we can restore the vow.

XI. The Means of Regaining Bodhichitta Once it is Lost. There are three main categories of vows, the pratimoksha vows (the vows of individual liberation, vows that have to do with moral ethics), the bodhisattva vows and the Vajrayana vows. Among these, two are very difficult to break because they involve definite physical and verbal rules of conduct. These are the Vajrayana vows and the pratimoksha vows. Because the rules are quite precise and involve physical and verbal aspects it is very easy to follow them and to avoid breaking them. But when it comes to the bodhisattva vows, it is a different matter since they are concerned with our attitude. The counterpart to this is that since the bodhisattva vows are of a mental nature they can be restored very easily. Just as they can easily be spoiled and broken, they can also be easily restored.[55]

The Buddha said that the vows of pratimoksha and Vajrayana can easily be kept and are like a cup. Once the cup is broken it is difficult to repair it, but the bodhisattva vows are like a gold vase. If a gold vase falls onto the ground it will have a dent, but any expert goldsmith can fix it again quite easily.

From this section that teaches us how we can generate the wish to accomplish enlightenment for the sake of all beings we have now covered eleven of the twelve points.

This concludes the explanation of the ninth chapter,
on cultivation of bodhichitta, from
The Jewel Ornament of Liberation.

Chapter 10
Training in Aspiration-bodhichitta

XII. The Training. After cultivating bodhichitta comes the twelfth point which is very extensive because it covers many topics. It is called "what is practiced" and "the methods for practicing bodhichitta." This will cover two aspects:

A. Training in aspiration-bodhichitta, what one has to practice when aspiring for bodhichitta and
B. Training in action-bodhichitta, what one has to observe when practicing bodhichitta, which deals with the six paramitas.

Now we will look at the first part of the methods of training, the ones that have to do with the aspiration and intention to reach enlightenment.

A. Training in Aspiration-bodhichitta. Here there are five practices to train in. The first point says that we shouldn't give up sentient beings, the idea of helping beings. This means that the wish to help and benefit beings should constantly be present in our mind. The second point is that we should remain aware of the great benefits of that state of mind. As already mentioned, that motivation may not be very strong in us at the moment, but still we know that it is bound to develop and grow. We have to be aware of just how beneficial it is. The third point discusses how to gather the two accumulations, that of virtue and that of insight. The fourth point will deal with how to cultivate bodhichitta more and more; we need to become very familiar with that very pure state of mind, that pure motivation. The fifth point will show how to cultivate four positive things and how to eliminate four negative things.

1. Not Forsaking Sentient Beings from our Heart: *The Method for Not Losing Bodhichitta.* The first training is never to stop caring for other living beings, never to give up our concern for them. This is the way to prevent the pure motivation of bodhichitta from degrading, from spoiling. It is easy to keep that wish for people we like because it comes naturally, so we don't really run the risk of losing bodhichitta in connection with those we are close to. The risk arises with people we don't like and are angry with. With such people there will always be the danger that we may stop caring and that we may stop wanting to help them. In connection with such people, it is important to keep compassion in mind, to think in terms of compassion, so that we avoid that danger.[56]

2. Recollecting the Beneficial Effects of Bodhichitta: *The Method of Not Decreasing Bodhichitta.* The second training is that we should try to always remember the benefits of bodhichitta. This is meant to prevent bodhichitta from diminishing. If we know that this is very special then we will make sure that we don't create obstacles to that feeling, to this state of mind. On the contrary, we will do everything in our power to make it increase and develop more.

In many sutras the Buddha spoke about the powerful nature of this pure motivation. From among all the different things he said, we can say that this pure motivation of bodhichitta is like the spear that can defeat all the enemies of negativity. It is also like the axe that will fell the tree of suffering. It is also like a wish-fulfilling gem that will grant each and every wish. This is just referring to some of the benefits of bodhichitta. Here it is said that we should try to remain very aware of just how beneficial and great this state of mind is, so that by being aware of how precious it is we don't let it go down the drain, we don't lose it.

3. Gathering the Two Accumulations: The Method of Strengthening Bodhichitta. The third instruction tells us how we should gather the two accumulations because they are the way to make our motivation grow more and more and to help it develop. These two accumulations are virtue or meritorious actions and wisdom.

The accumulation of virtue means that when we speak about practicing the dharma it isn't just an intention or an idea. Rather it is in terms of doing something practical and real with our body, speech and mind. With our body, speech and mind we should act as positively as possible. This is what is called "gathering the accumulation of virtue." This accumulation is done within a conceptual frame of reference.

The other aspect of the accumulation is wisdom, which is beyond any conceptual frame of reference. This means that while we gather merit, while we try to act positively, at the same time this wisdom will help us to understand that there is no need to feel proud about the goodness of our practice or to cling to the idea that it is something real. It is to do wholesome practice while at the same time being immersed in the understanding of the ultimate nature of things. This aspect is the accumulation of wisdom beyond any conceptual or objective reference.

The accumulation of these two will make it possible for the pure motivation of bodhichitta to increase and develop further.

*4. **Practicing Bodhichitta:** The Method of Increasing Bodhichitta.* The fourth training concerning the bodhichitta of aspiration to reach enlightenment is that we should cultivate that state of mind again and again. This is another way to help it develop. The third training to develop the positive state of mind is to gather the two accumulations, which is one way, a temporary means, enhancing bodhichitta through positive actions, through virtue. But, now the long term way of increasing the strength of bodhichitta and developing it further is through getting very familiar with it, through cultivating it again and again. We have to make it our second nature; it has to become a habit. The way to make it a habit is threefold; we have to work in three different ways.

The first is to develop the cause of this positive state of mind of bodhichitta. What is the cause of that state of mind? As explained already, it rests on two qualities, loving-kindness and compassion. Loving-kindness is the wish that beings be happy and have the causes of happiness, and compassion is the wish that beings be free from suffering and the causes of suffering. We have to cultivate these two causes because when they are present the mind of enlightenment will also be present, the pure motivation will be there. That is why the first way to become very familiar with bodhichitta is to become very familiar with its causes, loving-kindness and compassion. When we cultivate these two qualities they will become very stable. If they are very stable then bodhichitta will also become very stable.

The second way is to work on bodhichitta itself. It is to realize that what we want to achieve is not just short term happiness or the short term freedom from suffering. Of course, it is very nice to be happy for some time and to be free from suffering for a while, but this won't last forever. It won't go on for millions of years. What we are aiming at is something far greater. We are working for the long term, towards the ultimate level, Buddhahood, because that is the only way to find total freedom from suffering, the state in which suffering will never again appear and the only state in which happiness is permanent. That is why, since we want to work for Buddhahood, we have to generate the wish, the state of mind that wants to accomplish Buddhahood and that is prepared to work for that goal. This is the way in which we should try to become very familiar with this state of mind, to cultivate it again and again, thinking, "I want to accomplish Buddhahood in order to really be able to help beings in the very ultimate sense."

The third way to cultivate bodhichitta is to try to train ourselves in actions that are conducive to enlightenment. This has two facets. One way is to try to really help others directly and the other way is to really examine ourselves. As for the first aspect, it is developing the habit of helping others. It will only be on a very small scale in the beginning and we won't be able to do much at all. But the main point is to try, to try to really help others. It could be through our way of acting, it could be through giving things we own, it could be through dharma, it could be through whatever way possible. But at first it doesn't need to be big. If we can try to help on a very small scale then later this will develop. If we find that we can't help even in small ways there is a very clever instruction given by the Kadampa teachers. They used to say that when you need to train your mind, when you need to try to develop this bodhichitta motivation, at first you give what you have in your right hand to your left hand and you give what you have in your left hand to your right hand. This is a way to train ourselves gradually. Once we achieve this we can aim at something on a larger scale. Once we develop this habit properly it will become real in the end. That is one way.

Besides trying to help others directly we can also form the habit of examining our own mind. This means that daily we should try to evaluate our own practice. We should try to check how much we are progressing every day, asking, "How much have I been able to do in connection with the pure motivation today? How many positive things have I achieved? How many negative things have I done?" We should try to do this every day in order to eliminate what hinders us and to cultivate what is positive. That will also be a way to reinforce this motivation.

We have seen that the state of mind of bodhichitta has two aspects, one is the intention and the other is the actual practice, so there is the aspiration and the practice for enlightenment. We know that the rules of training to develop the intention to reach enlightenment are explained in five ways, of which four have now been covered. The first was to show how to prevent losing the pure intention to reach enlightenment. The second was to show how to prevent it from diminishing. The third showed us how to strengthen it. And the fourth showed us how to expand it. The fifth tells us how not to forget it and how to keep it alive, which we will look at now.

5. Rejection of the Four Unwholesome Deeds and Acceptance of the Four Wholesome Deeds: *The Method of Not Forgetting Bodhichitta.* The fifth instruction of this section tells us what we must do in order not to forget bodhichitta and how to keep it alive.

Bodhichitta is essentially a state of mind, a form of motivation. As such it contains one danger, namely that we can forget it; we may lose this state of mind through not thinking of it or through forgetting it. In order to prevent this from happening there are two things we can do. The first way to avoid forgetting it is to give up four kinds of negative actions. The Buddha in the sutras, and many others in the shastras, called these four kinds of actions we must get rid of "the four black actions." In addition there are four things we must develop within ourselves, which are the right actions we need to develop, these are called "the four white actions." In other words, there are four negative actions we should try to abandon and four positive things we should try to practice in order not to forget bodhichitta. So, there are eight things we need to remember in order not to forget bodhichitta. In the *Kashyapa-Requested Sutra* (Tib. *Odsungkyi Zhupai Do*), the Buddha addressing one of his main disciples Kashyapa, said, "Kashyapa, if a bodhisattva does four things he will forget his bodhichitta, and if he practices four things he will never forget bodhichitta." What are they? The first four are the negative actions that cause one to forget bodhichitta and the second four are the remedies that cause us to keep bodhichitta. Each will be explained together with its remedy.

a) The First Unwholesome Deed and Its Remedy

The first is to lie with the intention to deceive someone, like our teacher, people who have been very kind to us, our parents or even extending such behavior to others. When we tell a lie with the intention to deceive someone else it is a negative action because it comes from an impure motivation. It is said that if someone lies in this way, whether the other person has actually heard the lie or not, and whatever the result, if we haven't remedied the lie within one session (four hours), then it is said that our bodhichitta has deteriorated. This is because the pure motivation of bodhichitta has been changed into an impure motivation, the reason why it has diminished.

The remedy for this first negative action is the corresponding first positive action of having the pure motivation that refuses to consciously lie. This doesn't mean lying in the sense of telling something that is not true because we are mistaken. For example, we say something because we think it is true while it isn't; we deceive someone because we have been deceived. Here we are speaking about a conscious lie, having the deliberate intention to deceive somebody else with a lie. The pure or white action is to think and resolve that we will never deceive someone else, even at the risk of our life. Once we keep this strong resolution in our mind we have the pure motivation and this constitutes the first pure action. This pure intention will definitely lead us to not deceive someone else because we won't have the element of deceit in our mind that ponders cheating others. Also, as our actions will correspond, it is a double benefit, in terms of our attitude and in terms of our actions. Instead, we will spontaneously be able to act in a very honest, truthful and beneficial way.

There is one exception to lying and that is when we have to lie in order to help others or to protect them. This may happen when someone is in danger or may lose his or her life. In that case we may have to lie to help them, so it is a different situation. Sometimes it may be the case that a lie is necessary in order to lead someone towards the dharma. In those cases our words are not true and are a lie, but this isn't counted as a lie insofar as the intention of deceit is not there. We are not trying to deceive someone but instead out of a pure motivation we speak words that are not true because we want to help and benefit them, that is why we spoke words that are not true. So, those are not counted as lies that we are speaking about here.

b) The Second Unwholesome Deed and Its Remedy

The second negative or black action is causing someone to regret something positive, something they have done out of a pure motivation and which they have accomplished in a pure way. The way to make them regret it is speaking in the following manner for example: "Well, what you are doing is fine now but you may have lots of trouble later on." We try to induce the person to regret having done something very good and positive. It is said that whether such words are heard by another person or not, or whether they feel regret or not because of what we said, in any case, we have the negative motivation and (unless remedied within a session) this breaks the bodhisattva vow.

The remedy to this is the second white or positive action and this is not to cause someone to feel regret about their good actions. On the contrary, the white action is to help people who do not do anything positive, to do something positive and to influence them and instill in them the wish to follow the path of Mahayana.

c) The Third Unwholesome Deed and Its Remedy

The third negative action is to lack respect for a bodhisattva. A bodhisattva is someone who has really entered the path of Mahayana and who has really generated the pure state of mind of bodhichitta. Somebody who has done this is somebody who has far better qualities than ordinary beings; they are outstanding people. This is because most other people are only concerned about their own benefit and only think about what is nice and pleasant for them. A characteristic of being a human being is self-centeredness, thinking about what is pleasant for oneself. This is a very narrow-minded attitude and isn't a noble way of thinking. Generally, this can only give rise to inferior behavior because only thinking about oneself involves hurting others in order to achieve one's own personal aim of happiness. It certainly isn't a motivation that deserves respect.

Bodhichitta is a very pure, good and wholesome motivation. If we are together with people who have that motivation, then there is no need to doubt or fear whether these persons are good or bad for us. There is no reason to be afraid of them because all they intend to do is to help others without thinking of themselves. It is similar to what happens to someone who has to be in the midst of wild animals; they would experience much fear because they know that these animals are very aggressive and can jump at them any minute to attack and bite them. In the same way, if someone has to be in the midst of very selfish people, there is always the risk and possibility that they would try to harm and deceive us. It is very justified to be cautious of people who are self-centered.

If someone were to be in the midst of very gentle animals like deer, that are very peaceful and timid, then there would be no possibility of experiencing fear. In the same way, if someone were to be among bodhisattvas who have truly turned their mind towards enlightenment, then they will always experience a benefit and there would never be the occasion to experience suffering. Bodhisattvas will always do everything to accommodate others; they will bring about the cause for immediate and ultimate happiness. If we are among such people there is no need to worry or be afraid. This shows why someone who has turned their mind towards enlightenment is a very special person and as such we should appreciate their goodness and should respect them. If we are spiteful towards such persons and speak about their faults then this will have a very bad effect, not on the bodhisattva, but for us because we are speaking out of anger. Particularly, it means that we have no respect for the value of bodhichitta; we don't appreciate that quality enough since we cannot respect someone who has that quality.

It is said that whether we speak about the faults of such a noble person directly or indirectly in a very angry or smooth way, in whatever way it is done, it is something that (unless remedied in a session) breaks the bodhisattva vow because it shows a lack of respect for bodhichitta.

The remedy to this third negative action is appreciating the qualities of bodhisattvas and speaking nicely about them. Bodhichitta is something very special because it is a completely pure motivation. When there is the pure motivation then our actions are automatically very pure. It doesn't matter whether the direct result of this motivation is small or big in the short term, what matters is that at any time, and always, the results of a positive motivation will be positive and never harmful. Every small or big result of bodhichitta will be positive, never negative, and it is because everything is done out of an altruistic motivation, out of the genuine wish to help.

On the other hand, when someone acts out of a selfish motivation then this person may be doing something that looks like a good action in the short term but in the long term it can never be good, it can only bring pain and trouble because it springs from an impure motivation. A person who acts out of a selfish motivation will always try to get some kind of selfish profit or benefit and there will be an element of deceit in their behavior. Sakya Pandita once said, "When you see a dog that seems to be smiling at you he may be smiling because in the next moment he will jump and bite you." The dog smiles because it is happy about the prospect of jumping and biting you, not because it wants to make friends with you. This exemplifies that what seems to be nice may not always be nice; underlying is the expectation of personal gain or profit. As soon as there is a selfish motivation behind an action, even though it may look like a nice action, it is necessarily tainted by something negative.

We should realize the great value of bodhichitta, the pure motivation that only comes from the wish to help other beings. Acknowledging the value of this motivation we should try to appreciate the qualities of bodhisattvas, speak about these qualities and let others know about the qualities of bodhisattvas.

d) The Fourth Unwholesome Deed and Its Remedy

The fourth negative action is having a deceitful intention towards others, whether they are enemies, friends or neutral persons. Whenever we have a deceitful intention it breaks the bodhisattva vow. It is because a deceitful intention is rooted in a self-centered way of thinking and this self-centered way of thinking is the opposite of bodhichitta. So, whether we actually do something to hurt others or not, whether the others come to experience our deceitful intention or not, it makes no difference. Once we have a deceitful attitude, our mind breaks the vow.

In which way does this differ from the first negative actions, which also imply deceit? In the first one it is deceit that is actualized; it is when you tell a lie with the intention to deceive. In the fourth case it refers directly to the intention to deceive, to the negative state of mind of deceit.

As long as we have failed to remedy this negative action (within a four hour session) the vow will be broken. This is easy to understand because the bodhisattva vow implies a positive and pure motivation. As long as the motivation is pure then

everything that ensues out of it is bound to be positive and pure too. Anything that arises from a pure motivation will be good, like a good root has good branches and leaves. As soon as the opposite is present, as soon as there is a disposition that isn't pure and intends to harm others, then what follows will be negative. The remedy against the harmful intention is to try to get rid of self-centered motivations and instead try to cultivate the wish to help others as much as possible.

This is the description of how we should try to eliminate the four negative actions through practicing the four positive actions.

This concludes the explanation of the tenth chapter,
on training in aspiration-bodhichitta, from
The Jewel Ornament of Liberation.

Chapter 11
Training in Action-bodhichitta

B. Training in Action-bodhichitta. The training for enlightenment, or the practical application of the pure attitude, action-bodhichitta, which we have been defining, is found in the practice of the six paramitas: generosity, moral ethics, patience, diligence, meditative concentration and wisdom-awareness (prajna).

The six paramitas[57] actually constitute the way to overcome our negativity and cover three types of training: training in superior conduct, training in superior thought and training in superior wisdom. In order to overcome desire, we try to practice generosity and moral ethics. In order to overcome anger and aggression, we try to practice patience. These three paramitas are the training of superior conduct. In order to overcome ignorance and delusions, we practice meditative concentration and try to develop the deepest kind of understanding, prajna or wisdom-awareness. These two paramitas cover the training in superior wisdom. And diligence is the quality that fosters all three types of trainings. So this is the function of the paramitas, to help us overcome our different kinds of problems.

Each paramita is explained in a separate chapter, but before this is done all paramitas are considered together and in general. Gampopa explains this in six points: definite number, definite order, characteristics, definition, division and grouping.

*1. **Definite Number.*** The first group of three paramitas – generosity, moral ethics and patience – provides the right kind of life, the short term function of right livelihood.[58] The last three paramitas – diligence, meditative concentration and wisdom-awareness (the spiritual and highest form of understanding) – help us achieve liberation and omniscience, the final and ultimate goal of the path.[59]

*2. **Definite Order.*** The order of the paramitas corresponds with the degree of difficulty accompanying the practice. The first are the easiest to practice and the latter are the more difficult to practice and understand.[60]

*3. **Characteristics.*** When we speak of generosity or moral ethics we are not talking about ordinary qualities but the finest form. This is shown through four characteristics that apply to all paramitas.

(i.) The first characteristic is that the six qualities can destroy their opposite defects. For instance, ultimate generosity can remedy and eliminate avarice. In the same way, moral ethics can eliminate all the faults that come from not having proper discipline and so on. So, each paramita is the ultimate remedy to the opposite defect.

(ii.) The second characteristic is that these qualities are not just in terms of emotions or thoughts of what things are, but they actually imply realization of emptiness. These qualities are practiced while one understands the empty nature of the action and the quality.

(iii.) The third characteristic is that the six paramitas are qualities that can benefit others; they are intended to help others and have the power to do so.

(iv.) The fourth characteristic is that through the paramitas one can actually benefit beings. Whoever has these paramitas can mature other beings; they can help them develop and progress on the spiritual path.

4. Definition. Paramita is the Sanskrit equivalent for the Tibetan "pa-ro-du-chin-pa" which means, "gone to the other side." The "other side" is a word used to describe the other side of a river, crossing over to the other side. In the present case it means going across to the other side of existence, so one leaves existence (samsara) behind and goes to the other side, which is beyond existence, (Buddhahood). It says, "gone to the other side" in the sense that one has already arrived at the other side, is not in the process of going, rather in the state of having arrived there.

So, when we speak about any of the paramitas this does not refer to worldly aspects of generosity, etc. Generosity as a paramita is not the ordinary generosity practiced by people in worldly existence. Instead, it is the generosity of those who have already arrived at the other shore, those who have gone beyond the world. This is also true of all the paramitas, so this definition applies to them all.

5. Division. How can one reach these qualities that have gone beyond existence? Of course, at first it is a matter of motivation. These qualities are not practiced in order to achieve something in worldly life, such as wealth and personal success.

Furthermore, they are not practiced in order to gather virtue. They are practiced exclusively for the sake of reaching enlightenment, in order to help all beings. That is one aspect, that of motivation. The other aspect is considering the actual nature of the paramitas, which are practiced without any involvement or clinging to what is being practiced. In brief, it means that we are not practicing these qualities or paramitas within a worldly frame of reference, but it has to do with what is beyond existence.

6. Grouping. The paramitas are also grouped into the two accumulations. Generosity and moral ethics are the accumulation of virtue, and wisdom-awareness (prajna) is the accumulation of insight or wisdom (jnana). Patience, diligence and meditative concentration are included in both.

This concludes the explanation of the eleventh chapter,
on explaining the six paramitas, from
The Jewel Ornament of Liberation.

Chapter 12
The Perfection of Generosity

There is one chapter for each paramita, and each paramita is taught in seven points: reflection on the faults and virtues, definition, classification, characteristics of each classification, increase, perfection and result.

The first paramita is generosity. The reason generosity is taught first is because bodhisattvas need to act in a way that is beneficial to other beings. In order to really help other beings they must first establish the right connection with others; they must have a positive relationship with people. What makes a relationship positive is to help in different ways, to help temporarily through giving them things they need, through giving them protection from fear and through giving them the teachings. These different kinds of gifts or different ways of being generous will bring happiness and satisfaction to others. Once this feeling is established it is possible to gradually lead them on the path of dharma and finally to guide them until the achievement of the ultimate result, which is Buddhahood. That is why generosity is taught first, since it provides the means to achieve this.

I. Reflection on the Virtues and Faults. The first point is about the benefits that arise from practicing generosity and the faults that arise from not practicing generosity.

The basis of any practice is the wish to do the practice. As mentioned, Buddhism is not just a matter of a way of thinking or of speaking. We have to actually practice, the reason we are now at the point about the six paramitas. In order to practice generosity there must be the wish to do so. It isn't sufficient to hear that one has to practice. Even if our lama tells us, it doesn't mean that we will be able to practice. So, what can help us? It is important to know that if we practice generosity many qualities will arise and that if we don't many faults will arise. This comes from the nature of generosity: if we are generous many benefits will ensue and if not many faults will be there. The Buddha showed that lacking generosity makes it difficult to understand and progress and we will not be able to accomplish Buddhahood. The Buddha himself saw the disadvantages of not practicing generosity and he advised his disciples to practice it in order to avoid those mistakes. When he advised them he wasn't being authoritative, rather he pointed out that if they did practice generosity many benefits and qualities will be there and that if they didn't practice generosity many disadvantages and shortfalls will be there. We too have to recognize the advantages and qualities of practicing generosity and the shortcomings and disadvantages of not practicing generosity. Once we know this it is easy to practice and we will want to practice it spontaneously because we see how useful and beneficial it is. We will be inspired for this reason. This is the reason we now learn about the qualities that come from practicing generosity and the defects that come from not practicing it.

What are the benefits that come from generosity? With respect to the object of generosity it is explained in two aspects.

If we consider the object as being an animal, we see that animals suffer in many different ways, due to hunger, thirst, sickness, fear and we see that we can help them in many different ways by protecting them from their suffering.

If we consider the object as human beings, we see that human beings are subject to the four kinds of sufferings typical of human existence. These are the sufferings of birth, old age, sickness and death. In addition there are two specific human problems, the problem of excessive activity and the problem of frustration. Excessive activity is the feeling that we are always in a hurry, that there is never enough time for anything and that we are always busy from morning to night. It is the constant feeling that there is no time, that every moment of the day, every hour and every minute is filled up and that there is never a moment for relaxation. It is the constant feeling of having to rush and feeling that nothing we want to do is ever finished. We never find the time to complete what we intended to do and this causes considerable worry and difficulties. This problem of excessive activity is due to the fact that we have no control over our life. We can't say, "Hang on, I don't want to die now because I haven't finished what I started." When death comes, whether we are finished or not, it will happen. That is why we always have the feeling of rushing and that time is passing, which we can't hold on to. We feel that we can't finish anything. That is one problem of the human condition.

Another problem is that of frustration. Even though we are rushing about as much as we do, even though we work very hard physically, verbally and mentally, we never really feel that things are complete, there is always a feeling of dissatisfaction, that it isn't enough, that it isn't right, it's too little, or too small, or not good enough. There is always frustration in our mind that things aren't quite as they ought to be.

These two, excessive activity and frustration are a worldwide problem of mankind regardless of if they are rich or poor. People have to put up with these difficulties. So, how can these two aspects of human difficulties and causes of anguish be eliminated? The very best remedy for these two problems, at least in the short term, is generosity. Generosity is what can really alleviate that kind of suffering.

Overactivity comes from the feeling that we are missing something. So, if we give something to diminish the feeling of need and frustration, then automatically it reduces the suffering of overactivity, which is a result.

If we do something for someone then at least for a while that person will feel relieved from the feeling of constant frustration and deprivation; the cause of such feelings are taken away through acts of generosity and then the mind of that individual will be relieved and feel happy. That person will therefore benefit from our generous gift. That is why it is important to practice generosity, which is very beneficial because it relieves the other person of their pain and anguish.

Also for us, our wish to help other beings does not remain theory; rather it becomes an actuality because we are actually doing something to help others. By the same token, we are gathering a lot of virtue that will take us to Buddhahood very quickly. Once there, we can of course help beings further and in a much greater way. This is why the Buddha pointed out in sutras the great advantages, the great qualities that come from the practice of generosity.

In the *Householder Drakshulchen-Requested Sutra* (Tib. *Chimdag Drakshul Chengyi Zhupai Do*) the Buddha listed the qualities of practicing generosity and the defects from not being generous. The Buddha said, "What you give away is really yours and what you keep is not yours." This means that what we give away is truly ours because it will always bring good results for others and us, whereas what we keep will not be enjoyed by anybody but ourselves; when we die we will have to leave things behind and they will then not be useful at all. When we keep something we also have all the worries of looking after it; we worry that it will be stolen, wasted or will rot away. If we give something away then there is nothing to worry about; we needn't worry that it will be stolen, wasted or rot away. If we keep something for ourselves because we are very attached to it or we are miserly then it is only going to be useful for us for a short while, since it will eventually pass into another's hand.

If we give something away, it not only benefits the person who received our gift but will also benefit us because the result of generosity will bring us very close to Buddhahood. Whereas if we keep things for ourselves out of attachment, it will likely be the cause of pride, jealousy, hatred, all sorts of negative feelings. So, keeping things for ourselves means falling into the side of negativity rather than gaining anything.[61] Therefore, "If we give things away," the Buddha said, "then you really possess it because the goodness of gift becomes inexhaustible, whereas if you keep it, the goodness of the object becomes small and exhausts quickly." This is how the Buddha showed the goodness of generosity and the shortfalls of miserliness.[62]

II. Definition. The definition of generosity is the pure wish to give somebody something in order to help him or her; this wish is not tainted by any attachment for what you are giving. Generosity doesn't depend on the size and quality of what you are giving; generosity only depends upon the pure intention of really wanting to help the person receiving your gift without being attached.

III. Classification. There are three different aspects of generosity: giving wealth (the gift of material things), giving fearlessness (the gift of protecting others) and giving dharma, the gift of the teachings.

IV. Characteristics of Each Classification

A. Giving Wealth. Concerning material generosity, it is generally said that we should be generous and give things to others. Not all forms of such generous acts are however beneficial because there are impure gifts which we should not give. We should only practice the pure forms of generosity.

1. Impure Giving. There are four impure types of material gifts. They are impure due to four factors: when the intention is impure, when the gift itself is impure, when the recipient is impure and when the way of giving is impure. So, we should only consider generosity that is not spoiled by any of these four impure factors.

a) Impure Intention

The first impure factor is when the intention is not correct, when we give something with the intention to harm. For example, with such an intention you think, "If I give this person this then they will get into a lot of trouble and will have lots of pain." We may give something away intending that the receiver lands in jail or be banished from a country or be harmed or be killed. These are all very impure and negative intentions. We shouldn't give with such an intention.[63]

b) Impure Objects

The second impure factor is when the gift itself is improper. This means giving poison for example, poison given to hurt someone. Or it can be fire, which is meant to burn someone, or weapons, which are meant to kill others. The gift itself is then improper and will make the act of generosity improper and impure. However, there may be exceptions. We can give something that may look improper but actually helps, for example, if a poisonous snake has bitten someone's finger and the only way to save the victim was to amputate the finger. In that case, the action becomes generous because we saved that person's life.

c) Impure Recipient

The third aspect of impure generosity concerns the recipient of the gift. There are two kinds of improper recipients for gifts. The first is somebody who asks you for something with the intention to harm you. They know that by asking you for this object that you will experience many problems. Since the motivation of the receiver is impure it is not proper to give the gift to them. The second type of person is somebody who is mentally disturbed. If you have a mentally disturbed person who asks you to offer your life by chopping off your head, it would be very improper because that person is only mad and the act would benefit nobody.

d) Impure Method

The fourth factor of impure generosity concerns the way you give. This means that you give something away but really feel like hitting that person instead or you give something away in a rough and unfriendly manner. Giving in such a way will make the recipient feel unhappy and sad and will cause anguish in their mind, which doesn't help them at all. This makes generosity impure.

Those are the four aspects one should avoid and abandon so that generosity is pure.

2. Pure Giving. Pure giving has three aspects: pure objects (whatever is appropriate), pure receiver (our spiritual guide, the Three Jewels and whoever is in need) and pure method (giving with a pure motivation, with devotion, with respect, without bias and whatever is required).

B. Giving Fearlessness. The second gift of fearlessness means giving protection. It is even better than the first type of generosity because it means protecting someone from fear, such as from fear that arises from wild animals, sickness, fire, water or any form of fear. This form of generosity is said to be like the gift of life because you protect someone's life from what causes fear.

C. Giving Dharma. The third is the gift of dharma. This is the highest form of generosity since it brings very great benefits. Again there are four aspects that define a proper dharma gift: the recipient, the motivation of the giver, actual dharma and the method dharma teachings are given.

a) Recipient

Let us consider the recipient of the gift. To whom should we give the dharma? Not to people who are not interested in the dharma because it will not benefit them if they are not interested. It should be given to people who are interested and who have some faith and a certain degree of appreciation for the dharma.

b) Motivation

Concerning the motivation of the giver, we shouldn't give dharma to others in order to become famous or successful or for personal gain of any kind. It should be done out of a pure and exclusively good motivation. Dharma should be given when we are convinced that the receiver wants to know about the dharma when they don't know, when the receiver wants to know how to practice when they don't know, when the receiver wants to know how to become free from suffering when they don't know, and when others want to know how to achieve happiness and don't know how. In order to help them find out about all this we make the gift of dharma. Basically it means that we should only give dharma out of the wish to help and only with a compassionate motivation.

c) Actual Dharma

What should we teach when spiritual generosity applies? We shouldn't teach something we have made up for our self, for example the thought, "Well, I'm quite clever, have good understanding and realization in my meditation, so I can just make up some nice teaching." Of course, this is wrong because we shouldn't make up our own ideas of the teachings. Even if we are very clever, or even if we have a lot of understanding and realization through meditation, it is still possible to make mistakes. Therefore, we should only use the teachings of the Buddha because they are the only ones that cannot mislead, that are faultless. It is the stainless, immaculate words of the Buddha that should be used for spiritual generosity. We can also use the teachings of the very great beings who composed the shastras, the teachings that elucidate what the Buddha said. Either way, we shouldn't make up our own teachings.

When we use what the Buddha taught we shouldn't alter the instructions. We shouldn't try to use the teachings to suit our own needs. We should teach what is there. Furthermore, teachings shouldn't remain words only. Others should come to be able to practice through our explanation. We don't remain on the level of theory and speculation but put explanations in practical terms so that we actually show what can help, what can directly and practically be useful. If we speak about what needs to be eliminated, we are able to explain how it can be eliminated. If we speak about what one has to realize, we should be able to show the way to realize it. Then, what we teach the person becomes directly useful.

d) The Method of Showing Dharma Teachings

Concerning the way in which the dharma gift is made, when we are speaking about dharma it shouldn't be an ordinary conversation; we aren't speaking about dharma in order to have a chat or to impress and overwhelm others with our knowledge. We should speak about the dharma in order to help the other person to find out and recognize what the way to practice the dharma is. The way we should explain the dharma is to benefit the other person for practical purposes. We shouldn't teach in a way to impress others or to make a display of what we know. Rather, we should teach with the thought that it is intended to help the other person so that after we have spoken the other person has experienced a beneficial stimulus in their mind, that the other person can feel devotion for the dharma due to what we have said, that the other person can progress in their meditation practice, that they can feel more compassion, that they can really turn their mind towards enlightenment, that they can develop more diligence and so on. What it really means is that our explanations on the dharma should be beneficial for others and not for the purpose of impressing others.

V. Increase. From the point when we begin the practice up to the point when we accomplish the ultimate result of enlightenment we need to cultivate generosity. This means that we have to generate a very great amount of generosity; we have to practice generosity to a very large extent. Here we are provided with a means to increase our generosity and to make it much greater. This can be done in three different ways: through jnana (insight, primordial wisdom), through prajna (wisdom-awareness) and through dedication.

First it is said that through the power of pure wisdom or the finest form of intelligence we can make generosity outstanding. This refers to the absence of the three thoughts when we give something: when we give something we do not introduce the ideas of someone giving something, of someone receiving the gift and of the action of giving. Once we do not introduce this three-fold division, which comes from thoughts and concepts, then generosity is extremely pure. This type of generosity brings the greatest fruits and finest results. This is why it is said that through the power of the purest wisdom generosity is made to be outstanding.

The second way to increase generosity is through the power of prajna, through the power of spiritual understanding. It is said that through the power of understanding, generosity is brought to expand. This special understanding will help us expand generosity in three ways: it will help us in the beginning through the right motivation (to bring all beings to Buddhahood), it will help us while we are making the gift through not being attached to the object of the gift and finally it will help us in the end through not having any hope or expectation as a result of our generous action. Once we have these three positive actions then our action is not ordinary; it is special because it is accompanied by deep understanding. This will make our generosity very great; it will increase our accumulation of virtue. This is done through deep understanding.

The third way to increase generosity is through dedication. Dedication means that when we are practicing generosity we do not do so in order to benefit ourselves, but instead with the thought in mind to benefit all other beings through our actions. These thoughts of dedication will also be something that will increase the results of generosity tremendously.

VI. Perfection. Generosity can be made pure in two ways: through practicing generosity while at the same time having the understanding of emptiness and having compassion. When compassion and this understanding permeate generosity then it is pure generosity.[64]

VII. Result. Generosity is essentially a quality of not clinging; it is the ability to give things away. This shows that we are not very involved with things; we aren't very attached to worldly things. This means that since we don't have great attachment to things we can actually practice dharma with great strength; our practice will be very powerful because of the fact that we aren't attached to worldly things. If our practice is very powerful and strong through full dedication, it means that we will consequently be able to help others tremendously.

One of the temporary results that come from generosity is that we will become very affluent. We will have many material things in our life because we have been able to give away a lot. Once we have all these good things in our life we will be able to use them to help many other beings. So, there are really great benefits coming from generosity.

Perhaps many of us regard generosity as something that has to do with objects, with what we give. But this isn't the case. It is much more a matter of mentality than a matter of the object. If it only referred to external objects it would imply that only somebody who is very rich could give away a lot and that somebody who is very poor has no chance of practicing generosity and thus would not be able to accumulate virtue. If generosity only referred to power, then only somebody who has a high position in society would be able to give protection and somebody who does not have a high position would not. It would also mean that only if someone were very clever, they would be able to give dharma and somebody with little intelligence would not be able to give the gift of dharma. However, it isn't like this because generosity doesn't have to do with outer things; it is inner. It is a matter of thought, a state of mind. It depends upon how we think. It is a state of mind that really wants to help others through giving. It is the feeling that we really want to help others through giving something in whatever possible way. Even if the opportunity doesn't arise, it doesn't matter, because it is the state of mind that is most important. It is the feeling of readiness to do anything we can to help someone by giving him or her whatever they need. So, whether or not we actually have the opportunity to give or not is not so important. What is important is our pure motivation.

Since we are speaking about a state of mind we see that generosity should be a positive state of mind. Therefore feel this state of mind, rest within this state of mind for a few moments.

As already explained, one of the main topics of *The Jewel Ornament of Liberation* is bodhichitta, the mind wishing for enlightenment. Bodhichitta is basically the very pure kind of motivation, but it is not only that. It doesn't only stay a motivation but has to be put into practice. The way to practice the very pure motivation is to practice the six paramitas. We have now covered the first paramita, that of generosity.

This concludes the explanation of the twelfth chapter,
on the perfection of generosity, from
The Jewel Ornament of Liberation.

Chapter 13
The Perfection of Moral Ethics

Moral ethics has the same seven points as in the chapter on generosity: reflection on the virtues and faults, definition, classification, characteristics of each classification, increase, perfection, result.

I. Reflection on the Virtues and Faults. The first point of the chapter will speak about the benefits that come from observing moral ethics and the harm that comes if we don't. In fact, this provides us with the reasons why it is necessary to have moral ethics.

When we speak about moral ethics we are not speaking about something hard and harsh, like something that would tie us down to fetters. It isn't like a child not allowed sweets when it asks, like the situation when the child keeps nagging for sweets that are there and we forbid it. Furthermore, it isn't like a situation when the child wants to go out to play and the parents don't allow this, saying, no you have to stay at home. Moral ethics isn't like an order forbidding things. Moral ethics also doesn't prevent us from enjoying whatever nice things or pleasures we may have in life. Also it isn't trying to put us in prison or intended to give us a hard time, preventing us from having any kind of fun, like putting someone in a straightjacket. That is not moral ethics. Rather, the purpose of moral ethics comes from the fact that our mind is always occupied with desire, wanting things. We always have the feeling, "I want this and need that."

If we chase after the object of desire, whatever it may be, we are never going to be satisfied. It is the nature of desire that it is never satisfied. No matter how much we are involved with pleasing our desires we will actually never find satisfaction, and desire never stops. It is compared to drinking salt water to quench our thirst. If we drink a glass of salt water, the more we drink the thirstier we get. We will drink one glass after the other because we will become thirstier with each glass. In the same way, no matter how much we get, we always want more and that is the way we relate to all pleasures or to all objects in general. Before we start taking something, we thought, "Well, if I have this, then I will be very happy." But once we have it we want more. Desire goes on and on and produces more and more frustration and more and more suffering. We shouldn't make the mistake and think that following after each thought of desire and the pleasures that ensue will provide us with the feeling of peace and happiness that we are actually looking for.

If we allow desire to take its own course and to increase on and on, then this is an endless process; it will never stop. We may even reach the point at which the whole world is at our disposal but still we won't feel happy or content. We will never reach the point at which we think, "Okay, it's enough now, it's all right now. I am satisfied." It is the very nature of desire to generate dissatisfaction. We think that desire brings satisfaction, pleasure and so forth, but it really only brings on more dissatisfaction since the mind never feels content, it never thinks,

"I have enough," rather it feels, "I want this. I want that. I want more. It's not enough." There will never be satisfaction.

If we can make limitations on desire and can stop the flow of desire then things will get better. For example, if we have a mosquito-bite that is very itchy and we think that we can relieve the pain by scratching it, the itch gets worse and we have to scratch more; it will never stop itching by scratching and will get worse in the end. We may finally scratch out our skin, but we still have the itch and it won't get better. On the other hand, if we are able to control the itch of the bite, then slowly the itch will diminish and will disappear completely. In the same way, when we want things and enjoy them our desire grows stronger and stronger, we never feel content. As our desire grows greater, our frustration, pain and problems become greater. But, if we can put a limit to desire, if we can stop becoming involved with desire all the time, then in the end it will decrease and with that suffering, pain and problems will decrease.

The reason why the Buddha called the quality of moral ethics "shila" in Sanskrit is because shila means "cool." This describes how when we stop following the ideas of desire we can find coolness and happiness. Coolness here is a simile for living in a very hot country and experiencing a cool breeze from which we immediately feel relieved from the burning heat. If we can sit under the shade of a tree we feel cool, nice and relaxed because we are sheltered from the burning heat. Our situation is that the fire of desire is constantly burning us. What can alleviate the burning heat of desire is very pure moral ethics, very pure conduct. This is compared to a cool breeze or stepping into a very cool house and automatically feeling peaceful, refreshed and relaxed. The particular quality of moral ethics is "coolness," which is right conduct.

Another word describing the quality of moral ethics is "pratimoksha" in Sanskrit, which means "rules of discipline." Some explanations of this are not quite accurate. For example, often this word is explained in terms of liberation: if you keep the vows properly then you gain liberation from samsara. This isn't really an accurate explanation. The true explanation is that by keeping the vows you will be free of the sufferings that arise when you don't keep them; the particular suffering that comes from a particular negative action is removed by keeping the vow that prevents you from doing this. For instance, if you have taken the vow of not killing, not stealing or not engaging in sexual misconduct, then you are automatically liberated from all the pain and suffering that arises from killing, stealing and engaging in sexual misconduct. In this sense, the name "pratimoksha" means, "liberated from the specific difficulties associated with each vow."

When we speak about becoming free from suffering and pain, what does this actually mean? If we examine what the source of our happiness and goodness we experience in life is then we see that it comes from having control over what we do, from having free will, a free choice to do what we choose. If we follow our desires and get lost in the objects of our desire then we lose control; we lose our free will and become a slave of our desire and the objects of our desires. For instance, if somebody is very fond of drinking, they lose their free will to do this or that; they are totally the slaves of alcohol. As this is true of any form of desire, as soon as somebody is hooked on something they lose their own freedom and ability to choose. They are the slave of their desire and will have to suffer the consequences. That is why if we can break or stop the chain of desire and involvement, our own freedom is won, our own freewill is won and the power of our own choice is won.

So, from this first point, which shows us the qualities and advantages that arise from keeping moral ethics and the disadvantages that arise from not keeping moral ethics, we can see that it is really the source of our own happiness if we maintain the right conduct.

II. Definition. The second point of the chapter tells us about the definition of moral ethics. The definition of moral ethics is to refrain from negative actions out of a pure motivation.[65]

Here I should mention that the fact that we make a promise and take a commitment of observing a vow is very meaningful and important. For example, let us consider a person who doesn't steal for a whole day. You may ask, "Will they benefit from not stealing? Are they going to get any virtue out of doing this?" The answer is, "No, they won't because they didn't intend not to steal. It just happened that they didn't steal that day." There was no pure intention behind the fact that they didn't steal that day or motivation not to steal. When will we get the benefit of not stealing? We will get the benefit when there is the definite motivation, the determination not to steal. If somebody says, "Well, today I am not going to steal or kill," then they have committed themselves and there is an intention behind it. In that sense something positive and virtuous has been generated. It all depends upon what we are aiming at. We might say, "I am not going to kill or steal for one day, one month, one year or one life." According to what we are aiming at and fixed for ourselves in our mind, all the time that we have mentally chosen to hold the commitment will determine the behavior during that time. During that time our behavior of not committing a negative action will be producing virtue.

III. Classification. The third point of this chapter describes the different aspects of moral ethics. Another way of saying it would be the three different types of vows: moral ethics of restraint, morality of accumulating dharma virtue and morality of benefiting other beings.

The first type is moral ethics that is aimed at eliminating faults (and stabilizing the mind). The second type is aimed at producing good qualities (to mature or ripen the dharma qualities in our mind). The third is the moral ethics of helping other beings (to bring others to full maturity).

IV. Characteristics of Each. The fourth point describes the characteristics of each of the three types of moral ethics.

A. Moral Ethics of Restraint.[66] This first type of moral ethics that eliminates negative behavior doesn't mean to forbid doing what is pleasant and nice. It doesn't mean that we have a nice life, doing good things, and then the Buddha comes along saying, "You can't have fun. You have to stop because it contradicts the dharma." For example, instead of forbidding a child to eat sweets, it is more like stopping a child from putting poison in its mouth, so, more like pointing out what is dangerous and harmful rather than trying to stop what is nice and pleasant. The rules of discipline or conduct show us that if we engage in certain actions or fail to avoid others then both in the short term and in the long term this will result in only unhappiness and difficulties. That is why we are told, "This is what we should observe and that is what we should abandon."

We can go further than that and consider the nature of certain actions. If we do negative actions then suffering will ensue. If we avoid negative actions then we will not experience or cause suffering. Whether the Buddha said this or not doesn't change the truth that certain actions are the root of suffering and bring on pain. It is obvious that if we engage in negative actions that bring on suffering we will suffer and if we avoid negative actions that bring on suffering we will not suffer. Taking the example of a child again: If the child wants to put its hand in fire, the parents will respond, "Don't do that because you will burn your hand." But actually, whether the parents say this or not will make no difference to the fact that if the child puts its hand in the fire they will burn their hand because that is the very nature of fire. If the child doesn't put its hand in the fire, the hand will not burn. In the same way, whether the Buddha said these things or not makes no difference; we have to give up negative actions otherwise we will suffer. Their nature is that they cause suffering. That is the reason why keeping certain rules of discipline accords with the fact that certain actions cause harm.

B. Morality of Accumulating Dharma Virtue. The second type of moral ethics is that of practicing everything positive, everything virtuous. We are all seeking happiness, but what is the cause of happiness? It is goodness and positive actions. If we accomplish positive actions then we will not harm other beings and furthermore will be creating the cause of our own happiness. That is why one aspect of moral ethics has to do with acting in a positive way.[67]

C. Morality of Benefiting Other Beings. The third type of moral ethics is that of intending to help other beings. If somebody thinks, "I must be happy and find my own happiness," that person will find it very difficult to accomplish that wish. The reason is because they will always encounter others who automatically stand in the way of them achieving their personal preference of finding happiness. The best way to achieve personal happiness is to make others happy. If we try to help others, if we become friends with them, then they won't create any obstacles for us, so we will find our own happiness by making others happy. In general, this means that there should be no discrimination in help between beings, that we should help others to find their own happiness and in so doing we will find our own happiness. This is the very best way to find happiness for others and us. When we speak about benefiting others it refers not only to short term help but ultimate help, which is not just removing temporary suffering and bringing temporary happiness, but helping others find the ultimate type of happiness and freedom from suffering.[68]

V. Increase. The fifth point of this chapter, and for all the paramitas, is identical with the fifth point on generosity, which is to increase through the powers of primordial wisdom (jnana), wisdom-awareness (prajna), and dedication.The key point to increase moral ethics is having a pure motivation.

VI. Perfection. The sixth point is also identical for all paramitas. The way to make moral ethics pure is to have both compassion and the wisdom of emptiness. These are the practices that make moral ethics pure.

VII. Result. The seventh point of this chapter discusses the results of practicing moral ethics, in other words what benefits evolve. There are two benefits, short term and ultimate.

The ultimate benefit is, of course, to accomplish Buddhahood. This is accomplished through practicing dharma. And the practice of dharma means engaging, not just taking teachings, thinking about them and remaining stuck on a theoretical level, it actually means working on and practicing. So, how do we practice the dharma? In three ways: through abandoning all faults of body, speech and mind; through cultivating all virtues of body, speech and mind; and thirdly by doing this not only for ourselves but for the benefit of all beings. If this is done we will achieve the result, and if this is not done we will not. This is what can be achieved through the practice of moral ethics.

Let's now look at the short term benefits of practicing the dharma. The first is that all the Buddhas will be pleased and think of us. Actually, the very nature of a Buddha implies the total absence of selfishness; a Buddha is only concerned with the benefit of others. If Buddhas see beings acting in a selfish way and harming others, not thinking in terms of helping others, they will be displeased. If Buddhas see beings acting positively and intending to help others they will be very happy. So, someone who has moral ethics will make the Buddhas very happy and will be embraced by the Buddhas who will always look upon them.

Another short term benefit is that someone who has true moral ethics will be worthy of respect. If someone acts negatively and harms others then there is not much cause for respect. But if someone acts purely and helps others they become worthy of great respect. It is said that everyone in the world will respect them, even gods. These are the two short term benefits of moral ethics, which are to be added to the mentioned ultimate benefit.

This concludes the explanation of the thirteenth chapter,
on the perfection of moral ethics, from
The Jewel Ornament of Liberation.

Chapter 14
The Perfection of Patience

Patience[69] constitutes the remedy against anger. In the same way as for generosity and moral ethics, there will be seven main points explaining this paramita.

I. Reflection on the Virtues and Faults. The first point of this chapter tells us about the benefits that come from practicing patience and about the problems that arise when we cannot be patient and give way to anger. So this point provides us with the reasons why we should be patient.

First of all, if we lack patience that means that we become angry and anger is something that we should really try to eliminate because it is the source of many problems, both in the short term and in the long term. Considering the short term problems: if we allow ourselves to become angry then we are going to waste all the good things that we might have done before; it will destroy the virtue that we have generated previously. This is because anger by nature contradicts the spiritual path of the dharma. The very point of dharma is to avoid harming other beings and to try to help them find the path to happiness; it is to benefit and make them happy. If somebody is angry, then their motivation becomes the opposite; they are intent on harming and causing suffering instead of wanting to cause happiness. Therefore this state of mind, which is in contradiction with the very essence of spiritual practice, will destroy whatever goodness we have already generated.

The second problem that arises in connection with anger is that not only is virtue destroyed but also we will find no happiness. When anger arises in the mind it is like poison. If we eat poison we have a lot of physical pain and suffering. Once anger enters our mind it is the same. Once anger is in the mind there is no longer a feeling of peace, well being or happiness, everything becomes painful and there is constant stress created by the presence of anger, so much so that we cannot enjoy anything anymore and nothing is pleasant. In the end we might not even be able to sleep at night because anger is burning us out. To begin with we might be somebody who is very clear in the mind and who can think sharply and properly, but once we become a victim of anger we cannot even think properly because our mind will be so agitated by anger.

The third problem that is created by anger is that in the end it will part us from our friends. When we become angry then others around us will see it; our face will look angry and reflect the feeling we have inside. We won't look pleasant, open or smiling, instead we will have a frown on our face and look uptight. Our behavior will be the same: we won't be able to behave smoothly and we will instead behave roughly and unpleasant for others. When we speak we won't be able to speak nicely and gently, instead we will say things in a rough and aggressive way. Also we probably will insult others. So, once we have anger and aggression in our mind, even though we might intend to say something nice, we are going to say something very upsetting for others and even though we might want to behave smoothly, we will not be able to. Also, even though we might think that we want to smile and look friendly, we won't be able to because anger will be too strong in our mind.

Once anger arises, it will affect people around us, whether they are friends, relatives or relations; people will notice this unpleasant behavior that we have, the unpleasant expression in our face and our angry speech. This is going to upset others. Even though we might be nice to them, even though we do things to help them, in the end they will be upset by this kind of behavior because they know that all they can expect from us is angry words, an angry face and angry behavior. In the end, they will be so upset that they have to part from us. So, that is the third bad effect of anger: not only do we waste our virtue, not only are we not happy any longer, but also we lose our friends, relatives and those close to us.

The fourth problem that comes from anger is that we will encounter lots of problems, difficulties and obstacles. As soon as somebody is taken over by anger, then their whole being becomes very rough, coarse and aggressive so that immediately all other people feel this and there is no longer the possibility of harmoniously relating with others; it becomes very difficult in all directions. It is true even for those who try to follow a spiritual practice. Even though they do try to practice, once they have become an angry person then they will only encounter difficulties and can't really practice because others are giving them a hard time and making it difficult to practice. This is also true in ordinary life. If somebody is angry, then they constantly have problems and difficulties.

These four faults that arise from anger concern the short term and are very obvious. Then there are other faults that arise from anger which concern the long term or more in the ultimate sense.

If we have anger then patience is missing. In fact, patience is one of the most important qualities that we need to have in order to accomplish Buddhahood. The direct cause for Buddhahood is to have the right kind of attitude, the right way of thinking; this is the very positive motivation of wanting enlightenment for the sake of others. The opposite of this positive motivation is anger that intends to harm others. If there is anger then automatically our motivation to accomplish enlightenment for the sake of others is not there, so the cause for enlightenment is not there. That is why it is said that one of the most powerful obstacles to the accomplishment of enlightenment is lacking patience; without patience it is impossible to become a Buddha.

These are the five problems that arise from anger, four on the temporary level and one in the ultimate sense.

If we have patience, we will attain the qualities that are opposite to the faults just mentioned. First of all, virtue will increase more and more. Secondly, a patient person will not have unpleasant experiences in their mind. Thirdly, other people will have no reason to be upset about us; there will be a very harmonious relationship with others who will feel happy with us and will like us. Fourthly, there will be no obstacles to what we are doing, neither in terms of daily activities nor in terms of spiritual practice. Finally, it is said that Buddhahood will be achieved very quickly. Shantideva said, "There is no defect that is as crucial as anger, and there is no quality as precious as patience." We must strive diligently to eliminate the worst enemy inside, which is anger. Patience will be the source for happiness in this life and in the next and will bring us to Buddhahood very quickly.

II. Definition. The second point of this section speaks about the definition of patience, which is said to be an undisturbed mind and an absence of retaliating reactions. This is possible through a compassionate attitude towards others, towards one who is harming us.

In all the sutras the Buddha explains what patience is: it is the state in which the mind remains undisturbed, unperturbed. If someone has harmed us, we do not react, we just let the mind remain relaxed, without immediately thinking about taking any actions. Actually, what we have to consider is that whatever harm has been done is over and finished. It would have been better had the person not harmed us, but it has been done, so there is no point in reacting, retaliating and starting it again since it is done.

In order not to think about retaliating we must not keep a grudge in our mind and not think about it, just drop the whole issue. If we do think about it, we will harbor the thought for an entire day, an entire month or even longer, and while we are brooding over this thought our anger will become bigger and bigger. In the end this will be the source of many problems and suffering, both for us and the other person. So, the essence of patience is not to brood over what has been done to us and not to think about it, but just to leave it and to forget it.

III. Classification. The different aspects of patience are defined in terms of the object towards which we must have patience. We find three different kinds: the patience of not being disturbed by the harm done by others, the patience of accepting suffering and patience in understanding dharma.

These are quite simple to understand. The first is patience towards enemies or those who try to harm us. Second is patience in the face of suffering, problems and difficulties we have to go through due to our previous actions. Third is the patience we need when facing the difficulties involved with understanding the great depth of the dharma. It is hard to understand the deep meaning of dharma and sometimes we might feel discouraged and think it is impossible to understand. It is then necessary to have courage and to face these difficulties. This is also a part of patience.

IV. Characteristics of Each Classification. The fourth section tells us about the nature of each aspect of patience. In fact, this will show us practical means on how to practice the different kinds of patience.

A. The Patience of Not Being Disturbed by the Harm Done by Others: The Way to Practice Patience Towards Someone Harming Us. The way to practice patience towards someone harming us is based upon understanding what an enemy really is by nature, in his or her essence. We try to see that there is no point in harming such a person or in being angry; this will bring no benefit, whereas patience towards them will be positive and very beneficial. There are two sets of instructions from two sets of teachings on how to practice patience: In the *Guide to the Bodhisattva Way of Life* taught by Shantideva we find many different ways of practicing and meditating on patience and in the *Bodhisattva Levels* taught by Asanga five techniques for developing patience are taught.

From Shantideva's *Guide to the Bodhisattva Way of Life* there are nine ways to practice or things to examine.

1. Consider Those That Harm Us Have No Freedom

First, examine someone who is harming us. They are totally out of control and under the power of anger. The reason they are harming us is because they cannot stop the anger that makes them aggressive. That person does not cause the harm done to us rather it is the anger now manipulating and controlling that person. Our real enemy is the anger. What has to be removed is anger in any form, in ourselves, in others, wherever, whenever. The way to react when someone harms us is to understand that the source of harm is anger itself, not the person. In this case we should think that anger is the source of all suffering and problems and that we are determined to eliminate anger itself. Thinking in this way we try to remain relaxed and to be patient.

2. Consider the Harm as the Fault of Our Own Karma

The second way to practice patience is to realize that whatever is happening to us, any harm we experience, is the result of previous actions. In general, the source of all our happiness is all the goodness we ourselves have done in the past, whatever virtuous actions we have done that were inspired by a pure motivation. Whatever negative actions we have done that were inspired by a negative motivation are the cause of all our sufferings. So, presently it looks like we are suffering because of our enemy, but in fact this is the result of our own negative actions done previously. We should understand that our problems are not due to our enemies, rather they are due to our own previous negative actions. Thinking in this way, we realize that there is no point in being angry with others because the real cause is our own negative actions. With this thought in mind we try to practice patience.

3. Consider the Harm is the Fault of Our Own Body

The third way to practice patience is to realize that the reason we are suffering if someone is harming us is because we have a body. So here it is to realize that the fault lies in the fact that we have a body. If we can be hurt by someone else it is not that person's own doing, rather it is because we have a body. If we didn't have a body, then weapons, beatings and so on could not harm us. However, we have taken this illusory body made of flesh and blood, which we take as our own self and because of this we can now be exposed to pain. For example, if someone stabs us with a knife we will experience the pain of being stabbed because we have a body. It wouldn't be right to blame the enemy for the pain we experience. Of course, it looks like the enemy is causing the pain because they are hurting us with a knife or whatever, but really this is just due to the fact that we have a body in the first place.[70] So, it is not right to blame an enemy for the pain that comes from us. This should be another way to make us stop and think and have patience.

4. Consider the Harm is the Fault of Our Own Mind

The fourth way to practice patience is to realize that any pain we experience is the fault of our own mind. When someone hurts us the real cause is that in the first place our mind made a very big mistake. When our mind looks at the body and claims, "This is me! This is my body!" our mind took an inferior body. Instead of taking a tough body made of iron or stone that nothing could break or hurt our mind took this very fragile and sensitive body, one that can be hurt so easily. For example, the skin can be scratched so easily and so much pain can be felt. So, when someone hurts us, we have pain and this makes us angry, in fact, we should realize that this isn't the enemy's fault, rather our mind made a big mistake in the first place by taking this over-sensitive body that can now feel all this suffering. This should help us feel more patient.

5. Consider Both Have Equal Fault

The fifth way to try to develop patience is to try to think that really both the enemy and us are at fault; it is not only our enemy's fault but also ours. In the first place, the enemy made the mistake because they were angry with us, but we must have done something wrong too in order to make them angry. So, it wouldn't be right to get angry with them because really we are equally at fault ourselves. The best thing to do is to just forget about the whole thing because both were at fault to begin with. This is another way to practice patience in the face of any harm caused.

6. Consider the Benefit Received

The sixth way to try to develop patience is to think that the enemy is actually benefiting and helping us. It might not look like this. At first we think that they are causing us a lot of trouble and pain but once we can think about it in a clear and straight way then we realize that the enemy is actually helping us. The cause of all our problems and sufferings lie in our past mistakes. We have to stop making mistakes and purify whatever previous mistakes we have made. What can purify our mistakes are their opposites, virtues which will gradually eliminate the impure actions. So, presently anger would create more problems, more suffering and it is patience that can help us eliminate all the harmful effects of our previous anger; it will generate the virtue that can purify it. In this sense the enemy is someone who is doing us a favor, they are helping us to be patient; without an enemy we could not be patient. So, through the enemy we can have the patience that will generate the virtue that is required to purify our negative actions done in connection with anger. Therefore we should realize that the enemy is in fact doing us a favor and that will help us be more patient.

7. Consider Gratitude

The seventh way to develop patience goes even further. It says that we should think of the enemy as being extremely kind to us. In our attempt to practice the dharma properly we have to try to develop all the qualities of the six paramitas, so we have to try to be generous, keep good moral ethics, to be patient and so on. In connection with each quality we need to find the object that will enable us to develop that quality. If we take generosity as an example, it is very easy to find an object for generosity since there are lots of people who want or are looking for something, so it is very easy to give things away. But in the case of patience it is more difficult and a very rare occasion because normally we have to harm someone in order to make him or her angry at us. It is rare and seldom that someone we have not harmed will harm us. So, someone who harms us or who is aggressive towards us is doing us a very big favor because they are providing us with the opportunity to practice patience; we couldn't practice patience without that person. So, we should feel that truly this is a very rare opportunity, like finding an extremely precious jewel. If someone harms us we can practice patience and should feel, "This is great. Now I have the opportunity to practice patience because somebody else is giving me the chance. I am going to use it as best I can."

8. Consider How All the Buddhas are Pleased

The eighth way to try to develop patience is to think that patience will please the Buddhas immensely. The very nature of a Buddha is to have great kindness, love and compassion towards all beings. If any being is hurt the Buddhas are not pleased. If someone can refrain from anger and harm, the Buddhas are pleased. So, we should think that if we can manage to be patient it would please the Buddhas immensely. It will please them in two ways: first they will see that we are not harming the other person and secondly they will see that we are capable of being patient. We should consider our patience an offering to please the Buddhas.

9. Consider the Great Benefits

The ninth way to practice patience is to be aware of the great benefits that come from patience. If someone is patient it means that automatically all beings around them will be happy because that person won't harm them. Also, we have to remember that all the Buddhas in the past accomplished enlightenment because they practiced great patience. We should feel that if we also can practice great patience we will accomplish enlightenment and once we accomplish enlightenment we can also help other beings to do the same. In this way, being aware of all the goodness and benefits that come from patience we will be able to practice it.

That was the explanation on the way to develop patience in nine different reflections. Now we will consider the five different techniques of meditation on patience according to Asanga.

1. Thinking of Feeling Close to the One Who Harms Us

The first way is to think that the enemy is very dear to us. Presently this person is our enemy, but we have to try and realize that in many past lives this person had probably been our father, mother, dear friend, close relative, our child and so on. Again in the future it will happen that this person will have this close relationship with us. So, sometimes we are related to people in a way that is very close and intimate and sometimes in a way that is inimical. Sometimes people are our friends and sometimes they are our enemies. But we should realize that it is a mistake on our part to only treat people with love when they appear as our friends and then with hatred when they appear as our enemies. This means that we should always try to be kind towards people and there is no point in harming those who seem to be our enemies now. This thought should help us be patient.

2. Thinking that Everything Depends on Interdependent Conditions

The second way to think is that the enemy is not a real thing. The idea that another person is an enemy is only a thought; there is no real thing there called "enemy." It is only because we have fallen under the power of anger that we call this person "enemy." At another time, in the absence of anger and with a positive relationship, this same person was called "friend." So, "enemy" is only a creation of the mind, the result of a negative attitude. It is only a way of thinking, an idea that doesn't have an actual reality of its own. There is no such thing as "enemy" in reality. Thinking in this way we can be patient.

3. Thinking of Impermanence

The third way to be patient is to think that the enemy is impermanent. While we feel anger we try to harm the other person and maybe want to eliminate them or maybe even kill them. But we should realize that there is no need to do this. The other person is impermanent and will die one day; they will vanish of their own accord. This thought should help us be patient.

4. Thinking of Suffering

The fourth way to develop patience is to think of suffering. We have to realize that everybody, whether an enemy, friend or those we are indifferent towards are all exposed to suffering. As long as someone is subject to conditioned existence they will have to suffer in many different ways. Suffering is never something that we need to create because there is always too much suffering. Rather than creating suffering we should try to eliminate it. So, thinking in this way – that we must not add to the suffering there is enough of anyway – we shouldn't add more but eliminate suffering and we try to be patient.

5. Thinking of Fully Embracing All Beings

The fifth way is the thought of cherishing beings. When we took the commitment to accomplish enlightenment for the sake of all beings, we committed ourselves to help them in all possible ways; we committed ourselves to looking after them. If now we were going to harm someone whom previously we promised to protect and help it wouldn't be any good. This also should help us to be patient towards the ones we think are our enemies.

Concerning this first type of patience – patience in the face of harm – imagine that someone hurts us. Our immediate reaction would be to retaliate, feeling that if someone has done something wrong we really have to do something about it and we must react by harming that person. But, we should think twice before we do this because if we retaliate and hurt the other person in return it won't take away the pain we have experienced; the pain remains whether we retaliate or not. Retaliating will not relieve us or erase the fact that someone hurt us in the first place. That is one point to contemplate. The other point is that if we retaliate, then we are going to arouse the other person's anger once again, and as long as their anger blazes like a fire they will continue hurting us all the more. That is why we should understand that retaliating is not the answer; reacting in such strong ways is not the right way to deal with problems. The right way, as I discussed earlier when I defined patience, is not to think anything about it, just drop the whole issue completely. If we can do this, if we can stand not retaliating and be patient, then gradually the other person's anger will decrease and this will take away the heat from the situation. You just let things cool down. This is the first thing to do, not reacting and retaliating to harm done to us.

In the teachings of Shantideva there is a very good example to illustrate the effect of patience. Shantideva explained that if we need to travel through many different places, going on paths, roads and over hills barefoot, we would have to walk over stones, sharp pebbles, thorns and objects that hurt our feet. In the end our feet will be worn and blistered. What is the solution? One solution would be to pave every inch of road we cover with a leather carpet and then we wouldn't feel any pain. However, the fact is that at the end of that paved road sharp stones and thorns would prick our feet upon our continuing, so we would need another carpet. If we had to do this we would have to cover the whole earth with a leather carpet and all the leather in the world would not suffice. But maybe there's a better solution. Instead of covering the world with leather we could cover our feet with leather. Once we had leather shoes and soles, wherever we went automatically our feet would be protected from the thorns and stones pricking and stabbing at our feet. This solution would be the same as covering the whole earth with leather.

In the same way, if we try to use external solutions against the problem "the enemy," if we have an enemy we want to get rid of and manage to do so we will find ourselves with another enemy whom we will have to fight. Once we have dealt with that enemy the next is waiting in the endless process. We will end up having to kill everybody because there will always be someone who is our enemy. So, the solution is within ourselves:

it is the anger within the mind that has to be overcome. That's the enemy we must get rid of. Once we have eliminated this enemy then there is no reason to fear external enemies. Everything becomes very smooth, like when we wear leather shoes with which we can walk where we want. Nothing hurts us; neither stones nor thorns will cause pain. So we need patience, which is the root cause to overcome enemies. If we have patience then no matter what happens there is no anger or retaliation.

This finishes the section on the way one has to practice patience in connection with the first type of patience, which is to put up with harm that is done.

***B. The Patience of Accepting Suffering:** The Way to Practice Patience by Enduring Suffering with Appreciation.* Generally, suffering is something we want to get rid of; nobody wants to suffer. Unfortunately, suffering is the universal problem of all mankind, more than that, of all beings in conditioned existence. As long as someone is part of conditioned existence then suffering befalls him or her because it is an intrinsic part of existence. In fact, whoever says "existence" says "suffering." We can suffer in all sorts of different ways, due to illness, poverty, age or, in general, the problem common to all mankind, that of excessive activities and frustration, the all-pervasive suffering explained earlier. This applies to everyone in all different walks of life. Take someone very wealthy and famous or someone who doesn't have any wealth and fame, both have the same problems; they have suffering which comes automatically because they are part of existence. When suffering arises we shouldn't think it is something exceptional befalling us personally or that we are a special case and that we must be incredibly unlucky to experience those problems. If we take suffering personally we will increase the pain by our way of thinking. We would increase it to the degree of it becoming unbearable, so much so that we could even think about committing suicide; it can lead us to that extreme. But, there is no need to do that. Suffering does happen, it is part of existence, but we shouldn't take it personally. We aren't an exception when we suffer; suffering is the lot of all beings in existence. Everybody seeks happiness and nobody wants to suffer. But rare are those who find happiness and freedom from suffering.

We should understand that since suffering is part of existence there is no need to aggravate it by thinking negatively and fatalistically. The best thing to do in the face of suffering is to accept it and to think that there are ways to go beyond suffering and to gain freedom from it. We should try to work in that direction.

We have to endure suffering, and, as said, it is not a personal experience. It is the lot of everybody in cyclic existence since it is an intrinsic part of conditioned existence. In the face of this suffering, we should use it. If we can be patient when suffering arises then we know that we can use the opportunity presented to go beyond suffering. We can use the little problems we have now in order to become free from all the great problems of existence. That is, if we practice in order to achieve liberation from suffering, then while we practice it will certainly be difficult and at times will require tremendous effort and diligence in order to accomplish enlightenment, but we have to try to bear these problems and difficulties. If we compare these little problems with the endless sufferings of existence, then our problems are very small and are really worthwhile putting up with in order to gain freedom from all the great suffering existence entails.

It is similar to what we have to do when we have a severe illness. We may need an operation, and the operation is something painful. We have pain for a few days, but we put up with the pain from the operation because we know that it is what can release us from the much greater ongoing suffering coming from the sickness. In the same way, we can put up with suffering and the difficulties involved with practice, knowing that this will lead us to liberation from suffering.

This second aspect of patience refers not only to putting up with pain and suffering, but even more than that, using suffering to go beyond suffering. How can we use suffering to go beyond suffering? If we are presently going through pain, difficulties and suffering, we have to try to understand what the cause is. Let us take the example of someone thrown into prison. Why was that person imprisoned in the first place? Maybe they became involved in a fight because of their anger or maybe they stole something out of desire. In any case, they are suffering in prison because they did something arising out of a negative state of mind. So now this person has to put up with the difficulties in prison because of desire or anger. If they want to avoid experiencing this suffering again they will have to do whatever they can to prevent the same cause which led them into prison before; they will have to make sure that their desire and anger won't lead them into the same situation of being locked in jail again.

Likewise, if we have suffering we should understand where it comes from. If we had no negativity in our mind there would be no opportunity for suffering to arise. The first thing to do is to overcome the inner enemy; the real enemy isn't outside of us, it is within us and is the negativity that leads us to do negative things that cause suffering. If we can overcome this inner enemy then we will really be heroes who can find happiness and who can go beyond suffering.

Normally people think that others are the enemies and they think, "That person is my enemy, so I have to fight them. I have to buy a weapon and kill them." But it is no accomplishment to kill someone; there is nothing heroic to that because killing an enemy is like killing a corpse. The enemy is just as mortal as everyone else and whether they die now or later doesn't make that much of a difference, they are going to die anyway. It is much more beneficial to kill the inner enemy of our negativity. If we do it will be the source of great happiness.

***C. Patience in Understanding Dharma**: The Way to Practice Patience by Wishing to Contemplate on the Nature of Reality.* The third kind of patience needed is the patience to understand the dharma. Some people may feel that the dharma, the teachings of the Buddha, are so deep and subtle that they won't be able to understand them, let alone practice them. Of course, if someone feels like this they won't progress and won't be able to achieve any results. Discouragement is the feeling that we can't understand the teachings, can't practice and can't get anywhere, even if we tried. But there is no need to be discouraged in this way. Even if we want to achieve something on the ordinary level of life we put some degree of effort into accomplishing it because we know how profitable it will be in the long term. In the same way, we have to try to practice the dharma because we know that it can lead us to happiness.

As mentioned in the chapter on moral ethics, the Buddha's teachings on what to practice and what to give up aren't intended to make us suffer. The Buddha did not say, "These are nice things and you have to give them up because they are no good for dharma" or "These things will really bring suffering and you have to practice them because they accord with the dharma." What the Buddha did was to point out what the cause of suffering is, so that we can eliminate suffering, and what the cause of happiness is, so that we can experience happiness. In the same way, we should understand that although some things in the dharma may be difficult to understand and practice in the short term, it is worth trying because the benefits that arise will be great. So, knowing that Buddha taught the truth of things, which leads us to happiness, we should feel enough courage to face any difficulties involved with understanding and practicing the dharma.

V. Increase. The fifth point discusses how we should increase patience, and it is increased in the same way as the other paramitas, through the powers of primordial wisdom, wisdom-awareness and dedication.

VI. Perfection. The sixth section says that we should make patience pure. It is made pure both through the understanding of emptiness and through great compassion for all beings, as with the other paramitas.

VII. Result. There are two results that come from practicing patience, ultimate and temporary or short term results. The ultimate result is said to be unsurpassable enlightenment. Patience is very powerful and once this quality is there it will go on by itself. In the beginning, it may be difficult to practice patience but once we get used to it, it becomes easier and easier until it is something natural, like a second nature. It is said in some instructions, "There is nothing that doesn't become easier once it is a habit, once it is a second nature." So, although at first it might be difficult to practice patience, it will become easier and easier, until it grows all by itself, up to the point when one accomplishes Buddhahood. This is the ultimate result.

The temporary or short term result from practicing patience is that we will have a long life, no sickness, fame and so on. We can interpret this as being valid for the next life but it could also apply to this life. If somebody is very aggressive, then they will have many enemies and will therefore experience many problems. These problems are enough to ruin our reputation; they are enough to make us sick and to shorten our life. On the other hand, if we are patient then we will have the benefits of living a long life, of being free of illness caused by anger or worry and will probably have a good reputation. Spontaneously things are better and more positive if we have patience.

This concludes the explanation of the fourteenth chapter,
on the perfection of patience, from
The Jewel Ornament of Liberation.

Chapter 15
The Perfection of Diligence

We must know that one thing is required to practice the paramitas and that is diligence, the fourth paramita. All the paramitas are very beneficial but their benefit can only be attained if we practice, and the capacity to practice depends upon diligence. Without diligence we will not be able to achieve the powerful and beneficial results of the paramitas. That is why diligence is very essential among all paramitas. We will now look at the chapter on diligence, again dealt with in seven points.

I. Reflection on the Virtues and Faults. We should know why it is necessary to have diligence. Therefore the first point discusses the reasons why we need to have diligence. If we know the reasons then it will be easy to practice diligence; we will know why we need to have it and we will want to have it, otherwise we wouldn't feel motivated to have it. So, the first point tells us about the qualities that arise from having diligence and the faults that arise from not having diligence.

Somebody might be generous, have moral ethics and be patient, but if they are not diligent they will fall under the power of laziness, which is always possible. If someone is lazy they will not be able to achieve any real results through practice or be able to accumulate much virtue, so they will not accomplish very much. Also, they will not be able to do much to help other beings. Finally, in the long term, they will not be able to accomplish Buddhahood. So, if somebody wants to gather great virtue, to help other beings and to reach Buddhahood, they need to eliminate laziness, which is done by cultivating diligence.

In many sutras the Buddha spoke about the benefits of being diligent and the faults of being lazy. He spoke about this extensively in the *Sagaramati-Requested Sutra* (Tib. *Lodro Gyatso Zhupai Do*). The Buddha said that somebody who is lazy couldn't have true generosity, cannot really have moral ethics and cannot have patience and so on, for all paramitas up to prajna. Somebody who is lazy cannot really help other beings and for such a person Buddhahood is indeed very far away. On the other hand, if somebody has diligence, they will automatically be free from all those mistakes, which means that they will be able to have generosity, moral ethics, patience and so on, all the paramitas up to prajna. They will be able to help other beings and for such a person Buddhahood will be very near. In the *Condensed Perfection of Wisdom Sutra* (Tib. *Shechen Dupe Do*), the Buddha said, "Perseverance will not obscure all the virtuous qualities. One will achieve the treasury of limitless primordial wisdom of the Victorious One." This means that once someone has diligence, their virtue will never diminish and they will be able to find the great treasure of the Buddha's wisdom.

Now we are aware of the benefits of diligence and of the fact that it is indeed very harmful not to have diligence. Once we know this, we need to know what diligence actually is, what we are really talking about. The answer to this is given in the second point, which speaks about the essence of diligence.

II. Definition. When we use the word "bilja" (in Sanskrit) or "tsondhu" (in Tibetan) for diligence, it doesn't mean that you can use this for something negative. For example, if you invest all your effort in killing or stealing, this is not the diligence spoken about here. When speaking about the paramitas, diligence only applies to a high quality, something worthwhile.

Another definition of diligence is taking delight in what is good and wholesome. Taking delight in what is good and wholesome means that when you are doing something that is proper and correct, it will always be beneficial and will only bring on positive results. Also, it can never be the cause of any harm to oneself or others. This is true for whatever *yana* you consider. If someone is practicing virtue either in terms of the Hinayana or the Mahayana, this goodness will only be the cause for progressing from good to better. It will never be the cause for going from good to bad and will never involve harming others. So, we are not speaking about worldly effort which can also refer to harmful things, rather we are speaking about diligence which only refers to wholesome things and accordingly only brings on positive results. This is diligence defined as delighting in what is good and wholesome and as being the remedy to laziness.

Now, if we want to practice diligence we will have to eliminate laziness. This means that first we must be able to identify laziness so that we can eliminate it.

There are three kinds of laziness: the laziness of apathy and sloth, the laziness of discouragement and the laziness caused by being involved with lower aims.

A. The Laziness of Apathy and Sloth. The first type of laziness is apathy or sloth, which means a total absence, an unwillingness to act in any way; you are not prepared to do anything at all and remain disinterested. All you want to do is take it easy, lounging around and sleeping. You enjoy feeling at ease and rest in your body and mind and you remain involved with the pleasure you get from this. This kind of laziness really has to be abandoned. Not because it is pleasant, but because, as I mentioned earlier, now is the most precious time for us. This is a special opportunity for us. It is a time when we have the right body with all necessary freedoms and accomplishments to realize the greatest goal. Also, this is a time when we have a mind that is intelligent enough to know and understand what we need to understand. This is really a golden time. And this time shouldn't be wasted; it should be used properly, it should be used for practice. It would be completely pointless to waste this time by sleeping too much or by lying around and doing nothing.

The Buddha said that in the future the precious body that we have now would end; this very precious opportunity will not last forever. Now is the time when we can work towards Buddhahood. Now is the time when we can practice. Now is the time when we can help other beings. One day this time will run out, so we have to use it now. We also have to consider the fact that the teachings will not be here forever. Now that they are present we must make good use of the opportunity.

So, we have all these precious opportunities, we have the right body and mind and the Buddha's teachings are here. Why can't we practice? Why don't we practice? This is the time to make an effort. This is the time to be diligent. If we don't practice it is very stupid. So, we should really try to be diligent and give up this first kind of laziness.

Since our time is so precious – it is such a fortunate juncture in our existence – we must use it properly and with diligence. Even a very short moment is important and to waste even an instant is a great loss. So avoid wasting even one minute since it can be used in a very beneficial way. If we meditate for one minute or recite a *mantra* or do a prostration, these short minutes will not be wasted but will bring great results, whereas if we just waste these minutes, nothing will come about at all. In the same way, if we use one hour positively, either to meditate or to recite mantras or to do prostrations or anything valuable, it will bear great results. We should consider that even though we may not be able to be diligent all the time, every hour that can be used diligently will produce great results. So, we shouldn't postpone being diligent, we shouldn't think, "Okay, I'll start tomorrow" or "Okay, I'll start next year." We must start now because time is running out. This precious time is here now but it won't be here forever.

How should we go about eliminating the laziness of apathy or sloth? A few examples are presented to illustrate the way. The first example is that of a very cowardly man who suddenly sees that a snake has crept onto his lap. He immediately jumps up because he realizes the danger. He doesn't wait one minute. In the same way, we should start practicing right away because time is running out. Another example is that of a beautiful girl whose hair has caught fire. She immediately stops doing what she had been doing and extinguishes the fire. In the same way, we should immediately stop doing what we are doing and engage in virtue and being diligent.

That is the first kind of laziness and how to eliminate it.

B. The Laziness of Discouragement. The second kind of laziness arises from discouragement, which happens when you belittle yourself, thinking, "I am useless and no good. I can't manage to do anything. There is no point in even trying because I won't succeed. I can't work towards enlightenment and get rid of my negativity. There is no hope for me to help others. I can't meditate. Maybe bodhisattvas can do all this, but I can't." When you put yourself down in this manner and without any reason you will be in a state of great discouragement that will paralyze you to the point of total inability. This is a wrong way of thinking though because whatever the Buddhas and bodhisattvas accomplished we too can accomplish. We know the reason behind this, which is the topic in the first chapter on the Buddha potential.

We all have the same potential to accomplish enlightenment; the Buddha-essence is within the mind of each and every sentient being. That is why whatever Buddha Shakyamuni accomplished, so too can we. Besides having this wonderful potential within, we also have the perfect opportunity of the right life endowed with all necessary freedoms and qualities. And we have the teachings of the Buddha to help us accomplish the goal of enlightenment. So, there is absolutely no reason why we cannot do what Buddha Shakyamuni managed. And there is no reason why we can't accomplish what the great masters of the past, like Marpa, Milarepa and Gampopa, accomplished.[71] We have the same potential and the same teachings they received. So, there is no reason to be discouraged. We should try to eliminate this feeling of discouragement and instead practice diligently.

If we have all the good conditions just described, the potential for enlightenment and the right life, is there a guarantee that we will accomplish Buddhahood? No, not necessarily, because we still have to work for it. Whoever tries to accomplish Buddhahood will accomplish it, but if someone doesn't even try they will fail. So, whether we accomplish Buddhahood or not depends entirely upon ourselves, upon our own efforts. If we work to accomplish enlightenment, we will accomplish it and, if we don't, we won't. Even the greatest person will fail if they don't try. That is why it is important to give up the laziness of self-discouragement and to work diligently towards Buddhahood.

C. The Laziness Caused by Being Involved with Lower Aims. The third form of laziness is the laziness of involvement with lower pursuits. As mentioned, diligence here doesn't refer to negative activities. If someone is skilled at doing negative things it happens automatically because they want something so much. If somcone visits the pub in the morning and returns at night, drinking all day long, it wouldn't be proper to say that they are diligent at drinking because that is not the meaning of diligence. Diligence doesn't refer to automatically satisfying ones craving for negative things, or to harming others, or to striving to become rich, famous or the like. Rather, diligence only refers to doing things worthwhile and beneficial, for others and us, and not only in the short term but ultimately. That is when we may speak of diligence.

One of the greatest examples for diligence is the story of Naropa, who was able to practice so diligently that he didn't even care about food or clothes. He was able to undergo tremendous hardships and difficulties for the sake of his practice. Earlier I had pointed out that Milarepa hadn't practiced austerity for the sake of austerity; he wasn't depriving himself of food and clothes as a goal, rather he realized how precious his time was and didn't want to waste a minute running after food and clothes. For instance, it would have been very tedious for Milarepa to go to the village to get food, clothes and other comforts of life. He preferred spending his time practicing dharma because he knew that the benefit is greater than the feeling of physical comfort. He didn't make the mistake of going through hardships for the sake of it, rather he wanted to devote all his time to practice and was able to put up with physical difficulties because he so strongly wanted to accomplish the ultimate result. He knew that there wasn't much physically to lose, but it would have been a tremendous loss to waste the opportunity to accomplish enlightenment. Nothing could stop his diligence. In this way, Milarepa was able to overcome the three kinds of laziness. He didn't have sloth; he didn't have the laziness of discouragement because he knew that he would accomplish enlightenment if he practiced diligently, so he wasn't lazy by being involved with lower pursuits because he didn't even look for food and clothes. It is entirely due to being free of these three kinds of laziness and to being devoted to his practice diligently that he was able to accomplish enlightenment in one life.[72]

The first two kinds of laziness need to be eliminated by the practitioner himself or herself. Others, especially the spiritual friend and dharma friends, can give us instructions to eliminate the third kind of laziness. For instance, if the problem comes from having no trust and faith in ourselves, others can help us get rid of that kind of laziness, nevertheless in the end we will have to work at it ourselves. It is essential to understand why we shouldn't feel discouraged and why we should be diligent because if we don't understand there is no way to get out. We have to keep on reading and contemplating the instructions until the meaning has penetrated us, which then leads us to the point of actually putting the teachings into practice.

III. Classification. The third point in this chapter tells us about three different kinds of diligence: armour-like diligence, diligence of application and insatiable diligence.

The first describes the best and most positive motivation. The second, diligence in action, is when we actually act and really work for something. It describes the power and capacity of diligence allowing us to achieve our aim. The third applies to when we never have the feeling that we have ever done enough; it keeps us going until the task is totally completed.

IV. Characteristics of Each Classification. The fourth point discusses the nature of each of the three kinds of diligence.

A. Armour-like Diligence. Armour-like diligence is described in an example. If someone is wearing armour, then their body is protected by something strong and tough, so this person can pass their enemies unharmed; they needn't be afraid because they know that they are well protected. In the same way, the armour of our determination can protect us. So here we are speaking about the finest kind of motivation, which is great determination.

If there is great determination, then automatically the other kinds of diligence will be present. If we have decided to do something and have really set our mind upon it strongly, then we will definitely do it, which is diligence in action. We will definitely carry on until the end, which is insatiable diligence. So, the armour-like diligence, the determination and motivation, conditions the birth of the other two kinds of diligence. If we wear the armour of diligence, then automatically the other two will be there. Whereas if we are discouraged and don't have determination, then of course we will not be able to do anything.

To illustrate this point, in the days of Marpa, Milarepa and Gampopa, there was no need to do any preliminary practices (Tib. *Ngondro*) because in those days people had a very strong determination, they had a very outstanding wish to practice and tremendous diligence. So, there was no need to measure diligence through the preliminary practices. But as time went by people's diligence weakened so that they didn't have enough determination to even take refuge. That is why these kinds of measures had to be laid down (engaging in the preliminary practices) of having to do 100,000 prostrations, 100,000 recitations of the Vajrasattva mantra and so on. These were laid down in order to help people develop the armour of diligence, to help them form a determination that would be strong enough to practice. Once we have the right kind of determination we would be willing to do 1,000,000 prostrations. So, if we are prepared to practice, it means that we will be able to accomplish 100,000 prostrations. But if we do not have sufficient determination, then we will not be able to finish even 100,000 prostrations. This is the description of the first kind of diligence, armour-like diligence.

B. Diligence of Application. The second aspect of diligence is diligence in action, which refers to when we are actually able to do something practically. Diligence in action has to be applied in three ways: diligence to eliminate *disturbing emotions*, diligence to practice virtue and diligence to benefit other beings.

1. Diligence to Eliminate Disturbing Emotions

First of all, diligence in action must apply to eliminating negativity. We may begin with the feeling that there is very little we can do about our negativity, feeling that it is impossible to get rid of desire, anger or whatever. If we feel like this then of course we will be totally overpowered by these negative feelings and if we are overpowered we cannot do anything about it. But, in fact, we can do something. Taking the example of anger, whether anger arises or not depends upon us. It is our own doing if anger arises or not. There is nobody else controlling our mind, saying, "Well, if you don't get angry now, I will beat you up." It is entirely up to us. If we decide to be angry, we will be angry, but if we do not want to get angry, we can also overcome anger. So, we have to become responsible for our own mind, we have to become the boss of our own mind and we can do it if we try. So, if we try to apply diligence to eliminating negativity, then it will definitely bring results.

2. Diligence to Practice Virtue

The second way to apply diligence in action is practicing something that is positive and virtuous, which in this case means to apply practice to the other five paramitas.[73]

3. Diligence to Benefit Other Beings

The third way to practice diligence in action is to benefit other beings. It is thinking, "I must help other beings. I can help other beings." Once we have this determination and this diligent effort, we will be able to help other beings.

C. Insatiable Diligence. The third kind of diligence is insatiable diligence. When we do something without achieving anything, we don't think, "Well, now I have done enough. It's all right, I will stop." Instead, we must carry on until we actually achieve the goal of our efforts. The very meaning of diligence is to bring us to the point of achieving the result. So, we should carry on practicing diligently until we do achieve the result. If we only apply diligence from time to time, we won't achieve anything, there won't be a proper result. That is why diligence should be practiced until the full result is achieved.

V. Increase. The fifth point discusses how we should increase diligence. It is increased in the same way as the other paramitas, through the powers of primordial wisdom, wisdom-awareness and dedication.

VI. Perfection. The sixth section says that we should make patience pure. It is made pure both through the understanding of emptiness and through great compassion for all beings, as with the other paramitas.

VII. Result. The seventh point explains the result of diligence. There are two sorts of results, the ultimate and the short term. The ultimate result of diligence is the accomplishment of Buddhahood. And this is so important that it makes diligence worthwhile. Even in the short term, diligence is very beneficial. For whatever we attempt to achieve, even in daily life, we will need diligence in order to achieve a result; without diligence we won't achieve anything. All this shows the great importance and value of diligence.

This concludes the explanation of the fifteenth chapter,
on the perfection of diligence, from
The Jewel Ornament of Liberation.

Chapter 16
The Perfection of Meditative Concentration

In our quest for liberation and omniscience, which means Buddhahood, we travel the path and on the path we try to eliminate all the mistakes that presently separate us from enlightenment. These mistakes are to be found in our mind. But if we can eliminate these mistakes then all the various qualities of our Buddha-essence can manifest. The mistakes that are present in our mind are the three poisons – ignorance/bewilderment, desire/attachment and anger/aversion – the three negative mental mistakes that cause all our problems and sufferings. As explained, all of the instructions on the paramitas are remedies to help us get rid of these negative mental states.

The antidote to desire is what was taught in the paramitas of generosity and moral ethics. The antidote to anger is what was taught in the paramita on patience. The root of both desire and anger is ignorance. Ignorance here means not knowing, not properly understanding what is actually there, not understanding things as they actually are. This is basic ignorance, not recognizing or not seeing.[74] From not seeing, all the other negative mental states arise. For instance, we become attached to an object that isn't worthy of being attached to. This comes from bewilderment or delusion of what the object actually is, from not understanding that the object is not worthy of attachment or involvement. It is the same for aversion or anger, which are pointless and harmful for both others and ourselves. If we don't understand this we think it is all right to let ourselves go into the feelings of anger and aversion. Again, this is due to delusion, not understanding what we should really do. Behind all this we find ignorance, which is the root of all negative states of mind. Where is ignorance? It is in our mind.

Since ignorance is a basic state of not knowing, then how can we get rid of it? Through knowing of course. We learn what is true through eliminating what is mistaken, through replacing mistakes with the absence of mistakes, by replacing not knowing with knowing. In order to know things as they truly are, the mind must first become clear and stable. At the moment our mind is completely agitated and obscured by the presence of many kinds of different thoughts. Therefore, first we have to make the mind stable, and once the mind is stable we gradually come to see what is truly there. What will help make the mind stable is meditative concentration or mental tranquility. Once we have basic stability of mind, then we can come to gain insight or prajna. Once we have gained insight, then we can see the mistake, abandon it and see what is truly there. This is the way to eliminate ignorance. Once ignorance is defeated, automatically all other negative states of mind will be eliminated. This is how we will gradually come to accomplish the ultimate realization. We will now look at the chapter on meditative concentration, again dealt with in seven points.

I. Reflection on the Virtues and Faults. The first point speaks about the advantages and disadvantages, in this case the advantages of having a stable mind and the disadvantages of not having a stable mind. This is presented in order to point out the importance of developing meditative concentration.

In order to consider the disadvantages of not having a stable mind we must first reflect on the condition of our mind. As said many times previously, the actual nature of our mind is the very same nature as that of the pure mind of the Buddha. Our mind possesses the essence of Buddhahood, which is the union of lucid clarity and emptiness. Although our mind is lucid clarity and emptiness, by nature it is like this, for a very long time we have acquired many bad habits, particularly the habit of following after our thoughts so that these habits dominate the mind. We have lost power and control over our mind, so much so that if we decide to concentrate upon something, we aren't able to and our mind just goes its own way. Therefore, if we decide to try and avoid the negative states of mind, we can't. For example, even if we think, "I don't want to get angry," we are not able to prevent ourselves from getting angry because we have lost control over our mind. In a way it doesn't make sense because we are talking about our own mind. If I think it is my mind then I must have control of it, but the power of habit is very strong. And through our bad habits we come to lose control over our mind.

The mind has gone its own way and is ruling the show. That is why it so difficult to make our mind stable and to direct it towards something wholesome. This loss of control over our mind, the fact that our thoughts are controlling us and not vice versa, constitutes the root of all our suffering and all of conditioned existence.

To gain control over our mind is very simple because it is "our own mind," and there is no reason why we shouldn't be able to control our own mind. The only reason why we have lost control is because we acquired bad habits. What we need to do is to get rid of our bad habits and develop good habits until we can gain control over our mind.

Gaining control over our mind and cultivating the right kind of habits will be the root of all forms of joy and happiness. How we accomplish this is to practice meditation. What does meditation mean? The actual word for meditation, or practice, means to become accustomed, to become familiar, or to cultivate the habit. This means that we try to form a good habit; we put some effort into cultivating the same thing over and over again. Out of this effort to cultivate the right habit we will gain familiarity and we will have acquired qualities.

So, from having lost control of our mind through bad habits we train in good habits to reform our mind and gain control of it. Then this will be the root for all happiness and goodness. This shows us the advantages of having a stable mind, the disadvantages of not having a stable mind and should incite us to try to develop a stable mind.

II. Definition. The definition of meditative concentration is the ability to control the mind and to have power over our mind so that we are able to do whatever we need to with the mind.

Another way of describing meditative concentration is with a similar word often used in this connection, tranquility, "Shinay" in Tibetan and "*Shamatha*" in Sanskrit. This is a state in which the mind is neither disturbed nor tied up like in a straightjacket. It means leaving the mind peaceful and tranquil, peaceful in that the mind is relaxed, pleasant, positive and happy.

It is the opposite of a disturbed state in which the mind is so agitated by thoughts and negative mental states that the mind feels very unpleasant and loses control. But here we are talking about the moment when we gain control over our mind and we just allow it to remain in a state of peace and tranquility.

The meaning of this state of tranquility is described in an example of the way we should look after a cat. If we have a cat, the right way to relate to it is to treat it smoothly, gently and in a relaxed manner. If we have a cat and we lock it up inside our house, closing all the doors and windows, it will never settle down. It will try to find a way to get out, running up and down, screaming, jumping around and trying to escape, but it will never want to settle down. If we just leave the door and windows open, the cat will walk about a little, won't go far and will always return. Also, if we think that beating the cat up and giving it no food will make it stay at home we are very mistaken; the cat will never stay under such conditions. But instead, if we are very nice to the cat and give it milk and meat, pat it nicely, it will stay without any problems. In the same way, when we try to gain control over our mind we shouldn't do it forcefully or roughly. We just have to let the mind relax and be in a very peaceful, pleasant state and then it will want to remain in that peaceful state. We won't have to force it because it will remain in the state that is very natural.

When we try to keep the mind peaceful there will be obstacles, different adverse conditions. Some will be our mental states of mind and some will be thoughts in general. However, all can be described as distractions or thoughts that constantly agitate and distract the mind. It is very important to try to eliminate these distractions because once they set in we completely lose control. When we try to eliminate distractions it won't be of any use to think, "Well, I must give up distractions now" because this won't help, on the contrary, more thoughts will follow. The way to give up distractions is two-fold: first to isolate our body from distractions and second to isolate our mind from thoughts.

A. Isolating Our Body from Distractions. This means solitude, avoiding distractions by isolating our body from physical agitation. This has six topics: the primary characteristic of agitation, the cause of agitation, the faults of agitation, the primary characteristic of solitude, the cause of solitude and the good qualities of solitude.

1. The Primary Characteristic of Agitation

It is to be distracted because you are in the company or among your family, friends and possessions.

2. The Cause of Agitation

Agitation arises in connection with a mind that is very attached and involved. It is when we think, "I need this. I want that. If I don't get those things, I can't go on." Such thoughts lead us to do anything in order to get what we desire and we put all our energy into getting just that. Once we think like this we will constantly follow those thoughts and, in fact, all our thoughts will focus upon those desires. It could be trying to get food or clothes, fame or recognition, trying to find a wife or to have children and so on. Once we look for all these things our mind is strongly agitated by all these different thoughts and this creates a deep disturbance in our mind so that it cannot rest in a peaceful condition.

3. The Faults of Agitation .

Once our mind is agitated by different thoughts we have lost control over it, and once we lose control over our mind we lose control over our body. This means that we will lose control over our actions and consequently we will lose control over our own fate. For example, we might want to be happy and not want to suffer, but once we lose control over what we are doing then we also lose control over what is going to happen to us. So, once we have lost control it causes all mental and physical unhappiness and we won't be able to achieve what we want. If we want to get rid of all these problems, first we have to get rid of the agitation that causes all of them.

The objects to which we get attached and that prevent us from finding sufficient tranquility in our mind to meditation can be many. But the main obstacles have to do with either trying to help and protect people who are close to us, our family members and close friends, or trying to harm those we dislike. It can also have to do with trying to acquire more wealth and possessions. All of these are actions that create a disturbed mind so that it cannot be concentrated and peaceful. Even if we try to help our family members or those close to us we are not really able to benefit them greatly because what we do is of an impermanent nature. The same is true of trying to harm our enemies who are also impermanent. Another obstacle is through being involved with our own reputation and becoming famous. We should realize that all these actions are not very beneficial. There is no guarantee that we will succeed; even if we find fame it isn't certain how long it will last, most likely things will go wrong and the final outcome isn't definite.

Once we get rid of strong involvements with worldly activities, which create a disturbed mind, we should first try to work for ourselves, to learn to gain control over our mind. We shouldn't misinterpret this and conclude it is a Hinayana attitude and very selfish. In fact, this isn't what is meant. Of course, we are trying to work for other beings, which is our goal but first of all we have to be able to do this. If we try to help others but can't even help ourselves – we have no control over our own life and mind so we don't know where we are going and can't find happiness for ourselves or become free from suffering – then how can we really help others while in that kind of state? So, first we have to come to a point of gaining qualities through meditation and by maturing spiritually then we can really help others. Of course, at that point we will do what we can to help others. But, first you should help yourself; then you can help others properly.

4. The Primary Characteristic of Solitude

This is to be free from the above-mentioned agitations. .

5. The Cause of Solitude

We can eliminate the fault of agitation by staying in solitude, which literally means remaining in a solitary place. Although it doesn't necessarily mean to go to a desert or remote site, primarily it means to practice meditation, to try to eliminate the negative states of mind and to try to practice dharma. For many people it would mean mostly trying to go to places where the dharma is practiced, like going to a dharma center where most activity isn't directed towards ordinary life but towards spiritual life. Of course, we can practice dharma at home while doing ordinary work, but usually it is quite difficult because we find that our meditation is invaded by thoughts about work and preoccupations. That is why it is very beneficial from time to time and while not giving up ordinary activities, to take some time off and to practice in a dharma center.

You can take a week or month off and go to a dharma center where you try to practice as much as you can. During that time, you can learn to stabilize your mind more. Actually, you will learn to cultivate true solitude of mind, which makes your mind more stable. You will learn how to gradually eliminate or leave the negative states of mind that usually torment you aside. So, it can be very beneficial to do this. You will find that this will help you develop your meditation.

6. The Good Qualities of Solitude

The Buddha said in sutra that if people make offerings of flowers, incense, food and so on to the Buddhas, or to a representation of a Buddha with faith and devotion, then of course this would bring great merit. But as far as the Buddhas are concerned this is not the most outstanding kind of offering. The Buddhas themselves have no need for flowers, incense, food and the like; they are not deprived of these things, so it makes no difference to them if someone makes an offering or not. The wishes of the Buddhas are that all beings be free from suffering and that they come to accomplish enlightenment. So the Buddhas rejoice if they see somebody like us going to a place of solitude to practice meditation. Therefore, the Buddha in the *Moon Lamp Sutra* (Tib. *Dawa Dronmai Do*) said: "The Victorious One is not honored by offerings of food and drink or, likewise, of clothes, flowers, incense and garlands. One will make greater merit by taking seven steps towards a monastery in order to benefit sentient beings by renouncing evil, composite phenomena." The reason is that this person is now really intending to work towards Buddhahood, towards full enlightenment. They are taking active steps towards practicing in order to achieve that goal.

B. Isolating the Mind from Discursive Thoughts. It is not enough to isolate the body from agitation. We must also isolate our mind from thoughts. Imagine that you have arrived at a place of solitude where you are going to meditate. First, we have to examine our mind and our whole being to see whether we are really engaging in the practice of meditation or not. We have to see what we are really doing with our body, speech and mind. With our body, we must check whether we are acting negatively or not. In itself, being in solitude isn't necessarily good or improving our physical behavior; for example, there are lots of wild animals and robbers who live in solitude. So, if we find that we are acting negatively then we must realize that what we are doing with our body is not of much benefit. Then we have to examine our speech. What are we doing with our speech? Are our words wholesome or not? If we find that we are speaking negatively then we should realize that it is of little use, just like what parrots or birds in the wilderness mutter. They are in the wilderness all the time and this doesn't make their speech any better. So if our words are not used properly, staying in solitude will not make them better. Finally, we must examine our mind to see whether it is falling under negative states or not. If we find that our mind has become negative then we must realize that staying in solitude is no more beneficial than it is for the wild animals or monkeys that live in the wilderness all the time. They live there all the time but it doesn't mean that the negativity in their mind is cured. So, if we don't work at it, remaining in the wilderness is useless.

Once we have carefully examined ourselves in this way we should resolve to try to use our body, speech and mind in a positive way and encourage ourselves to do what we can to transform negativity. As mentioned, the point is to get rid of the bad habits that we have formed in our mind and not follow after these bad habits and succumb to their power. Instead we should think, "I will try not to do this and, instead, I will try to gain control over my mind."

If we can develop stability of mind through concentration and meditation then we will regain control over the mind and automatically it will become stable again.

When we speak about a stable mind, the word "mind" refers to the way the mind is, the way in which the mind functions. Normally we allow ourselves to chase after the various thoughts that arise in our mind, but these thoughts are not part of the true state of the mind, the natural condition of the mind. We just create these thoughts and follow after them in all directions. It is like having clear water that you stir up so it then becomes agitated and unclear. To begin with, the actual nature of the mind is very clear and contains no thoughts. But the way to realize the clear and natural state of the mind is not to think, "I must give up the thoughts." On the contrary, it is to just let the mind be, let it be what it is. Just let it go back to its natural state and let it rest within that natural state. The second word in this context, "stable," means to settle, to let the mind settle. We let the mind be in its natural state, its normal mode. This is really the meaning of meditation, to relax perfectly, to let the mind go back to what it is.

When we speak about meditation, or cultivating meditative concentration or letting the mind go into an even state, we do not mean that the mind should be forced or controlled; we mean to let the mind relax and just be. This is what we should try to do.

If we consider the original nature of the mind, it is very blissful, joyful and peaceful, because the very essence of the mind is emptiness and its nature is clarity. However, somehow we cannot manage to find the way to happiness. This is because the mind is disturbed by negative mental factors that prevent the mind from finding rest, peace and happiness. When the Buddha described the negative mental factors he called them disturbing mental effects or disturbing emotions.[75] Disturbing emotions make you feel distressed and unhappy; they create all our problems and all our difficulties. He gave this name to desire, anger, jealousy, ignorance and so forth because these are the negative factors of mind that make us feel unhappy, disturbed and upset; they prevent our mind from being in its natural state. That is why we learn to meditate, in order to get rid of these disturbing emotions that distress our mind.

C. Through the Isolation of Body and Mind, Distraction will not Arise. In order to achieve freedom from disturbing emotions that distress the mind we first have to look at the mind and see what the strongest distressing factor is. For some people it will be desire, for others it will be anger and for others it may be ignorance. When we discover the main problem in our mind we have to learn about the corresponding remedy. We see that there is a given technique of meditation to eliminate each particular afflictive problem.

In fact, there are three different ways of dealing with the distressing factors that are present in our mind. One way to eliminate them is the general way taught in the sutras. A second way is the particular Mahayana aspect of the sutras, which is to try and transform these negative aspects. The third way is taught according to the special instructions that come to us from Marpa, Milarepa and Gampopa. They taught that there is no need to eliminate or transform the negative factors; they just need to be allowed to vanish of their own accord. We will see the successive three ways of dealing with our negative mental factors.

Eliminating the Disturbing Emotions

If we try to stop the negative factors of mind, we will fail. The way to get rid of them is through knowing what they are, learning to recognize their nature, and then they will vanish. The *Jewel Ornament* gives six different meditation techniques that help eliminate the five main negative factors of the mind: to remedy desire, meditate on the unpleasant; to remedy anger, meditate on loving-kindness; to remedy ignorance, meditate on interdependent origination; to remedy jealousy, meditate on the similarity of self and others; to remedy pride, mediate on exchanging self for others; and if the disturbing emotions or discursive thoughts are equally present, then meditate on the breath.

1. To Remedy Desire, Meditate on the Unpleasant

What is the cause of desire? Basically, desire is rooted in our attachment to ourselves, to our own body. Because we are very involved with our body, we are therefore involved with outer objects as well. The inner form of attachment conditions the outer form of attachment. It comes from the idea we have that our body is very beautiful, very pleasant and very special. Once we have this attachment towards our own body then automatically we will want to acquire the outer objects or have the persons around us who will satisfy our body; our desire and attachment concerning our own body will generate desire and attachment to outer objects and people to satisfy the basic involvement with our body. Such attachment is really a mistake since there is nothing there that is really worth being attached to. If we consider our body, we will realize that there is nothing there that is permanent, durable, pure or pleasant. If we analyze the body we will find that it is just made up of different substances that aren't particularly pure or pleasant. The body consists of flesh, blood, skin, bones and things that are of a rather impure nature. Also, the body is not permanent or solid; our flesh can rot, our bones can break and our whole body can change and degrade quite easily. So, it is really a mistake to think that the body is something durable, pure, pleasant and worthy of attachment. By meditating in this way, if we can manage to diminish or stop involvement with our body, then automatically our attachment towards outer things will also diminish and stop.

When we are taught to meditate on the impurity of the body it isn't an idea made up just to help us counteract desire alone. It isn't as though our body is pure and we have to create an artificial idea that it is impure in order to get rid of desire. We meditate upon what is actually there; we have to think of the way the body is and to recognize how it is. Once we do this we realize that the body we are so involved with is not really anything worth remaining involved with. We should know that our attachment to our body is not worthwhile. Once we know this we will automatically be able to reduce and eventually to get rid of this attachment. As is said, attachment to the body is the root of all other forms of attachment. If we can counteract attachment to the body, then automatically all other forms of attachment will be counteracted.

2. To Remedy Anger, Meditate on Loving-kindness

This basically means that we stop considering the person we dislike as an object of anger or aversion, instead we consider this person as an object of loving-kindness. Actually, nothing additional is taught here other than what is taught in the chapter on loving-kindness and compassion; it is the same meditation.

3. To Remedy Ignorance, Meditate on Interdependent Origination

When we speak about the other negative factors that distress our mind (such as desire, anger, pride and jealousy) it is very easy to identify them. We can see them easily because they are very alive and active. But ignorance isn't that easy to identify. We can't really point to something and say, "This is ignorance or delusion." Sometimes the word ignorance is used in different ways. In one way it is called "ti-mug," which is ignorance or delusion, in other ways it is called "ma-rig-pa," which is not knowing, not recognizing, which is also ignorance. Whatever word is used, it refers to the same thing. Sometimes ignorance is spoken about as being on its own and sometimes as being mixed with the other negative factors.

If we consider the other negative factors, they never come on their own, they are always accompanied by ignorance; it is due to ignorance that they can manifest in the first place. For example, desire; when we have desire it isn't because the object of our desire is worthwhile, it is not worthy of bringing on desire. But we do not know this, we do not recognize this fact properly and we make the mistake of thinking it is worthwhile. Because of our mistake – our delusion and illusion concerning the object – we get into all the problems and sufferings that come from desire. But, desire is basically caused by our not understanding, by our mistake, so it is desire mixed with ignorance, or it would be better to say, ignorance mixed with desire.

Let us consider anger. When we get angry it involves ignorance. If anger were beneficial there would be nothing wrong with it. But anger basically involves a misunderstanding, an element of delusion and mistake. We don't realize that anger is not worthwhile and is not beneficial, so here we have ignorance mixed with anger. In the same way, this is the case for pride, jealousy and all other negative factors.

So, ignorance is going to taint our approach to all things. This is what will stop us from relating to things in the right way and making a mistake about their nature. We could say that from the very moment thoughts and concepts set in, from that very moment we are already divorced from understanding the very nature of things. This is due to the presence or the play of ignorance.

Ignorance can also be very lively on its own, for instance when someone has wrong views and takes the opposite stand against truth. When ignorance is very strong then automatically all other negative factors will be very strong. But if ignorance can be reduced then all other negative factors will diminish; they will lose their power and intensity. That is why it is very important to come to control ignorance and to gradually eliminate it. This is done by means of meditating on interdependent origination.

When we say "ignorance," it means not knowing. The remedy against not knowing is learning to know. Here it means to know things as they really are, to know the actual nature of things. What will help to understand this is to learn about interdependence, how things arise interdependently, with one thing conditioning the next. If we can understand this, we can gain some understanding of the nature of things and gradually this will diminish our ignorance and make the other negative aspects decrease.

4. To Remedy Jealousy, Meditate on the Similarity of Self and Others

Jealousy is caused by excessive care for oneself, an egocentric concern, in which case we always want the best for ourselves and don't care what happens to others. For instance, we want to be happy and content, but if somebody else is happy we are upset. Also, we want to be free from suffering and difficulties, but if someone else is free from these problems we can't bear it. This is the feeling of jealousy. What is behind jealousy or what is the root of jealousy comes from not thinking at all of others and only being interested in our own happiness and well-being, being totally egocentric. This prevents us from seeing that others are, in fact, in the same boat as us; they also want the same things as we want.

When we say that the remedy against jealousy is to realize the similarity of others and ourselves it isn't making up a remedy to rid us of jealousy, but it is to become aware of the way in which things are. We want happiness but so does everybody else. We don't want to suffer and nor does anybody else. Everybody wants to be happy because that is nice and this is why we want it and why all others want it too. Nobody wants to be unhappy because that is painful and unpleasant and this is why we don't want it and all others don't want it either. With this meditation we should come to realize that everybody is after the same thing and that there is no reason just trying to find our own happiness without thinking that others want the same. Also there is no reason just trying to get rid of our own suffering without thinking that others also want the same.

5. To Remedy Pride, Meditate on Exchanging Self for Others
The Tibetan word for pride is "I, the king." Pride means that you consider yourself as being the most important, being better than everybody else and as possessing qualities that nobody else has; you have an inflated feeling of your own value, whether justified or not. In fact, what we have to realize in this meditation is that this form of egotism only brings lots of trouble and

problems, whereas if we have concern for others, good things and good qualities will come.

If we consider the Buddhas, their main concern is others, not themselves; they always act to help other beings and we can see all the qualities this brings. The opposite: if you consider people like us, ordinary beings in the world, we are only interested in ourselves; we are very egocentric and only concerned with ourselves. Look at the mess this has put us in. So, we need to see that when someone acts with concern for others many good things arise and when someone acts selfishly a lot of trouble and pain arise. This we can even see in a very simple way in the world around us. Whenever someone achieves any form of goodness, happiness and some fame, it is usually based upon the fact that they have done something (even if it is small) that has benefited others; they have had some concern for others. If we consider any problems and sufferings in the world, it has to do with selfishness and someone only concerned about themselves and their own profit.

So, it is quite clear that egotism is the root of all problems and sufferings and that altruism is the source of many great advantages, benefits and qualities. That is why we learn to meditate in this way, substituting others for oneself. Instead of only being concerned with oneself, we learn to be concerned with others, so we substitute self-concern with concern for others.

6. If the Disturbing Emotions or Discursive Thoughts are Equally Present, then Meditate on the Breath

As explained earlier, thoughts are not a natural part of the mind; they come out of our bad habits. The reason we find it so difficult to get rid of our bad habits and can't do it quickly is because our bad habits have been going on for so long. In order to form new habits, good habits in the mind, and to bring it back to its natural condition we learn how to stabilize the mind through using an object of concentration. If we were to use an outer object it may be too coarse, therefore that isn't the means chosen here to gain freedom from thoughts. The means chosen here to enhance concentration is the breath, which is very subtle and not material. If we learn to meditate on the breath, which is always moving, it will be very helpful to learn to control our thoughts. There are very many different techniques of breathing meditation, such as counting the breath, following the breath and so on. All of these techniques are intended to bring us to the point that we learn to control our mind. When we gain control over our mind it doesn't get carried away.[76]

Transforming the Disturbing Emotions

In addition to the six techniques of meditation to eliminate the negative effects that plague our mind as taught in a general way in the sutras, there is a way to transform these negative factors using the Mahayana aspect of the sutras. This transformation is usually affected with the help of the purest altruistic motivation, which is the mind wanting enlightenment for the sake of all other beings, bodhichitta.

The Special Instructions from the Lineage of Marpa

In the special approach developed by Marpa and his lineage of spiritual sons, we neither try to eliminate, follow or transform the negative factors of mind. What we simply do is to let the mind be within its own nature and to let the mind rest in its natural condition. Then we look inwards and try to see and face what is going on in the mind. For instance, we look for anger.[77] But when we look for anger we don't find anything or see anything. This is because there is nothing there that has any reality. The essence of the mind is just as it is; it never stops being there and is at all times empty. Within this emptiness there is no real thing as anger or any other negative factors; they are just like reflections in a mirror. If we look into the mirror we will see a reflected image, but if we try to find the image, we won't find it. The image is not inside the mirror, nor is it not in the mirror, nor is it outside the mirror, it is merely a reflection that has no nature of its own and no independent reality.

In the same way, when negative factors arise in the mind, we must learn to let the mind remain in its natural state, within its original emptiness. Within this, all negative factors vanish because they have no actual reality. This is what we learn to do for all negative factors that come up in the mind, for anger, pride, desire or whatever occurs. When it is said that when we look for thoughts we cannot find them, this doesn't imply that we aren't looking good enough, but it is because there is nothing to find since those things have no reality. We simply learn to let the mind be within itself, within its natural condition. If we can do this, all negative factors disappear automatically.

III. Classification. After the point describing the techniques of meditation, we turn to the aspects of meditative concentration. There are three aspects of meditative concentration: meditative concentration which gives one happiness while it is practiced, meditative concentration which produces all good qualities, and meditative concentration that can accomplish the good of beings. Those are the aspects of what meditative concentration can do.[78]

IV. Characteristics of Each Classification. The fourth point describes what each aspect can do.

A. Meditative Concentration which Gives One Happiness while it is Practiced. As already explained, most of our problems and sufferings are of a mental nature. Of course, we do have physical pain and difficulties, but mostly our pain and troubles are of a mental nature. This is because we do not have control over our own mind. When we practice meditation we learn to gain control over the mind. Once we have gained control over our mind then automatically all sufferings of the mind will disappear and we will find a state of happiness and peace. This is why here one aspect of meditative concentration is that it places us in a state of happiness and peace while it is practiced.

B. Meditative Concentration that Produces All Good Qualities. The second aspect of meditative concentration is that it produces qualities, which is a direct consequence of the first aspect. Once we regain control over our mind then this will be the source of all good qualities to become manifest.

C. Meditative Concentration that can Accomplish the Good of Beings. The third aspect of meditative concentration is that once we have gained control over our mind then automatically we are able to accomplish the good of other beings. This is the third aspect of what meditative concentration can do.

V. Increase. The fifth point discusses how we should increase meditative concentration. It is increased in the same way as the other paramitas, through the powers of primordial wisdom, wisdom-awareness and dedication.

VI. Perfection. The sixth section says that we should make meditative concentration pure. It is made pure both through the understanding of emptiness and through great compassion for all beings, as with the other paramitas.

VII. Result. The seventh point of this chapter discusses the benefits and advantages that come from having a stable mind. As already pointed out, the short term advantage is that all the various qualities will develop automatically once we have a stable mind and have control over the mind. In the long term, on the basis of a stable mind, we will gain all the qualities of meditation and will develop prajna (wisdom-awareness), the deepest form of understanding. Finally, through all this we will accomplish Buddhahood.

This concludes the explanation of the sixteenth chapter,
on the perfection of meditative concentration, from
The Jewel Ornament of Liberation.

Questions

Question: When you say that you must examine your mind to see which is the strongest negative characteristic, how do you do it?

Thrangu Rinpoche: I don't think that this is particularly difficult. Normally we are quite aware of our main problem, even without looking at our own mind. You should be able to see what the main problem is today, whether it is anger or desire. Just through thinking about it you should know.

Question: You experience a self that is very active and you experience as well a spontaneous being; they are together yet not one.

Rinpoche: We are not really sure about the question. But about the aspect of mind which is always very discursive, very active and very agitated, that is the one we are talking about here and the one that has to be purified, of which we have to remove all the negative aspects and bring it to peace.

Question: Did Rinpoche give an explanation about the transformation?

Translator: He said it very briefly, just in terms of applying the purest form of the altruistic motivation, working through bodhichitta.

Rinpoche: There is an example in a short story that many of you probably know. In one of his previous lifetimes as a bodhisattva, Buddha Shakyamuni was the captain of a ship. There were 500 traders on the ship and there was also someone who was called "the nasty little black man." This nasty little black man had a plan to make a hole in the boat so that everyone would sink and die. The Buddha, through his clairvoyance, saw this and knew that he had to do something to stop the little man from doing this, otherwise the 500 people would die and the little black man would be reborn in a hell realm. Transformation takes place in the way that the Buddha decided to kill the nasty little black man. He took an axe and broke the little man's head. By doing this he saved the man from negative karma and he saved the lives of 500 people. Transformation happens when we take something that would be a very negative action, such as killing, which is motivated by hatred and aversion, and transform it by the presence of compassion, by the presence of bodhichitta. The Buddha killed in this case in order to save the lives of 500 people and to save the little black man from the hell realms. What is technically very negative becomes very beneficial and virtuous because of the pure motivation behind it.

Question: Was the Buddha angry?
Rinpoche: It is as in the example. We are not talking about anger in that story. It is like a form of anger, anger in the sense that you actually have to take the decision to kill. When you make that decision, it is very violent and grows into anger. But, as we said, it wasn't real anger since it was inspired by the wish to help.

Chapter 17
The Perfection of Wisdom-awareness (Prajnaparamita)

First of all, we should try to put our mind in the right disposition in order to receive these teachings. This is the precious mind intent upon enlightenment, the precious bodhichitta.

In our study of the six paramitas we have now arrived at the last and sixth one, which is the perfection of wisdom-awareness. It will be described in seven points, just as with the previous paramitas. The seven points will be identical, except for two. For the other paramitas, the fifth point dealt with increasing and the sixth point dealt with making the paramita pure. The force to increase and make the previous five paramitas (perfections) pure was prajna itself, so this does not apply for the prajnaparamita itself. In the fifth point we will consider the fact that prajna has to be known and in the sixth point the fact that prajna needs to be cultivated.

I. Reflection on the Virtues and Faults. If someone has the prajnaparamita, then automatically the practice of the first five paramitas will become extremely fruitful, in the sense that it will lead to Buddhahood. So, with the prajnaparamita our practice of generosity up to meditative concentration becomes a cause for Buddhahood. It automatically transforms the five practices into spiritual practices, something that goes beyond the world. They become the cause for going beyond the *three realms* of conditioned existence,[79] for reaching true liberation. On the contrary, if someone doesn't have the prajnaparamita, then the practice of generosity, moral ethics up to meditative concentration will produce very great meritorious results, but it will not bring that person to liberation; they will not reach the other shore ("paramita" means "arrived at the other shore"). If the five qualities of the first five paramitas are not accompanied by prajnaparamita they will not be real paramitas, in the sense that they won't be a cause for arriving at the other shore, the other side of existence, which is liberation.

In the *Condensed Perfection of Wisdom Sutra* (Tib. *Shechen Dupe Do*) the Buddha said, "If millions upon billions of blind people are without a sighted guide and do not know the road, how can they enter the city? Without wisdom-awareness, the five eyeless paramitas, being without a guide, will not be able to reach enlightenment." A blind man wanting to go somewhere will not be able to do so because he cannot see the way. If someone who is also blind wants to help him, they won't manage either. If a third person, who is also blind, wants to help the other two, still all three won't arrive at their destination. You could go on like this, four, five, six, up to one million and more blind men, they won't get there because they cannot see where they are going. But just one person who can see properly can lead all these blind people to their destination. In the same way, if there is no prajnaparamita, the other paramitas are not real paramitas in that they do not represent the final arrival at the other shore of samsara. It is the prajnaparamita which makes the other paramitas part of the path to liberation. This is the reason why that among all the paramitas the prajnaparamita is really the most important, the most vital.[80]

Knowing the enormous advantages that come from having this great quality and the disadvantages that come from not having it, we see the need to understand and develop the prajnaparamita.

II. Definition. The second point explains the essence of the prajnaparamita. The essence of the prajnaparamita, its very nature, is the exact discerning, the exact understanding and appreciation and the exact discrimination of phenomena. It is seeing and understanding things as they truly are, in a very exact and discerning manner, discerning in the sense that we are not mixing up everything. Whatever is the actual nature of an object of consideration, we appreciate it as it is and without confusion. If something is white, we understand and appreciate that it is white; if something is yellow, we understand and appreciate that it is yellow; if something is red, we understand and appreciate that it is red; and we don't mistake white for yellow or yellow for red. We have a concise appreciation for what the object really is, without mistake and without confusion. If the object has such and such characteristics, we know it and do not add something to it. It is appreciating what is actually there while and as it is there. This quality of understanding is the very best means to gain liberation from all the states of suffering of conditioned existence.

III. Classification. The third point discusses the different aspects of prajna. The Tibetan word for prajna is "sherab," which consists of two syllables. "She" means, "to know, knowledge, understanding, cognition" and "rab" means "best." So it is the best form of understanding, the best form of cognition, the best mind and the best knowledge. This is explained in three aspects: wisdom-awareness of the mundane, wisdom-awareness of the lesser supramundane and wisdom-awareness of the greater supramundane.

The first aspect of this understanding is a worldly form of understanding and the second and third aspects are the two forms of spiritual understanding, one being inferior and the other being superior. The two spiritual aspects will be called prajna because very often there is confusion in translations, so I will use the Sanskrit term.

IV. Characteristics of Each Classification. The fourth point of this chapter describes the nature of each aspect of prajna.

A. Wisdom-awareness of the Mundane. Worldly understanding is what allows us to find the best form of satisfaction, contentment and well being in this life. It is the capacity to know, to understand; it is a form of intelligence and knowledge that enables us not to be ignorant as to how things are and function. This is the worldly form of understanding, intelligence or knowledge.

B. Wisdom-awareness of the Lesser Supramundane. The second aspect is inferior prajna, the inferior form of knowledge and understanding that is gained in connection with the practice of the Hinayana path.[81] If this path is practiced properly and without mistakes, if there is no ignorance of this path, then the inferior form of prajna is gained.

C. Wisdom-awareness of the Greater Supramundane. The third aspect of prajna is superior prajna, which is understanding beyond the world, the highest level of spiritual knowledge. It is prajna that is developed in connection with the Mahayana path and denotes the absence of ignorance concerning the nature of all things. In this particular chapter, the first two forms of knowledge are not dealt with, only the third highest form of prajna is explained.

As mentioned, the fifth and sixth points are specific to prajna; they aren't discussed in the other chapters on the paramitas. First we need to know what prajna is and then we need to cultivate it. Let us consider the fifth point, the need to know what prajna is.

V. What Needs to be Known: Wisdom-awareness. We need prajna because we need to go beyond conditioned existence and all its sufferings, problems and all its difficulties. A good reason for wanting to go beyond conditioned existence is suffering. Another reason is that even the happiness we find in cyclic existence is not stable happiness, is not permanent happiness. Of course, it does happen that sometimes things go very well, we are very happy and things are nice in our life. But this happiness that we might experience is not permanent and unchanging. It is not unchanging because it is always tainted by the presence of the various forms of sufferings, which are typical of our existence. There is the suffering of change; whatever happiness we have will turn into something else. There is also the universal suffering which is inherent in the very process of existence and so on. There are all kinds of different forms of suffering, so much so that even if we are happy, this happiness does not last and is soon replaced by unhappiness and suffering. That is why we must try to go beyond ordinary existence, to get rid of suffering, but also to find true happiness, the one that will not change all the time, the one that will not be lost. In order to find this, we cannot be ignorant concerning the nature of things. This is the reason why we need prajna. We need to understand things as they are.

Why is prajna so effective and so beneficial? We know that there are lots of difficulties, problems and sufferings in our existence. But what is the root of all these problems? The root is that the world is not real, but we take whatever is there as being real. Although something is by nature unreal, we take it as true. Because of this we will encounter many difficulties and sufferings. For instance, if we have real gold it will remain gold as long as we have it and it won't change. But, if we have something that isn't real gold, and mistake it for gold, then at some point we try to use it as gold, we won't be able to and then we will realize that it isn't real. In the same manner, no matter how much we try to convince ourselves or try to think that existence is happy and pleasurable, that we can find happiness and satisfaction in existence, no matter how much we try to think in those terms, we will not be able to achieve this because it is only a self-deception; there is no truth in it at all. The only way to cut the root of suffering of samsara is to know that all of this is only a deception, a self-deception.

Let us refer back to one of our classical and favorite examples of mistaking a rope for a snake. If the light is not good or it is dim in the room, we enter and see a rope lying on the floor which we mistake to be a snake; we think that we have seen a snake and are very frightened and terrified that the snake might bite us and harm us. How can we remove the fear that arose by thinking it is a snake? If we try by getting a weapon or eating medicine or wearing a coat of arms it will not help to remove the fear. The only way to remove the fear is to understand that there is no snake there in the first place, that it's only a rope. Once we know this, there is no need for any other cure; once we know that it was only a deception, then automatically all fear vanishes. It is the same with samsara. Once we understand that the nature of samsara is only illusory then all the sufferings that come along with samsara will disappear automatically. Once we know the real nature of samsara, then everything else will vanish of its own accord.

A. The Refutation of Grasping Things as Being Existent. The remedy to dispel the deception of the reality of things is meditation on emptiness. The way to meditate on emptiness has two aspects: we meditate on the non-existence of the personal self and on the non-existence of the self of phenomena.

The Non-existence of a Personal Self

Why do we have to meditate on the non-existence of a personal self? If we consider all the problems we have in our life and all the problems and difficulties that we experience in our mind, the root of all these problems rests in all the negative factors that disturb our mind and which bring a feeling of distress in our mind. These are the feelings of desire, anger, pride and ignorance. Behind all these feelings there is something deeper, which is the very feeling of "I," the very idea of "self." The idea of self is when we feel "I" or "me" or "myself." As soon as we have this feeling of an "I". or self, then we want something and this wanting is desire. Desire means, "I want," "I need" and it relates to the "I" or "self" that we feel we are. Once the cause is present within us then all the problems begin. For instance, this "self" feels hurt and that is the birth of suffering. The root of all problems is this idea of a self. If we can remove the idea of a self, then automatically all the negative factors that disturb our mind will stop, and all suffering will come to an end.[82]

So, how can one stop this idea of a self? We have to understand that this idea of a self doesn't have any reality. It is in itself an illusion, a delusion, which is why it can be eliminated.

When we have the idea of a self, we apply it to something that isn't there. There is no such thing as an object which we could identify as "I," nor has there ever been such a thing there that could be called "I." However, although there is no self there, we think in such terms and this is the root of all our problems. If we come to understand that there is no real self, then we do not have to suppress the idea of a self; it will just vanish of its own accord. It is much like the example of mistaking the rope for a snake. We don't have to remove the snake, we just have to understand that it is only a rope and not a snake. In the same way, when we understand that there is nothing there that we could call "self" or "I," then automatically the idea is gone since this notion loses its basis of support. That is why we need to meditate on the non-existence of a personal self.

What kind of idea do we have about this self? What is this idea of self all about? Sometimes we think that our self is our body. Sometimes we think it is our mind. Sometimes we think it is our name. But when we investigate closely we discover the self cannot be found in any of those aspects.

Our idea of the "self," the "I," is that it is a single and solid entity. But looking at our body we find that it is made up of a collection of different things. If this "I" were our body it would also be our hand, our leg, our head, our organs, the intestines and the skin. This means we would have many selves if it were the body. If our hand were cut off that would mean that the self is gone, but we would never come to that conclusion because we conceive of the self as being the whole. Therefore the self isn't the body because what we call "the body" is not one thing, so there is no "I" there. Could this "I" be the mind? When we look to find the mind we can't find anything. The mind isn't inside or outside the body, because the mind has no true existence, so the mind cannot be the self either. Finally, we might think that the "I" or "self" is within a name, but our name is given to us, there is no ground for it to be a "self" or the "I." Our name is something temporarily assigned; we can receive another name but that would make no difference to our "self" or "I." It is really a mistake on our part to believe that our body, mind or name is the "I." There is nothing really there that we can call the "I." When we come to understand that there is no such thing as an "I" or a "self," then that will automatically counteract the idea of a self. The result will be that all the negative mental states will vanish. The consequence of this will be the end of all suffering.

In addition to thinking in terms of "I," we also think in terms of "my." We say "My clothes, my things, my friends." Actually the combination of "I" and "mine" is the cause of all our negativities. Let us look at the example of a cup. If someone throws a cup on the ground, it will break and this will make no difference to us. But if we think, "This is my cup. This cup belongs to me," we have labeled the cup as our property and then if someone throws it down and breaks it we will be angry. Why? Because we think, "That is my cup." Attaching "my" to the cup will generate anger. But if we look closely, there is no difference between "a cup" and the cup we call "my cup," it is still a cup. If we look at it there is nothing in the cup itself that indicates that it is "my cup." But as soon as we put the idea of "my cup" on the cup, it generates all kinds of negativities. We have to realize that the "my" we attribute to the cup doesn't really exist, it is not part of the cup, it is only an idea we have put on the cup. We have to understand that there is no real thing we can call "mine" or "my" which exists, they are only labels and fabrications of the mind. What we will feel in connection with the idea of "my" or "mine" is the cause of all negativity and is why we have to understand that there is no real "mine."

When we meditate on the absence or non-existence of a self it is to understand that the idea of "I" and "mine" doesn't really exist. We are not trying to think that what is really there is not there. For instance, if you know that you have a head and think, "I have no head," it would be pointless. We are not trying to do this. It is not as if the "I" and "mine" are really there and we are trying to brainwash ourselves into believing they are not. Rather, we have to understand that the "I" and "mine" are not really there as we believe, but that we have made the mistake to believe that they are there as we think they are. It is this mistake that we have to stop because it is causing suffering. If this mistake didn't cause problems, if believing in the "I" and the "self" were beneficial, then there would be nothing wrong with that. But because this way of thinking generates so many problems for us, we have to learn to see it is a mistake. As long as there is the belief in "I" and "mine," we have negativity and negativity is the cause of all sufferings. The beginning of this is very small, a slight misunderstanding; the idea of "I" and "mine" is very tiny, but it is the root of great suffering. That is why we have to come to understand that they are non-existent.

This concludes a brief explanation on one of the ways to meditate on the absence of a self-entity, which is the way to practice in order to understand the non-existence of a personal self.

The Method of Meditation

Before I discuss how to understand the non-existence of the self of phenomena, let us first look at the practical way of doing the meditation in terms of the prajnaparamita. What do we meditate on? Emptiness. How do we meditate? There are two different approaches. One approach is called "the reflective approach" and the other one is called "the immersing approach." People who like to study the meaning of emptiness apply the first approach. It is a way of meditation through which one thinks about emptiness by trying to really understand what it is. Once you have gained an understanding of what emptiness is you contemplate it. This is a form of discursive contemplation, which is a long path. The second type of meditation is the approach cultivated by yogis and is called "the do nothing approach" since it refers to those who do nothing but rest in the natural state of their mind. It is the immersing aspect of meditation in which you don't think about emptiness, wondering whether it is like this or like that. You just rest within the essence of the mind; you allow yourself to be immersed within the mind's nature, knowing that it is not a real and solid thing and you remain within this natural condition of the mind.

The Non-existence of the Self of Phenomena

We come to know what prajna is through two means, through meditating on the non-existence of a personal self-entity and also on the non-existence of the self of phenomena. We now know we should meditate on the absence of a personal self-entity which leads us to understand that there is no "I" or "self" as we believe. That leads to understanding its non-existence. Now we must take the next step and understand the non-existence of phenomena.

The belief in a self of phenomena is the idea that things truly exist in a real and substantial way. Whatever object we take into consideration we think it is real and substantial. This is the belief in the existence of a self-entity of phenomena. We have been in samsara for a very long time now. During this time we have probably experienced all sorts of different problems and sufferings. Everybody tries to escape from suffering and difficulties, but the way we try to remove suffering is only very superficial. We try to cut off the branches of the tree but they keep on growing again; we may be able to eliminate one problem but another one will arise again. This goes on all the time and it will go on until we eliminate the root of suffering. If we just cut away the branches of a tree new ones grow again, but if we manage to cut the root then nothing more can grow. In the same manner, we have to try and cut the root of suffering and then there will be no more cause for suffering to arise. The way to cut the root of suffering is to understand the nature of all things.

We may wonder if there ever will be a time when we can become free from suffering, a time when we can gain liberation from samsara. It is possible to gain liberation from suffering and samsara. The very reason for this is that conditioned existence and suffering themselves are not real. If they were real there would be nothing we could do about it. If something really exists then it would not be possible to change it or remove it. But since things don't truly exist, it is very easy to get rid of them. For example, if we see a tiger leaping at us there isn't much we can do about it. We feel frightened and this fear is justified because we can't do much about it; we can't think that all we have to do is wake up and the tiger will vanish. But, if we are dreaming, then while asleep we see a tiger leaping at us, there is no reason to be afraid because there is no real tiger; we know that when we wake up the tiger will vanish automatically. This is due to the fact that while dreaming there is no real tiger that has any actual existence. In the same manner, if the illusory appearances we experience in samsara were real there would be no hope. But we are lucky that these things are not real. Since they are not real it is possible to get rid of the illusory experiences and sufferings that we normally undergo. It is possible to get rid of them because they are by nature devoid of any actual existence. All it takes is the recognition, the understanding of the true nature of things. If we can understand this, then automatically all the illusory appearances disappear and with them all our suffering and problems. That is why it is so vital to meditate on the non-existence of the self of phenomena.

When we learn about the emptiness of all phenomena it is presented in two ways, emptiness of all outer phenomena (i.e. of all objects and forms we perceive and relate to) and emptiness of all inner phenomena (i.e. of mind, consciousness with its attributes of lucidity and cognition).

The Emptiness of Outer Objects

First of all, we must consider the emptiness of outer objects. If we consider this matter without having contemplated or meditated upon it, we would think that everything is very real and solid; the houses, hills, animals, people, water, earth, fire, air, all seem very real to us because they are in front of us. These things don't seem empty at all because they are there, clearly, and we can see and relate to these things. But that is before we examine things carefully. If I show my hand to somebody and say, "My hand is empty," the person will conclude, "That is rubbish. It doesn't make any sense because I can see a hand and I know that it functions as a hand. I can see that it's a physical object. There are flesh and bones." The person will think that I am talking nonsense and it won't make much sense to them to hear that the hand is empty. But when we consider the matter carefully it is easy to realize that there is no such thing as "a hand." Of course, when we look at it we see a hand and when we talk about it we mean "the hand," but consider this more carefully. We speak about "the hand," but what we see is a thumb, a first finger, a second finger, a third finger and a fourth finger. We can't say that the thumb is the hand; nobody would say that it is. We also can't say that the first finger is the hand, nor the second, nor the third, nor the fourth, nobody could validly argue that either part is the hand. If we continue investigating, it leads to the same result. There is flesh, there are bones, but we will never find the hand, we could never pinpoint the hand because the hand has no true existence of its own. Being naturally devoid of an own existence it is thus called "empty."

If we consider the hand, it is made up of the thumb and four fingers. As explained, there is nothing we could ever point to as "the hand." But, we collect all the parts and form the idea "hand." So "hand" is just a label for the collection of all the parts of the hand. But we can go further. Let's look at the thumb, that which we designate as "the thumb." In fact, it consists of two phalanxes. We can't say that the first is the thumb or that the second is the thumb, yet we call both together "the thumb." We can find nothing we could really call "thumb," only connected parts. This is how we relate to all objects. We consider a complex collection of many things an object and call it "a hand," "a man" or whatever. We attribute solidity and reality to what we designate, but in fact that object has no justified substance. In the same way as the hand and thumb are empty, so too are all phenomena. We aren't making up emptiness. Whatever object we investigate, we will never find that there is any "thing" there we could pinpoint as the object we designated. What happens is that our mind designates a name and an idea to a collection of parts, but the object itself is devoid of any real existence.

We may think, "This is all very well and we say that all things are empty. But why do we see things? Why do we perceive things? We see all sorts of different colors; white, red, yellow, green, blue. We see all sorts of places; we see houses, cottages and hills. We see all sorts of different things; people, animals, trees. If we discover that all things are empty, why do we see all these things? Why do we perceive all of them?" Well, in fact, things do not have to be real in order to appear to us or to manifest to us. They are actually the manifestation of our own mind. To understand that things don't have to be real in order to manifest to us we can look at our own experience when we sleep. When we sleep, we dream and see all sorts of things, a particular house, friends, people, animals, anything. Imagine that you see a big elephant in your dream. Probably you are sleeping in a small room and if the elephant were real it would not fit into the small room you are sleeping in. But it is your mind that sees the elephant and your mind does not see a real elephant, it only sees a projection that is a manifestation of your own mind. If the elephant really existed, you couldn't see it because it wouldn't fit into your little room. But the elephant has no true reality; it just manifests from your mind and appears to your mind. In the same way, we perceive and experience all sorts of things that have no true reality. We see them out of our delusion. As long as this deluded mind continues, we will project appearances. The very fact that all of these things are empty makes it possible for them to vanish. It is by virtue of the fact that all things are empty that suffering can be removed, both temporarily and permanently.

The Emptiness of Inner Mind

We have gone through the first step, which is the explanation of the emptiness of outer things. Besides these outer things being empty, the mind perceiving these things is also empty and unreal. Three reasons are given here for the emptiness of the mind: the mind does not exist when examined through momentariness, the mind does not exist since it has not been seen by anyone, and since there are no objects, no mind exists.

1. The Mind does not Exist when Examined through Momentariness

The mind is not one thing, it is a constant flow. It is a succession of instants one after the other, changing continually. There is not one thing we can call "the mind." For instance, the mind of this morning is no longer here now and the mind of the last hour is not the mind of this hour. We can even go further and say that the mind of the last minute is not the mind of this minute and even the mind of this instant will not be there in the next instant. It is just a continuous flow of instants of mind. One instant of mind goes and is replaced by the next instant of mind, so we can only find the mind within one instant. Then, considering the instant itself: if we say that the mind is of the nature of one instant, we will find that it is only a notion of time, and that there is nothing there even in that instant that we can point to and prove to be a real thing; it is only an idea of time. So, the mind has no true reality.

2. The Mind does not Exist since it has not been Seen by Anyone

We speak of the mind, but who has actually seen the mind? Have you seen it? Has anybody else seen it? When we try to look for the mind it is impossible to find it. You can never find where the mind comes from or where it is now or where it is going or when it stops. It has never been seen by anybody. Nobody has ever been able to claim, "Well, that's the color of the mind or that's the shape of the mind or that's where you find the mind." However, we keep on thinking that there is a mind, but when we actually look for the mind, it is impossible to find anything there.

In the *Kashyapa-Requested Sutra* (Tib. *Odsungkyi Zhupai Do*), the Buddha was speaking to his disciples about the non-existence of the mind. He addressed one of his disciples called Kashyapa and said, "Kashyapa, the mind is not inside, the mind is not outside and it is not between these two. The mind cannot be shown to others. The mind cannot be seen. The mind does not stay anywhere. There is no mind. The mind is only like a bubble on the surface of water. It looks like a bubble, but there is nothing there, it is completely empty inside. The mind is in fact like a puppet. It looks real, but in fact there is nothing there, it is completely false. Before we examine this, we think there is a mind, but once we look carefully, we find that there is no mind."

3. Since There are no Objects, no Mind Exists

The third reason coincides with what we have just established. All outer things have no reality. If the object is not real, the subject perceiving an unreal object cannot be real either. If the object were real, then the mind perceiving the object would be real, but if the object is unreal, then it follows that the subject is unreal too and cannot exist of its own accord. In this way, we see the emptiness of both outer phenomena and the inner aspect of phenomena, which is mind.[83]

B. Refutation of Grasping Things as Being Non-existent. Now we said that everything, mind and outer phenomena, are empty. What does this leave us with? Does it mean that everything is like empty space or the emptiness of a rabbit's horns, the total absence of something? No, we are not speaking about emptiness in this sense. If we consider the emptiness of space or the non-existence of a rabbit's horns, these are things that cannot be changed, they cannot take on a form. But when we speak about the non-existence of outer appearances and of the mind then this isn't like empty space because it possesses the quality of clarity. Here clarity doesn't refer to the clarity of sunlight, rather clarity is the fact that within emptiness everything can manifest, can appear and can take place.. While being non-existent, while being empty, everything can take place in the same way as a reflection can appear on the surface of a mirror. This is called "the very expression of the nature of phenomena." If we come to understand this, then automatically all of our negativity and all of our suffering will disappear.[84]

C. The Path that Leads to Liberation. If we meditate on emptiness in order to understand the emptiness of all things, then there is no need to try to fight suffering or to remove it. All we need to do is to understand that suffering is empty and non-existent. Once we know that it is non-existent, there is no need to suppress it; it will just go of its own accord through understanding. The same is true of the negative states of mind. We may first feel that they cause distaste in our mind, that they are a big problem for us and that we want to fight them. But once we meditate on emptiness, all we have to do is to see that in essence all the negative factors of mind are empty and non-existent. If we see this, they will disappear of their own accord and there is no more need to fight and to try to eliminate them. All we need to do is get used to the fact that they are empty in their own essence.

We have said that everything is empty, but through the play of interdependent origination things do appear and do manifest to us. But how can we come to the point where this stops and that the emptiness of all things manifests to us? If it were a matter of sleeping, we could just wake up and it would be all over. But we can't really wake up. What can we do? In fact, it isn't a dream, it is similar to a dream in many ways, but a dream is only a very short moment of experience, whereas what we experience now is the result of a very long accumulation of illusion. Since we have been in conditioned existence for an endless number of eons we have formed a very strong habit of illusion. The remedy to this illusion cannot take place through a moment of understanding. Understanding how things are is helpful, but more than just understanding is required; we must cultivate this understanding until it becomes completely manifest. That leads us to the sixth point of this chapter, which is the need to cultivate prajna.

VI. What Needs to be Practiced. Once we understand that things are empty then this understanding must be cultivated until it is there all the time. As explained already, the way to begin is to stabilize our mind. We practice tranquility meditation in order to make the mind very stable, very workable, to gain control over the mind in a very relaxed way. Once we have achieved this we learn to let our mind rest within the emptiness of things and come to experience emptiness just as it is. Another way of describing this is to meditate on Mahamudra according to the special instructions transmitted from Marpa.

In this way of meditation, it is simply a matter of resting within the mind as it is in itself. Since the mind is the very expression of the true nature of all phenomena, if we immerse ourselves within that state then the emptiness of all things is obvious and also the quality of the clarity of the mind is obvious. This clarity aspect of the mind contains all virtuous qualities, it contains the Buddha-essence that can unfold until it manifests as the perfect realized mind of the Buddha. So the technique of Mahamudra meditation is to let the mind rest within its own nature. Through doing this we will stabilize our understanding of the nature of the mind. The point is to develop that into a habit. Once it becomes a habit, we will have much more confidence in the nature of things and will be convinced of the way things really are. On the basis of such confidence and conviction we will gain direct experience of what it means. Once this experience is there it will automatically eliminate all impurities in the mind, all the faults and defects in the mind and all negative factors that disturb the mind. It will be like when clouds vanish in the sky, which happens naturally. Likewise here, there is no need to fight the defects or negativities of our mind and no need to go through many hardships in order to remove them. All we have to do is to immerse ourselves within the true nature of the mind. And within that great state of peace and bliss, all impurities will dissolve completely and naturally.

What happens when somebody realizes emptiness? Realizing emptiness does not mean that all of a sudden there is nothing at all, like complete annihilation. It is not the case that nothing is there, like when someone is poor and has no money. It is emptiness, but is intimately united with great bliss and clarity. This union of bliss and clarity with emptiness is due to the fact that emptiness is in essence blissful, in the sense that it is devoid of suffering and problems and it is pure of all stains. This is true happiness and beyond all fear. Whatever side it is on, there is no more reason to be afraid or to apprehend anything. This is the state of great bliss, but it is also the state of great clarity. Emptiness does not mean that the mind goes blank, rather the mind is in a very lucid and very clear state; it is emptiness with lucidity and clarity. When one realizes this bliss, lucidity and clarity of the mind, this will gradually lead us to the point where this is fully developed, just like the pure and perfect mind of the Buddha who has omniscient wisdom and perfect bliss.

VII. Result. Now we come to the seventh point of the chapter, which describes the results of practicing the prajnaparamita. There are two sorts of results, the long term and the short term results.

The long term or ultimate result is that we will become free from all negative disturbances of the mind and of all sufferings. This will happen spontaneously and naturally through understanding emptiness. At the same time there will be the development of all the virtuous qualities within the mind. We will acquire the qualities of great bliss and clarity. Ultimately, this denotes the accomplishment of Buddhahood, full enlightenment.

Besides the ultimate results, there are also short term results. If somebody understands emptiness then automatically this person will have compassion towards all beings. With an understanding of emptiness we spontaneously have faith in the dharma and a very strong intention to practice and progress in the dharma. In fact, even the short term benefits of understanding prajna are inconceivable.

This concludes the explanation of the seventeenth chapter,
on the perfection of wisdom-awareness, from
The Jewel Ornament of Liberation.

Questions

Question: You said that the understanding of emptiness automatically brings compassion. Is that different from the understanding that the pratyekabuddhas have?

Thrangu Rinpoche: Yes, there is a difference between these understandings. In the case we are talking about, the understanding is of all phenomena as being non-existent and as being unreal. The pratyekabuddha's understanding doesn't go that far.

Question: How does compassion come automatically from understanding emptiness?

Rinpoche: First it is said that emptiness itself possesses the very essence of compassion; it has in itself the essence of compassion. For example, if somebody sees another person suffering, they might think, "Well, it's the result of their own doing, so it's their own problem if they are suffering." But if somebody understands emptiness they will know that although the suffering of that person is not real, the person thinks that they are really suffering, so through that illusion that person must go through that suffering. This automatically brings about very strong compassion. Imagine somebody here was asleep and had a nightmare and they saw a wild and ferocious animal just about to eat them. In the dream they would be totally frightened and would be in a state of panic, they would try to escape and be undergoing tremendous fear and pain. But if a clairvoyant saw what was going on in the dream they would think, "Oh, the poor person. There is no wild animal there that will eat them, so actually there is no problem, but they think there is. Poor person!" The clairvoyant would try to wake them up so that they could see that there is no wild animal there threatening them, thus no reason to be in fear and pain. In the same way, if somebody understands emptiness, they can see that the suffering beings undergo are not real, they are really just an illusion and there is no real suffering there. This understanding brings a great feeling of compassion.

Question: I want to ask about inspiration in contrast to intention, the inspiration to make a strong intention. Do we have to have inspiration to make a strong intention? Does inspiration help you do things? I want to ask Rinpoche, if we lack inspiration what you can do?
Translator: How is that connected with prajna?
Same Student: With the prajna aspect, I think it is inspiration. If you know you have to do something you have to feel inspired. If your intention is an inspired intention then you can easily complete what you are doing. If inspiration is lacking you somehow have to make yourself do something and it is hard. How can you get those together?
Rinpoche: It seems that the function of prajna is not really to increase your inspiration or motivation to do things. Its function is to make you understand what the actual nature of things is so that you can be free from your illusory way of apprehending and experiencing things. It's like what I said about the snake and the rope. Prajna will help you understand that the rope is not a snake and then you will automatically be free from the fear and suffering that arise from believing that the rope was a snake.

Question: When you say, "rest your mind in its own emptiness," can you clarify that please?
Rinpoche: When one lets the mind rest within its own nature, within its own emptiness, we are not speaking here in terms of

thinking about it, but we are speaking of looking directly at the essence of mind. As in the earlier quotation from the *Kashyapa-Requested Sutra,* it said, "The mind is not inside, the mind is not outside and it is not between these two. The mind is in fact like a puppet. It looks real, but in fact there is nothing there, it is completely false." We make the mistake to believe that when thoughts come up in our mind that they are something real. It is like clouds appearing and covering the whole sky. We do the same with thoughts. We let them accumulate and obscure the whole mind. But in fact, there is no need to try to remove thoughts or to try to chase them away. What we have to do is understand that they are not real. If we look directly at thoughts, at their essence, they will automatically vanish because they are not real. Once we look directly at them, we will see they are not real. Once a thought is gone, we rest in the absence of the thought. That is resting in the emptiness of mind.

Question: When you are talking about meditative concentration you are talking about the mind as something you could control. Would Rinpoche please say something about the division between controlling the mind and the mind that tries to control?
Rinpoche: Actually, there is no need to think that the controller is different from mind itself. By nature, the mind is its own boss; it is in control of itself; it is independent. However, the mind loses control over itself, not because of its own way of being as it really is in itself but through a mistake, through illusion. As said before, an illusion is by nature something that does not exist, that is not really there. So, one has to see that this is only an illusion. Once we understand this then the illusion is gone. Then the mind is with its own nature, which is automatically in control of itself. When we look at the mind we find that we have all sorts of thoughts going on all the time. It

is an uninterrupted chain of thoughts from morning until night; from the moment we get up until we go to bed again, thought after thought follows. At first we have the feeling that there are all kinds of different thoughts, good thoughts, bad thoughts, but when we really look we will see that these thoughts have no solid reality, that the mind is by nature completely clear, completely lucid. There is no solid thing called "a thought." When we speak about gaining control over the mind it is like letting the mind be itself again. When the mind is itself again, when it is as it is naturally, then it automatically is in control of itself. So, we shouldn't see it in terms of doing something forceful or think that it is difficult to regain control, but rather it is allowing the mind be as it is, just letting it be. Once we let it be, then it automatically is in control of itself.

Question: If we were having a debate and you had already proved the non-existence of the mind and then you saw that although the mind is non-existent, the emptiness is blissful, then the other person would say, "If the emptiness is blissful, then it must be something." I am just wondering how the logic stands up?
Rinpoche: When we speak of bliss of the mind, of emptiness being blissful, it isn't the kind of bliss or happiness you would talk about when eating candies or something tasty or when taking drugs. Those kinds of things can generate a pleasant feeling within you that is very nice. But here we are speaking about a bliss that is beyond any sort of object, that isn't created by any object. It is the bliss that comes from the absence of all forms of unhappiness, suffering, fear and negativity. When all those have disappeared, then there is the presence of bliss within emptiness. Because it is not a bliss that is due to any thing, to any object, it doesn't make emptiness into a thing. It is just within the

emptiness, a characteristic or quality of emptiness. When there is the absence of any suffering whatsoever there is the presence of bliss.

Question: But the logic is that if it has qualities, then it must have an existence. Logic refutes the existence of the mind. You said that the mind does not have the qualities of color and shape, so if the emptiness does have qualities, then something is wrong.
Rinpoche: As I already pointed out, when we speak of the emptiness of mind or things, it isn't emptiness meaning a total absence, like when you speak about the horns of a rabbit. There is never a rabbit with horns, thus there is an absence or non-existence of rabbit's horns. But when speaking about the emptiness of phenomena, it is not a total absence or total non-existence. If we go back to the example of the hand, I said that while you can see the hand, at the same time in essence the hand is empty. Because the hand is empty doesn't mean that the hand becomes absent. You can see it, while at the same time it is empty in essence. The fact that you see it doesn't make it become anything other than empty.[85] In the same way, when we speak about emptiness and bliss, while it is blissful it is completely empty and while it is empty it is blissful.

Question: I think my real question is that the logic doesn't really bear up to something that is inconceivable. So when you are saying something through logical terms, they don't bear up to what one is trying to say, which is that you cannot think your way around it. You cannot grasp it with your thoughts.
Rinpoche: It can be proved through logic because if you are seeking to find the truth, then it can be demonstrated through logic. If you are talking about something false, then of course it

cannot be proved logically. But if we go back to the example of the dream it might make things a little bit clearer. Everybody knows through their own experience that there is nothing real in a dream, the essence of the dream is completely empty, but while you are having the dream that is completely unreal you do experience what you see, what you experience is really there for you. If you see a house, an elephant, a buffalo or whatever, you cannot say it is not there while you dream. So two things are happening, the fact that there is no reality to what is happening and the fact that it is happening, it is visible; so it is visible while empty and empty while visible. This is the same as what we are speaking about now. It is blissful yet empty, empty yet blissful.

Question: I do accept what you say. I believe it to be true. But on the other hand, if someone asks a silly question, I won't be able to answer it.
Rinpoche: I do think that it is possible to prove this through logic due to the fact that bliss itself is not real and emptiness itself is not real. We are not speaking about truly existent things. In fact, it should be possible to prove this because it is the very expression of the truth. If you are basing your argument on something that is true, then it can be proved through logic. However, sometimes when we ask questions I can say things to clarify things for you and that will help you eliminate your doubts, but sometimes I can't manage that. It isn't because the subject matter discussed is wrong or because the Buddha's teachings aren't clear, rather I myself cannot make them clear because I am not clear enough myself. Theoretically, through logic one could clarify all of this, but the person must be clear enough himself in order to do it.

Chapter 18
The Aspects of the Five Paths

Please try to take these teachings with a mind intent upon perfect enlightenment. These teachings will show us that once we have approached the spiritual friend, started relying upon their help and taken their instructions, then we can really make the decision and take the commitment to work towards enlightenment for the sake of all other beings. The way we work towards enlightenment is through the practice of the six paramitas. We saw how we should practice and develop the various qualities of the six paramitas. That was completed with the explanation of the prajnaparamita. Once somebody does that kind of practice, the result of that practice and what one accomplishes up until final realization is explained through the outline of the five paths and ten levels. First we will consider the paths.

There are five paths: the path of accumulation, the path of junction, the path of insight, that of cultivation and the path of accomplishment.

I. The Path of Accumulation. The first of the five paths is that of accumulation. It is really the way in which we truly enter the path to enlightenment. The main point of this path is not so much the practice of meditation as the attempt to achieve as much positive meritorious actions as possible through body, speech and mind because the accumulation of virtue will act as the necessary factor to increase all good qualities within us. It will help us develop more faith, a stronger wish to practice, more interest in the practice and more devotion. Once we have these qualities we will really be on the path. As a result, many good qualities will develop and meditation will become better. This is what is accomplished on the path of accumulation.

The path of accumulation is divided into three stages: lesser stage, medium stage and greater stage. For all stages, however, the main point is to do as many virtuous actions as possible because their effect will be to increase our faith, devotion, diligence and correspondingly this will increase our understanding, realization and meditation.[86]

II. The Path of Junction. The second path is called "the path of junction." Actually, when we speak about "path," we should distinguish between what is called "real path" or "the actual path" and what is called "the fictitious path." The real path is when we actually see the true nature of things just as it is. It is not a matter of just thinking, "It is like this" and aspiring towards that, but it is actually experiencing what it is. It is no longer a matter of ideas, but of actual experience, of actual realization of the nature of things. This is what we should consider "the real path." The path that comes before is artificial or fictitious because there is not the real experience of the path. However, it is very important because the experiences are the preparation for the real experience of the true path; in this sense the first path is very important. However, the real path is the third path of insight. The first two paths lead to this understanding.

On the path of junction, we do not just try to accumulate good actions, but we are concentrating on meditation. This path is also called "the path on which our practice is based on an idea, an aspiration" because at this point there is no true experience of the nature of things. However, through tremendous effort, through tremendous practice, through great devotion we are trying to go in the direction of that understanding. We think, "I am doing tranquility or *insight meditation*[87] and this is emptiness, this is clarity." It all concerns ideas, things we make up with our mind, the idea of meditation, the idea of emptiness, but it is not the real experience. Yet, through forming the aspiration and the idea, we will come closer to the point when we can really experience it. Although at this stage it is only make-believe and only an aspiration, this doesn't mean that it is useless. In fact, it is very useful because it prepares us for the real experience. That is the reason why this particular path is called "the path of junction," because although not the real experience or real understanding of the true nature of things, it is what joins us to the real experience; it provides the link with the insight that is gained on the third path of seeing.[88]

When we are traveling through the different steps of each path, there are different experiences that we can have in meditation. At that moment we are meditating on the mind itself and this can bring up all sorts of experiences. Sometimes when we meditate we will find that our meditation is very clear, very pleasant, very stable and very enjoyable. Within this meditation we may see all sorts of things; we may see light, we may see colors, we may even see deities. This can happen. But we may also have other experiences that are very unpleasant. We may find that our mind feels very uptight, very unhappy, that meditation is very unclear and difficult, that we hear and see things that aren't pleasant and maybe even see ghosts. All these are just experiences that may occur in meditation. Good or bad, it doesn't matter. All this is just a manifestation of our mind. We shouldn't feel the experiences are good and pleasant and think, "Oh, I am doing really well. In fact, I am doing better than anybody else." On the basis of such experiences we become very proud and blown-up with what we think is the value of our experience. This isn't the right reaction to have because what we are looking for is Buddhahood, enlightenment, and this has to be accomplished through a continuous and perseverant effort. We are not into just experiencing sounds and lights because that is just a way to develop more pride; becoming big-headed is not what is going to get us to enlightenment. Those are just experiences that occur in the mind.

As long as we follow the right path taught by the Buddha we don't need to have any worries. This path is not going to take us to suffering or more difficulties, so there is no need to worry. We just need to carry on with our practice, no matter what happens and regardless of whether our experiences are good or bad, pleasant or unpleasant. The point is to just go on with practice.

If we continue on with our practice then there will be two signs that indicate real progress on the path. One sign is called "the sign of purity" and the other is called "the sign of understanding or realization." Some instructions explain that the signs of success in study are that our mind becomes more peaceful, more in control, that our pride diminishes and that the wish to help others increases. Those are signs of successful study. The signs of successful meditation are that our negativities decrease to a great degree. As said, the purpose of the meditation is not to have all sorts of experiences, visions, sounds and the like. The point is to achieve success in getting rid of our negativity and the mind becoming more clear, having less and less pride, less and less anger and less and less involvement with negative appearances in the mind. These are the real signs of good meditation.

Concerning the aspect of the path of junction, which is also the path practiced out of aspiration, out of an idea of our goal, in terms of the qualities of purity, it is the stage at which our negativities will be reduced. This is because we aspire to the realization of the true nature of things and this aspiration will sustain our practice in such a way that it will reduce our negativity automatically. The other sign of success is realization. This means that at this stage our meditation progresses, our concentration improves and we find generally that our faith and devotion are much greater. These are the immediate qualities that come from practice on this stage of the path.

III. The Path of Insight. If we practice the path of junction, the result is the third path, the path of insight. When we have practiced with great inspiration, faith and diligence, then the path will bring us to a real result, a real sign of success, which is actually the insight into the truth. When we speak about the truth concerning the true nature of things or that we want to accomplish enlightenment to gain total insight into everything or that we want to accomplish Buddhahood, this doesn't mean going somewhere else or trying to find something new. Actually, the truth is always there, but it is temporarily obscured by impurities. What is unmistaken is distorted by mistakes, what is pure is veiled by illusion. The truth is not something that was made up by the Buddha or something that can be given to us by the Three Jewels. Therefore, what we need to do is to get rid of our illusion, get rid of the mistake our mind has made about the nature of things, then the truth will be seen.

We have within our mind this quality of understanding, of realization that can see and understand the truth about everything. If we practice meditation on what is called "emptiness" or "the true nature of the mind" or "the true nature of everything" or "Mahamudra" or "the Buddha-essence" or whatever other names it is given, if we practice meditation on this, then we will come to the point of actually experiencing it for what it is. Then, even if the Buddha were to appear personally and say, "It is not this," nothing would change our mind because by then we would have direct experience of what it is, we would taste it directly within our own mind. It would be like if someone was telling us about London and we had a fair idea that it must be there because we are being told it is. But if we actually went there and saw London for ourselves, then even if one hundred people said, "There is no such place as London," we wouldn't believe them. Nobody could ever make us think that there is no London because we have had the direct experience of seeing London ourselves. This exemplifies that once we have the direct experience ourselves, of what the truth is, nobody can disprove it because we know what the truth is. This is what is achieved through the path of insight.[89]

IV. The Path of Cultivation. As said, even insight into the truth is not enough because for a very long time our mind has formed bad habits. Therefore, it is still possible that from time to time we will fall under the power of deception and of illusory appearances. So, we have to cultivate the insight gained on the path of insight. This is done on the fourth path, which is the path of cultivation.

On this path we become very familiar with what has been seen on the path of insight. When there is the combination of insight into the truth and its cultivation, until it becomes a second nature, the result will be that all negative factors that plagued our mind before will automatically disappear. Because things are not real, they are only a part of illusion, when we see the truth, automatically all these illusions will vanish. This implies that the non-existence of an individual self will be seen directly. Once this is seen it will eliminate the idea of a self. Once the idea of a self has disappeared, automatically there are no more desires, no more anger and no more ignorance. The same applies to phenomena. Once we see the truth of all things, automatically the belief in reality, the solidity and the substantiality of all things will vanish.

Let us take an example to show how this insight really gives us an unflinching conviction concerning the nature of things. Using again the example of somebody mistaking a rope for a snake. This mistake will lead them to believe that there is a real snake there. However, once they understand that it is only a rope, even if somebody comes along and says, "I'll give you 100 ounces of gold if you say it is a snake" or "I will kill you if you don't say that it is a snake," it won't change their mind because they know very well that it is not a snake; they have seen the truth and know that it is a rope. In the same way, once we have seen the truth of all things, then even if somebody says, "Please, get some negativity going in your mind" or if we think to ourselves, "I should do that," we won't be able to because by then we have seen the nature of things and can't be fooled anymore. It is impossible at this stage to have any negativity in our mind.

So, through seeing the true nature of all things, through insight into the truth, automatically all things that have to be eliminated are removed and by the same token automatically everything that has to be understood, all the insight that one has to develop, the jnana (primordial wisdom) that has to become manifest happens naturally.[90]

V. The Path of Accomplishment. The fifth path is called "the path of accomplishment," "the final path" or "the path of Buddhahood." A common word used to designate the Buddha is "Tathagata" in Sanskrit and "De-shin-sheg-pa" in Tibetan, which means, "gone to thatness." The state of Buddhahood is not like going to a foreign place or something new that we fabricate. It is plainly and simply seeing what is there, seeing the truth as it is, the real nature of things. It is the "thatness" that is there. We just go into the path of what is there, which explains the name "Tathagata," "gone to thatness." When we follow the path that leads to thatness, to the "is-ness" of things, then there is no need to have fear or to worry because it is just going back to what is there.

Another synonym for the Buddha is "Sugata," in Sanskrit and "De-wa-sheg-pa" in Tibetan, which means "gone to bliss" or "gone to happiness." As already explained, the truth of all things is not just emptiness, it is empty and at the same time it is the very expression of great happiness and bliss. The Buddha is the one who has gone to the great bliss of mind. Our sufferings, our problems all come from our mind. They are generated in our mind by the negative factors that can disturb the mind. But all these problems and difficulties are only made by the mind. Once we are back in the true nature of things, there are no more problems and sufferings fabricated artificially by the mind. As the true nature of the mind is naturally blissful, when somebody has stopped all negativity in the mind they then automatically go back into the original blissful nature of the mind. This is what is accomplished at the end of all paths: perfect enlightenment, Buddhahood.

It is also said that at that stage there are two kinds of knowledge or awareness: awareness of exhaustion and awareness of non-arising. Knowing exhaustion means that the Buddha knows that everything negative, any mistakes or confusion in the mind have been exhausted. The Buddha also knows that all the faults and confusion will never ever arise again, they are permanently exhausted. This is the final path of Buddhahood.[91]

This concludes the explanation of the eighteenth chapter,
on the five paths, from
The Jewel Ornament of Liberation.

Chapter 19
The Levels of the Path

Following the chapter on the paths is the chapter on the ten bhumis or levels. The ground covered on the five paths and ten levels are the same, the ten levels are just presenting a slightly different aspect. All the levels are included in the five paths and the other way around.

Outline of the Thirteen Levels

The path of accumulation is called "the beginner's level," which constitutes the first level. The path of junction is the level that is practiced out of aspiration and it constitutes the second level.[92] The path of insight and the path of cultivation cover what are called "the ten bodhisattva levels." Finally, the fifth path of Buddhahood covers the level of Buddhahood. Altogether that makes thirteen levels, the beginner's level, the level of practice out of aspiration, the ten bodhisattva levels and the last, that of the Buddha.

The word "path" is used because by practicing that specific path we achieve a particular state. The word "level" is used because we move from one level to the next, like traveling from one place to the next, mile after mile, gradually reaching the goal. Here, after thirteen miles, thirteen particular steps, we achieve the goal, which is Buddhahood.

We will not go into details concerning the beginner's level and the level practiced out of aspiration because they have been described in the previous chapter on the path. But, I will go through the ten levels of the bodhisattvas.

1. Overwhelming Joy

The first level of the bodhisattva is called "overwhelming joy" because at this point the mind experiences great joy and happiness. There are many different reasons for this joy and happiness, but mainly it is because this is the first time that one comes to see the truth of everything, the true nature of things, which has never been experienced before. This, of course, is a great source of joy and one realizes that all efforts in trying to achieve this have become worthwhile and meaningful; they have led to this very great result. Another source of joy is that one can see that nearly all of the negative factors that previously disturbed the mind are gone; this is, of course, a great source of happiness. Consequently, one can also see that now it is possible to help a great number of other beings, which again makes one very happy. Finally, one can see that now Buddhahood is really close at hand. One can see that it is straight ahead and that there are no more obstacles or adverse conditions on the way that can stop one from accomplishing Buddhahood. All this causes great happiness in the mind.[93]

2. Stainless

The second level is called "stainless" or "immaculate" because at this level one has completely perfected the paramita of moral ethics. As a result, one has totally eliminated any sort of negative action.[94]

3. Radiant & 4. Luminous

The third and fourth levels are similar. On the third level one has perfected the paramita of patience, on the fourth the paramita of diligence. As a result, one's realization is greatly increased. The clarity of inner realization is signified by the example of light in the names each is given. On the fourth level the clarity of experience and understanding is even greater than on the third.[95]

5. Difficult to Practice

The word for this level has a double meaning, "difficult to practice" and "difficult to purify." This is because on this level one has completely perfected the paramita of meditative concentration. As explained earlier, the achievement of a perfectly stable mind is what determines the achievement of prajnaparamita, perfect understanding. However, there is a moment when it is very difficult to achieve that kind of understanding and insight, the reason why this level is called "difficult to practice or to purify."[96]

6. Obviously Transcendent

This is the level where one has completely achieved the prajnaparamita, so one's understanding is complete. At that point one gains an even sharper and more direct insight into the truth of all things, the reason why it is called "obviously transcendent"; the truth is very obvious, and one has transcended abiding in either samsara or nirvana.[97]

7. Far Gone

The seventh level is called "far gone" because at this point one has gone really a long way from conditioned existence. Before that there was still a slight distinction between self and others;

it has been an instinct within oneself to think in terms of "I" and "others," but on the seventh level this has disappeared, thus it is far gone beyond samsara.[98]

8. Unshakeable

From the eighth level onwards one enters what are called "the pure levels." It is because from this point onwards almost everything that needed to be eliminated has been eliminated; all negative aspects of the mind, in particular the belief in "I" and "others" have been eliminated. The eighth level itself is called "unshakeable" because at this point one is no longer shaken, moved or swayed by thoughts.[99]

9. Excellent Discriminating Wisdom

This is so named because at this point one can clearly see the way in which everything is and the way in which everything manifests. One's understanding really embraces all aspects of existence, on all levels.[100]

10. Cloud of Dharma

On the tenth level there is still a significant difference between the qualities of purity and realization of a bodhisattva and a Buddha, the next level. But in terms of actively helping others, it is similar to the Buddha's ability to helping beings and so the reason it is called "the cloud of dharma."[101]

The last level is the ultimate state, that of the Buddha. It is similar to what has been explained about the path of accomplishment.[102]

This concludes the explanation of the nineteenth chapter,
on the levels of the path, from
The Jewel Ornament of Liberation.

TOPIC 5: THE RESULT

The Result is the Body of Perfect Buddhahood

Chapter 20
Perfect Buddhahood

Please try to think very clearly that you want to accomplish enlightenment for the sake of all beings and that this is the reason why you are receiving these teachings now. In the study of *The Jewel Ornament of Liberation*, there are six main points that summarize the entire book. I have now covered four points: the cause for achieving Buddhahood is the Buddha-essence; the basis to accomplish this is the precious human life; the necessary condition is the spiritual friend; and what the means are to accomplish enlightenment and the instructions we receive from the spiritual friend. Now, the fifth point is about the result of this path, the result we will accomplish, which is the kayas[103] of the Buddha. Now we have the full outline of the path. First we begin with the resolution to accomplish Buddhahood for the sake of all beings. Then we practice the paramitas in order to accomplish this. By going through the paths and levels, finally we accomplish the ultimate result, which is the kayas of the Buddha.

What does the accomplishment of Buddhahood actually mean? As explained earlier, Buddhahood has two aspects, one is the aspect of purity and one is the aspect of realization. When full enlightenment is accomplished, all qualities of purity and realization are totally completed. So now we will examine the meaning of Buddhahood, the ultimate result of the path, by way of seven points: nature, significance of the nature, classification, definition, reason for the definite number, characteristics and special traits.

I. Nature. The first point discusses the nature of Buddhahood. In general, it seems that there is a contradiction between the worldly or mundane aspect of things and the spiritual aspect of things. In some scriptures it is said that a person cannot do worldly and spiritual things at the same time and that if we are trying to achieve something on the worldly level we cannot achieve something on the spiritual level at the same time. However, maybe this is a way of reinforcing our aspiration for the dharma, a way to make our diligence stronger and more stable. But in terms of the way things really are, it isn't quite like that. In a sense, on the worldly level, the objective or goal of people is just like the spiritual goal. Even on the worldly level everybody is trying to achieve the same thing, which is trying to find the best possible happiness, well-being and to be without problems, pain, suffering and difficulties. On the spiritual level it is the same: we are trying to achieve the greatest and final ultimate happiness for all beings. So, the goal of our worldly actions and the goal of our spiritual practice are the same; they both aim at finding happiness and goodness and try to eliminate suffering and problems. This isn't just something that applies to human beings, it is also true for animals, who automatically try to find what makes them feel well and happy and shun what makes them feel pain and suffering.

In fact, there won't be anybody who seeks pain, trouble and misfortune. Everybody is trying to be free from that and to find the opposite, which is happiness, wellbeing and so forth. The path of dharma is the one that leads oneself and all other beings to true happiness and freedom from suffering. If we call happiness and goodness "qualities" and suffering and problems "defects," then we will find that the objective of spiritual life and the goal of ordinary life are similar. In ordinary life we are trying to increase our qualities, our good sides – qualities being what lead to good results, – to something wholesome, good and joyful. Faults and defects are what cause trouble, suffering, misfortune and unhappiness. Then, also in the worldly sense we try to decrease our faults and mistakes.

In terms of the spiritual path it is exactly the same; we are trying to develop qualities more and more and to eliminate defects more and more. When we reach the completion of that process, when all qualities are complete and when all defects have been eliminated, this is what is called "Buddhahood." In ordinary terms, we would say "the fullness of qualities and the total absence of defects." In dharma terms we would say "the complete qualities of freedom and realization," freedom from all mistakes and confusion, which have been eliminated, and realization of all the qualities of understanding being complete. This is the nature of Buddhahood.[104]

In the *Jewel Ornament* there is a long discussion presenting the different positions various scholars have about the mind of the Buddha. Some say the Buddha has cognizance and others say he does not have cognizance. There are many arguments about this. Those who say the Buddha does not have cognizance consider accomplishing Buddhahood a process of annihilation, like a candle flame being extinguished. They say that in the same way, accomplishing Buddhahood means vanishing or dissolving and that there is no mind, no cognition left. The reason why this is said is not to show that there is nothing there at all, that would be complete extinction. Instead, this is said to show that the pure cognizance a Buddha has is not the ordinary form of mind of cognition that we ourselves experience. Our form of cognition is very coarse and gross because it is based upon the idea of self. Through the idea of self everything is experienced in terms of attraction and repulsion, attraction to what we feel is pleasant and joyful and repulsion against what we feel is unpleasant. The consciousness or mind of the Buddha doesn't have these coarse thoughts, the coarse mind that ordinary beings have. That is why in many sutras and in some shastras it is often said that the Buddha doesn't have cognizance so that we understand that cognizance is not the way we experience it, with all its very coarse forms of thoughts.

It is also stated in other scriptures that the Buddha does have pure cognizance. This is to show that Buddhahood doesn't mean complete extinction; there is a form of cognizance but it is extremely pure. Instead of the ordinary cognition with all the coarse thoughts that we have, the Buddha's is like a mirror within which everything can reflect, appear and can manifest. For instance, the Buddha can see all beings and out of his non-conceptual compassion he can help them because everything is reflected within this pure mind, but there are no thoughts there, no coarse form of mind as we experience it.

So although there are lots of arguments on this point, they are not contradictory because they describe the actual nature of cognition at the stage of a Buddha. The main point for us is to learn from all this, and the best presentation that is given is by Milarepa. Milarepa defines the cognition of a Buddha in a very simple way. He says that the pure jnana, the cognition of a Buddha is not something very far off or foreign, but it is the mind in its immediacy. It is the mind before it has been altered in any way, before it has been manipulated or changed. As said previously, when the mind is in its own nature it is not agitated by thoughts, our own fabricated thoughts do not modify the mind. Once the mind is agitated and modified, it loses control over itself and becomes over-powered and determined by negative factors. Normally and presently, we do not see the true form and state of our mind and that is why we cannot let it be as it is; we cannot allow it to be in control of itself and to be its own master. However, there is no need to improve the mind or to make it better and there is no need to remove anything from it; we just need to let it be what it is, this original form of mind, cognition or awareness. In fact, there is little need to say anything about it because whatever description we give is irrelevant because mind is nothing that can be labeled. Whatever we say will be a misassumption of the mind, it will be going into extremes either in terms of existence or in terms of non-existence. Really, the true state of the mind is beyond the sphere of thoughts and the intellect. But we use language to communicate and designate it, calling it "mind" or "jnana." In fact, this mind can only be understood through directly seeing its own nature, what it is in itself.

When purification and realization are complete, then the true nature of the mind, as it is in itself, is made manifest. The mind then is no longer disturbed by thoughts, it is in its initial and original clarity. It is an omniscient form of cognition. This is the form of cognizance that the Buddha has.[105]

II. Significance of the Name. The second point of this chapter explains the meaning of the word "Buddha." Buddha is the Sanskrit word and the way it was rendered into Tibetan is in two words, "Sang" and "gye." These two words describe the two qualities already mentioned about the Buddha, the quality of purity and the quality of realization.

The first aspect of the name Sangye, which is "sang," deals with the quality of purity. We do not need to think that outer objects are very solid and real and that in order to gain liberation we have to destroy all these things or burn them or smash them to pieces. All illusory appearances of conditioned existence are only an illusion; they are only the result of a mistake, of a misapprehension of the truth; they are only a delusion. So, there is simply this little mistake that the mind makes and therefore there is no reason to try to destroy external objects. The change has to come from within the mind. And within the mind it is not a hard and solid thing that we have to defeat. There is only a very small mistake, a misunderstanding, only a small illusion. When we speak about liberation, it means the end of all mistakes, the end of illusion. What we need to do is to awaken from this mistake, which is like sleep. Or we can also say we have to remove the mistake. That accounts for the first part of the name of the Buddha, which means, "awakened" and "purified" of mistakes. So, it is just a matter of awakening through knowing what was not known, knowing the mistake for what it was worth. So, we say "awakened" or "cleared away" rather than "to remove or eliminate" because it is not a matter of taking away an external object, but is a matter of understanding our mistake, our illusion.

The second aspect of the name for Buddha is "gye," which means "fully expanded." This relates to the qualities. All the qualities and wisdom blossom and are fully expanded, which is complete realization.

There is also another word for Buddha, which is Samyakbuddha. This means, "really and truly perfect Buddhahood." It means that the qualities of purity and realization are not just any degree of purity and realization, but are the very final and ultimate level of purity and realization; there couldn't be anything more realized or pure. The first part of the name, "samyak" means "true." This is in relation to the qualities that come from practicing the true path. And they are perfect in that all the qualities are complete. So, one achieves true and perfect Buddhahood when all qualities of purity and realization are totally complete.

III. Classification. The third point describes the different aspects of the Buddha. When we speak about Buddha, it is one state, but in terms of the value that Buddhahood has for oneself and others it can be divided into three aspects, which are the dharmakaya, the sambhogakaya and the nirmanakaya. I will explain them by using the well known words of prayer, in which it is said, "I and all beings as limitless as space take refuge in the Guru, who is the Buddha, the dharmakaya."

The Buddha himself is referred to as being the dharmakaya, which represents the very nature of the mind of the Buddha with all the perfections of purity and realization, purity in the sense that all defects have been perfectly removed and realization in the sense that all qualities of knowledge and perfect wisdom are complete.

The prayer continues and reads, "The most blissful sambhogakaya." This is the aspect of the Buddha that is made manifest after all suffering and hardships are gone. So the sambhogakaya here is the expression of that great happiness, that great bliss which comes after all suffering is gone.

The third aspect of the Buddha is the nirmanakaya. The prayer reads, "The most compassionate nirmanakaya." The nirmanakaya is the very expression of the non-conceptual compassion that the Buddha has for all beings. Through the nirmanakaya he takes birth in our world and does all sorts of things for the good of beings, for instance as explained by way of the twelve deeds of the Buddha.[106] So, these are the three aspects of perfect Buddhahood.

IV. Definition. The fourth point describes the system of presentation of the three kayas of the Buddha. What we call "Buddha" is the very expression of the ultimate nature of things and of the qualities inherent to that pure nature. The name given to that is "dharmakaya." The dharmakaya is really that to which we apply the name Buddha; Buddha *is* dharmakaya.[107] But, there are two other aspects of Buddhahood, which are the two form kayas. These form kayas manifest for the sake of other beings. The sambhogakaya manifests to beings that are already pure and it manifests in five particular and definite ways. The nirmanakaya manifests to beings that are more impure. Another way of saying this is that the dharmakaya represents the best possible value and benefit for oneself and the sambhogakaya and nirmanakaya represent the best possible value and benefit for others.

V. Reason for the Definite Number of Three Kayas. The fifth point tells us why there is the definite number of kayas of the Buddha; why there are particularly three.[108] What we need to achieve is twofold; we need to achieve the best value for ourselves and we need to achieve the best value for other beings. This kind of achievement must be the ultimate form of achievement, not just something that is beneficial in the short term, but ultimately beneficial, the best possible on all levels. So, the value that we must achieve for us must be the best possible and this is done through achieving the dharmakaya. This accounts for one kaya.

The value for others must also be the best possible. This can be accomplished by way of the two form kayas. Because there are two types of beings, those who are pure can be helped through the sambhogakaya and those who are impure can be helped through the nirmanakaya. That is why three kayas are necessary and the reason why it is this and no other number.

VI. Characteristics of the Three Kayas. The sixth point describes the particularities of Buddhahood, the specific characteristics of Buddhahood and this is in terms of the particular qualities that are accomplished at Buddhahood. For instance, the dharmakaya aspect is represented by the thirty-two qualities of freedom, such as the ten powers of the Buddha, the eighteen distinctive qualities and so on. In order to help other beings it is not enough for the Buddha's quality of mind to be perfect, for his jnana to be totally blossomed. There needs to be a form that manifests for others, for the good of other beings. That is why the form qualities, those that can manifest in a visible way, are represented by the thirty-two qualities of maturity. These are qualities that have to do with very special signs and marks on the body of the Buddha. Altogether there are sixty-four qualities, thirty-two qualities of freedom pertaining to the dharmakaya as far as the Buddha himself is concerned and thirty-two qualities of maturity that pertain to the form kayas and are for the good of others.[109]

VII. Special Traits. The seventh point of the chapter shows the particularities of the Buddhas. There are three special and distinctive attributes that are the same for all Buddhas: equality, permanence and appearance.

A. The Special Trait of Equality

In terms of the dharmakaya, it means that the dharmakaya of all Buddhas is the same within the *dharmadhatu*;[110] the dharmakayas of all Buddhas are one and not separate within the dharmadhatu. Concerning the sambhogakaya, it means that the mind and intentions of all sambhogakayas are the same. It is a form of mind that is turned towards the good of all other beings and it is a mind that similarly understands the true nature of all things. In terms of the nirmanakaya, it means that all activities of all nirmanakayas are the same, which is the activity to free all beings from the ocean of suffering.

B. The Special Trait of Permanence

The dharmakaya is permanent by nature insofar as it has no beginning, no middle and no end. It also never comes into being or ceases to be. The sambhogakaya is the permanence of continuity insofar as the sambhogakaya never passes away or disappears. The nirmanakaya doesn't have the permanence of continuity, but it has the permanence of never being cut-off. In other words, its activity never discontinues and in that sense it is permanent. This means that a particular nirmanakaya Buddha may pass away, but the activity of all nirmanakaya aspects goes on continuously. Therefore, it is permanent through its activity.

C. The Special Trait of Appearance

The third attribute is manifestation. When all obscurations are purified and all qualities and wisdom completely manifest, the dharmakaya appears. So the fullness of purity and realization of the dharmakaya is only experienced by the Buddha himself, it is only the domain of the Buddha. The sambhogakaya manifests to bodhisattvas on the levels through their purification of the disturbing emotions. Finally, the nirmanakaya, or the historical

Buddhas, manifests to beings whose karmic obscurations are purified to some extent.

That is the seventh point on the particularities of the Buddhas.

This concludes the explanation of the twentieth chapter,
on perfect Buddhahood, from
The Jewel Ornament of Liberation.

TOPIC 6: THE ACTIVITIES

The Activities are Benefiting Sentient Beings without Conceptual Thought

Chapter 21
Activities of the Buddha

Now we have come to the last point of this text, which describes the activities of the Buddhas. This point is actually very brief in the text itself. The two things that are pointed out concerning the activities of the Buddhas are that they are free of concept and spontaneous. This is explained in detail in the *Uttaratantrashastra* (Sanskrit), in Tibetan *The Gyulama*, by way of nine examples. Since it is dealt with briefly here, it is summarized in the form of three ways of activity: the activity of the Buddhas through the body, through the speech and through the mind. In these three ways they are able to help beings. This actually covers all the different possibilities.

I. Spontaneous Activities of the Body to Benefit Beings. The form of a Buddha is not an ordinary form like ours but is a form that is adorned with all the special marks and signs, in particular the thirty-two beautiful signs.[111] When somebody sees this form of a Buddha, it can inspire a strong wish in that individual to work on the spiritual path and to accomplish enlightenment. It has the power to inspire people with great devotion and with the wish to attain liberation. The reason why the Buddhas have such power in their body is that during the practice of the path they gathered very great accumulations of virtue. This virtue wasn't accumulated in order to achieve something for themselves – they didn't do this in order to get rich or powerful or with an expectation of personal profit or triumph – they accumulated virtue only with the wish to help other beings. From the moment they first resolved to accomplish enlightenment until the moment of actual enlightenment, there was only one thought in their mind, which was to help beings, both in the short term and ultimately, and to protect beings from suffering. So all along, with just that thought in mind, in the end this produced a result, which is the very embodiment of compassion. So when somebody sees the form of such a Buddha, automatically they can feel instinctively that this means great goodness and great benefit for them. This inspires people tremendously. This is how the Buddhas work physically in order to help beings. Just the effect of seeing their body has this tremendous power of inspiration.

II. Spontaneous Activities of Speech to Benefit Beings. The second aspect of Buddha activity is that of speech. The speech of the Buddha can help beings without a thought behind it and without any effort; it just happens completely and naturally. How is this possible? How does it really happen? As already said, the Buddhas are inspired by their non-conceptual compassion and this is what brings activity to help other beings. That is why the Buddha turns the wheel of dharma. He doesn't give teachings because he expects any kind of profit or reward or glory for himself; he turns the wheel of dharma in order to help all other beings according to their own possibilities, according to their own faculties, and that is why there are 84,000 different aspects of the dharma. If we ask, "For whom did the

Buddha turn the wheel of dharma? Was it for the Indian people because it took place in India?" No, it wasn't for the Indians alone. "Was it for the sangha?" No, it wasn't only for the sangha. "Was it for the Buddhists?" No, it wasn't only for the Buddhists. The Buddha turned the wheel of dharma for all beings, without making a distinction of race or any bias. He turned the wheel of dharma for all beings without excluding anyone in order to bring all beings to happiness. He also did it for each of us individually. If we ask, "For whom did he turn the wheel of dharma?" He turned it for you, for me, for us so that it could help us. He turned the wheel of dharma for each one of us specifically in a way that was appropriate for every individual and that could help each person realize the same thing he realized. That is how the activity of the Buddha's speech can help all beings.

III. Spontaneous Activities of Mind to Benefit Beings. The third point speaks of the mental activity of the Buddhas, the way in which Buddhas can help beings through their pure mind. Again, this aspect of their activity takes place without thoughts or concepts, without any effort, it just happens spontaneously. The Buddhas do not have to think, "Now I have to help beings and do this or that to help them." Without relying on thoughts, their help happens spontaneously. This is because the mind of the Buddhas has been set upon the welfare of beings a long time ago; it is already focused on the need to help beings. Once this focus is there and is free of any selfish stains then automatically non-conceptual compassion happens spontaneously and all the time for the sake of beings. Of course, that is quite different than what we are used to. We need to think, "Now I must meditate, now I must develop compassion, now I must help beings." As for the Buddha, there is no need for such intentions because automatically compassion is there without any thought and without any effort.[112]

This concludes the brief description of the activities of the Buddhas to help beings through their perfect body, speech and mind, which take place without any thoughts and without any effort.

This concludes the explanation of the twentieth chapter, on perfect Buddhahood, from *The Jewel Ornament of Liberation.*

Conclusion

Now we have finished the six points or the twenty-one chapters that make up this precious teaching of Gampopa, called *The Jewel Ornament of the Precious Liberation.*

Actually, when I taught this teaching, maybe I didn't use the best words or convey the finest meanings, but what is in the book itself is the fruit of the experience of the realization of Gampopa himself. Gampopa was one of the very extraordinary beings that were able to accomplish Buddhahood in one lifetime. This book is a sign or fruit of his realization. By showing us that, we can do what is taught here, we can also accomplish the same result. It is like giving us direct instructions on how we can also go about it and also accomplish the same result. There is a saying in Tibet, "If you have taken gold, purified it through fire and processed it properly, it will be pure gold and without any defects." In the same way, these teachings are very pure teachings because they were spoken out of the realization of Gampopa. This book contains within itself proof through realization. We therefore know that if we use it properly, it will lead to the same result.

It is part of the very nature of existence that everything has to come to an end because everything is impermanent, so this teaching has now come to an end. But, it is not just so for the teachings. Everything ends; our life will come to an end, our experiences and our impressions, everything that manifests to us. In a way, maybe impermanence is something that makes us feel sad, but maybe it is something that makes us feel very happy because the dharma is something that can really help us in the face of impermanence. What we have from these teachings is something each and every one of us should keep inside our hearts. Now it is up to us. Now it is our own responsibility to use these teachings and not to become lazy and forget them. Now we have this tool and can use it properly.

So, maybe impermanence is a good thing. Look at what happened now. We have managed to finish these teachings without any obstacles, without any difficulties. Actually, things go very fast. Presently it seems to us that the first bodhisattva level is miles away, is completely out of our reach and that it is impossible to get there. But, because time passes and things happen quickly, before you know it, one day you will be there and suddenly you will be a bodhisattva on the first level. Because things always change and continue happening, then one day, before you know it, you will be a Buddha too. So, impermanence is very good. Things are not static; they change. But, we just have to see to it that we apply enough diligence and then we can also achieve the same result. So, feel that what you have received is something you must use and do not become a prey to laziness. I want to request this of you.

Summary of the Text, The Jewel Ornament of Liberation

The Name of the Text

The Jewel Ornament of Liberation, the wish-fulfilling gem of the noble teachings.

The Homage

I prostrate to the noble Manjushri in youthful form. I pay homage to the Victorious Ones, their followers, the holy Dharma, and to the lamas who are their roots. This noble teaching, which is like the wish-fulfilling jewel, will be written for the benefit of myself and others by depending on the kindness of Lord Mila.

The Six Topics of the Book

The primary cause, working basis, condition, method, result, and activities. All discriminating beings should understand that these six comprise the general explanation of unsurpassable enlightenment.

TOPIC 1: THE PRIMARY CAUSE

The Primary Cause is the Essence of the Buddha

Chapter 1

Buddha nature

All sentient beings, including ourselves, already possess the primary cause for enlightenment, the essence of the Buddha.

Three Reasons Why Beings Possess Buddha nature

Because all sentient beings are pervaded by the emptiness of dharmakaya, because there are no differentiations in the nature of suchness, and because all beings have a "potential." For these three reasons, all sentient beings are of the Buddha-essence.

Five Categories of Potential

Those with enlightened potential can be categorized into five groups: the cut-off potential, the uncertain potential, the shravaka potential (listeners), the pratyekabuddha potential (solitary-realizers), and the Mahayana potential.

I. The Cut-off Potential. *Those with the cut-off potential are without the slightest weariness of samsara. Although they know of the qualities of the Buddha, they feel not the slightest faith, embarrassment, shame, compassion, or regret. Those who maintain these six attributes have no chance to work toward enlightenment.*

II. The Uncertain Potential. *Those with the uncertain potential depend upon circumstances. If they attend a shravaka spiritual friend, associate with shravaka friends, or study the different shravaka texts, then those persons will awaken in the shravaka family. They will study and follow that path and become part of the shravaka family. Likewise, if those persons meet with a pratyekabuddha or a Mahayana master, then respectively they will become part of the pratyekabuddha or Mahayana family.*

III. The Shravaka Potential. *The shravakas are those who fear samsara and yearn to achieve nirvana, but they have little compassion.*

IV. The Pratyekabuddha Potential. *The six signs of a pratyekabuddha are: they have fear of samsara, they believe in nirvana, they have little compassion, they have great pride, they keep their teacher's identity secret, and they like to be in solitude.*

V. The Mahayana Potential. *The Mahayana potential is summed up in six topics: classification, definition, synonyms, the reason why it is superior to other potentials, the characteristics, and the signs.*

A. Classification. *Classification is two: the potential that is present* *by nature, and the potential of perfect accomplishment.*

__B. Definition.__ The potential present by nature is the ability to bring forth the Buddha qualities which are there since beginningless time and which are realized through suchness. The potential of perfect accomplishment is the ability to bring forth the Buddha qualities obtained through former practice of the roots of virtue.

What is the potential that is present by nature? It is the nature of the mind, the dharmakaya.

What is the potential of perfect accomplishment? It is the sambhogakaya and nirmanakaya.

__C. Synonyms.__ It can be called potential, seed, nature or essence of the mind.

__D. The Reason Why it is Superior.__ Both the shravaka and pratyekabuddha potentials are inferior because when they have become perfected then only the obscuration of disturbing emotions has been removed. The Mahayana potential is supreme because when it has become perfected then the two kinds of obscurations have been removed, the emotional obscuration and the cognitive obscuration.

__E. Characteristics.__ The potential can be described as awakened and unawakened. Those with awakened potential have achieved the fruit perfectly and the signs are very obvious. Those with unawakened potential have not achieved the fruit perfectly, and the signs are not obvious. What causes the potential to awaken is freedom from unfavorable conditions and the support of favorable ones. If the opposite occurs, it cannot awaken.

The four unfavorable circumstances are to be born in adverse circumstances, not to have the tendency to practice, to be born on a wrong path and to have very bad obscurations.

The two favorable circumstances are outwardly that the holy dharma is being taught and inwardly to put one's mind in correct countenance.

__F. Signs.__ The bodhisattvas, even independent of a remedy, are by nature gentle in body and speech. Their minds have little deceit and they have loving-kindness towards sentient beings. If somebody loves sentient beings, this is a sign of them being a bodhisattva.

TOPIC 2: THE WORKING BASIS

As a Working Basis, the Precious Human Life is Excellent

Chapter 2

The Precious Human Life

All sentient beings have Buddha-essence. That being the case, do all beings in the five (non-human) realms have the capacity to work towards enlightenment? No. Only a "precious human life," which holds the two qualities of leisure and endowment, and a mind that holds the three faiths, is a good basis to work toward enlightenment. Of these five points, leisure and endowment are the two physical aspects, and the three faiths, trusting, longing and clear, are the three mental aspects.

Two Points of the Physical Aspect

The two physical qualities are explained in terms of the eight freedoms and the ten endowments..

I. The Eight Freedoms. *Freedom from being in hell, a hungry ghost, an animal, a barbarian, and a long-life god, holding wrong views, the absence of a Buddha, and being mute. These are the eight unfavorable conditions.*

The hell realm is unfavorable state of existence because its very nature is a tormented mind. Being a hungry ghost is an unfavorable state because its very nature is a tormented mind. Beings an animal is an unfavorable state because its very nature is complete obscuration. Being a barbarian is an unfavorable state because it is difficult for them to meet holy beings. Being a long-life god is unfavorable because one's sense consciousness is interrupted. Having wrong views is unfavorable because one cannot see that virtue is the cause of higher birth and liberation. Being born in a time devoid of Buddhas is unfavorable because there is nobody to teach what should and should not be done. Being mute is unfavorable because one cannot understand the holy dharma by oneself.

II. The Ten Endowments. *Five of the ten endowments that allow for dharma practice come from ourselves and five come from others.*

A. Five Endowments from Oneself. *Being human, being born in* *a central country, having all the senses, not reverting to evil deeds, and having devotion for the teachings.*

B. Five Endowments from Others. *A Buddha has appeared in this world, a Buddha taught the precious dharma, the dharma that was taught continues, there are followers of the dharma that continues, there is love and kind support from others.*

Examples Showing Preciousness. *Because it is so precious to obtain and because it is of such great benefit it is called "precious."*

Three Points of the Mental Aspect

Following the virtuous path requires faith. Without faith, virtue cannot develop in our being. There are three kinds of faith: trusting, longing, and clear.

III. Trusting Faith. *Understand that this faith occurs due to understanding the topic of "cause and result."*

IV. Longing Faith. *Understanding the extraordinary nature of unsurpassable enlightenment, one follows the path with respect and reverence in order to obtain it.*

V. Clear Faith. *Clear faith arises in one's mind by depending on the Three Jewels.*

TOPIC 3: THE CONDITION

The Condition is the Spiritual Friend

Chapter 3

The Spiritual Friend

Even though we have the excellent working basis, a precious human birth, if we are not encouraged by spiritual friends then it will be difficult to follow the path of enlightenment because of the power of the non-virtuous inveterate propensities of previous lives and the force of habitual tendencies. Therefore, it is necessary to attend spiritual friends.

The five topics summarizing the attending of a spiritual friend are reason, classification, the characteristics of each, method, and benefits of attending a spiritual friend.

*I. **Reason: Why We Need a Spiritual Friend.** There are three reasons explaining why we have to attend a spiritual friend: scripture, logic, and example.*

*A. **Scripture.** The noble disciple who has respect for the lama should always attend the wise lama because one receives good qualities from him.*

*B. **Logic.** One who wishes to accomplish the omniscient state should attend a spiritual friend because of not knowing how to accumulate merit or how to purify obscurations.*

*C. **Examples.** A spiritual friend is like a guide when traveling to an unknown place, like an escort when going to a dangerous place, and like a boatman when crossing a big river.*

*II. **Classification: The Types of Spiritual Friends.** There are four types of spiritual friends: the ordinary spiritual friend, the bodhisattva spiritual friend who has attained certain bhumis, the nirmanakaya spiritual friend, and the sambhogakaya spiritual friend.*

When one is a beginner one can attend and benefit from an ordinary being as a spiritual friend. When one has almost purified the obscurations of action (karma) one can attend and benefit from a bodhisattva on a high level as a spiritual friend. When one is above the great path of accumulation one can attend and benefit from a Buddha in his nirmanakaya being. When one is at a high level (on one of the ten bodhisattva levels) one can attend and benefit from the sambhogakaya as a spiritual friend.

*III. **The Characteristics of a Spiritual Friend.** The characteristics of the spiritual friend as the Buddha in his nirmanakaya being are complete and excellent abandonment and realization. If the two kinds of obscurations have been abandoned, it is complete and excellent abandonment. If the two kinds of knowledge are present, it is complete and excellent awareness.*

The characteristics of the spiritual friend as a bodhisattva on a high level are that he has the abandonment and awareness according to his level, from the first to the tenth.

The characteristics of the spiritual friend as an ordinary human being are: having eight qualities, having four qualities or having two qualities.

To have eight qualities means: having the ethics of a bodhisattva; having studied many of the bodhisattva texts; having realization; having compassion accordingly; having fearlessness; having patience; having a completely untiring mind; and having the right use of words. To have the four qualities means: having studied a lot he is able to teach expansively; by great wisdom he is able to cut away the doubts of others; having the conduct of a holy being his words are worth holding on to; he teaches both the origin of the kleshas and the purifications. To have the two qualities means: the spiritual friend is always well versed in the meaning of the Mahayana and not even for the sake of his life would he forsake the excellent behavior of a bodhisattva.

IV. How to Relate to a Spiritual Friend. *When this kind of authentic spiritual friend is found, there are three ways to attend him: through respect and service, through devotion and reverence, and through practice and persistence in the teachings.*

A. Respect. *Attending him through respect means doing prostrations, standing quickly, bowing down, circumambulating, expressing yourself with a feeling of closeness at the right time, gazing at him on and off without satiation, and so forth. Attending the spiritual friend through service means to offer him dharmic food, clothes, bedding, seats, medicine, and all other types of necessary things even at the risk of one's body and life.*

B. Veneration. *To attend him through devotion and reverence means that one should regard the spiritual friend as the Buddha. One should not disobey his teachings. One should develop devotion, respect, and a clear mind. Furthermore, one should avoid wrong view toward the skilful actions of spiritual friends. Instead one should respect them highly.*

C. Practice. *Attending him through practice and persistence in the teachings means to truly integrate and practice the teachings of the spiritual friend through hearing, contemplating, and meditation practice and through persistence. This will make the spiritual friend supremely pleased.*

V. The Benefits of Relying on a Spiritual Friend. *In Srisambhava's life story it is said, "A bodhisattva who is well guarded by spiritual friends* *will not fall into the lower realms. A bodhisattva who is escorted by spiritual friends will not fall into the hands of an evil person. A bodhisattva who is well guided by the spiritual friend will not turn away from the Mahayana path. A bodhisattva who is well guided by the spiritual friend will go beyond the ordinary person's level."*

TOPIC 4: THE METHOD

The Method is the Spiritual Friend's Instructions

The Teachings of a Spiritual Friend

We possess the Buddha potential. Since samsara is beginningless, we must have also obtained, from time to time, the working basis of a precious human life and met the condition of a spiritual master. So, what faults have prevented us from accomplishing Buddhahood in the past? The four obstacles have overpowered us.

Four Obstacles to Accomplishing Buddhahood. *1) Being attached to this life's activities, 2) being attached to the pleasures of samsara, 3) being attached to the bliss of peace, 4) and not understanding the method by which enlightenment is accomplished.*

The Four Remedies. *How can these four obstacles be dispelled? Practicing the instructions heard from the spiritual friend dispels them. What does the spiritual friend's instructions comprise? They can be summarized as four: 1) meditation on impermanence, 2) meditation on the faults of samsara, and cause and result, 3) meditation on loving-kindness and compassion, 4) and the cultivation of bodhichitta.*

Chapter 4

The Instructions on Impermanence

The First Remedy for Attachment to this Life

Three things summarize meditation on impermanence: classification, the method of meditation, and the beneficial effects of meditation.

*I. **The Classification of Impermanence.** The classification of impermanence is twofold: the impermanence of an outer world, and the impermanence of sentient beings as the inner essence. The impermanence of the outer world is also twofold: gross impermanence and subtle impermanence. The impermanence of sentient beings as the inner essence is also twofold: the impermanence of others and the impermanence of oneself.*

*II. **The Method for Meditating on Impermanence.** There are nine ways of meditating on death. There are three ideas to contemplate, each with three reasons: 1) I will definitely die, a) because there is no-one from the past who is alive, b) because this body is composite, c) because life is becoming exhausted every moment, death will definitely occur; 2) the time of death is uncertain, a) because lifespan is indefinite, b) because the body has no essence, c) because there are many causes of death; 3) there will be no help when death comes, a) we cannot be helped by our wealth, b) we cannot be helped by our relatives, c) we cannot be helped by our bodies (it cannot accompany us at death).*

*III. **The Benefits that Arise from Meditating on Impermanence.** Awareness of the impermanence of all composite phenomena leads one to release attachment to this life. Further, it nourishes faith and supports perseverance. By quickly freeing one from attachment and aversion it becomes a cause for the realization of the equal nature of all phenomena.*

Chapter 5
The Meditation on the Suffering of Samsara
The Second Remedy to Attachment to Samsara's Pleasures.

You may think that it is fine that impermanence causes us to die because you will be reborn again and, once you are reborn, you will then have an opportunity to enjoy all the glorious pleasures of gods and humans, and that will be sufficient for you. Such thinking typifies one who is attached to samsara's pleasures.

Three Types of Suffering

The shortcomings of samsara are summarized as three: all-pervasive suffering, the suffering of change, and the suffering of suffering.

I. All-pervasive Suffering. *The all-pervasive suffering is like unripened rice and is the feeling of indifference. This suffering will not be felt by ordinary people but will be seen as suffering by the noble beings.*

II. The Suffering of Change. *The suffering of change is like eating rice mixed with poison and is the feeling of happiness. This is so called because all the pleasures and happiness of samsara will eventually change into suffering.*

III. The Suffering of Suffering. *The suffering of suffering is like an ulcer due to eating poisoned rice and is the feeling of suffering. This is the appearance of all the greater suffering in addition to the suffering that pervades through having taken on the afflicted aggregates.*

Chapter 6
Karma and Its Result
The Remedy to Attachment to Samsara's Pleasures

You may wonder what causes the sufferings that have been explained. One should know that they come from the karma of tainted activity. Actions and the results created by their force are summarized in six points: classification, primary characteristics, the action ripening for oneself, strict result, great ripening arising from small actions, and the inevitability of actions.

I. Classification. *There are three classifications: 1) non-meritorious actions, cause and effect, 2) meritorious actions, cause and effect, 3) and cause and effect of unwavering meditative concentration.*

II. The Primary Characteristics of Each Classification. *1) Non-meritorious actions. Generally there are numerous non-meritorious actions, but they can be summarized as the ten non-virtues: there are* *three non-meritorious actions done with the physical body: killing, stealing, and sexual misconduct; four non-meritorious actions of speech: to lie, to use divisive speech, to use harsh words, and to engage in idle talk; three non-meritorious actions of mind: to covet, to have ill-will, and to hold wrong views. Each has three types of results: the result of the maturation of the act, the result similar to the cause, and general result of the force.*

2) Meritorious actions. Avoidance of the ten non-virtuous actions constitutes the ten virtues. Furthermore, living in accordance with virtuous activity means: protecting the lives of others, practicing great generosity, maintaining moral ethics, speaking truth, harmonizing those who are unfriendly, speaking peacefully and politely, speaking meaningfully, practicing the reduction of attachment and development of contentment, practicing loving-kindness and so forth, and engaging in the perfect meaning. Each has three types of results: the result of the maturation of the act, the result similar to the cause, and general result of the force.

3) Unwavering meditative concentration. By practicing the cause, meditative concentration of equipoise, one will obtain the results born of meditative concentration. The meditative concentration of equipoise has eight preparatory steps, eight levels of actual meditative concentration, and one special meditative concentration. The resulting birth in a state of meditative concentration is as gods in the seventeen form realms and as gods in the four vast formless domains. In general, all are based on the ten virtues.

III. The Action Ripening for Oneself. *You experience the results of the karma you create. Results will ripen in the aggregates related to the actor and not to others.*

IV. Strict Result. *One will experience happiness and suffering without mistake through the results of virtuous and non-virtuous karma. One will experience happiness through the accumulation of virtue. By accumulating non-virtue, one will experience the result of suffering.*

*V. **Great Ripening Arises from Small Actions.** For example, with respect to non-virtuous actions, it is possible that a single non-virtuous action can cause one to experience a kalpa in the hell realm. Similarly, by even a small virtuous action, a great result can ripen.*

*VI. **The Inevitability of Actions.** Unless a remedy is applied an action is not annihilated or destroyed, even if its effect does not ripen for endless eons. Even if the actions remain dormant for a long time, then at the time when they meet with certain circumstances, the effect arises.*

Chapter 7
The Instructions On Meditation On Loving-kindness & Compassion
The Remedy to Attachment to the Pleasure of Peace

What does "attachment to the pleasure of peace" mean? It is the desire to achieve nirvana only for oneself without an altruistic mind for sentient beings, and because of it, one does not benefit others. This is called the "lesser vehicle." But if one develops loving-kindness and compassion, then there is so much care for others that one could not bear to attain liberation only for oneself. Therefore, one should practice loving-kindness and compassion.

*I. **The Practice of Loving Kindness.** The study and practice of immeasurable loving-kindness is completely summarized in six points: the classification, the object, the identifying characteristic, the method of practice, measure of the practice, and the benefits.*

*A. **The Classification.** There are three categories of loving-kindness: loving-kindness with sentient beings as its object, loving-kindness with phenomena as its object, and loving-kindness without any frame of reference.*

*B. **The Object.** Towards whom is loving-kindness directed? It is directed towards all living beings without any exception.*

*C. **The Identifying Characteristic.** A mind that wants all sentient beings to meet with happiness.*

D. Method of Practice. *This practice depends on the memory of the kindness of all sentient beings, so recollect the kindness of sentient beings. In this life, your mother has been the most kind. How many types of kindness does a mother provide? There are four: the kindness of giving you a body, the kindness of undergoing hardships for you, the kindness of nurturing your life, and the kindness of showing you the ways of the world.*

E. Measure of the Practice. *When one does not desire happiness for oneself but only for other sentient beings, that is the perfection of the practice of loving-kindness.*

F. The Benefits. *One obtains limitless qualities by practicing loving-kindness. It is the source of all happiness for oneself and for others.*

II. The Practice of Compassion. *The study and practice of immeasurable compassion is completely summarized in six points: the classification, the object, the identifying characteristic, the method of practice, measure of the practice, and the benefits.*

A. The Classification. *There are three categories of compassion: compassion with reference to all sentient beings, compassion with reference to the nature of things, and compassion without any frame of reference.*

B. The Object: *All sentient beings are its object.*

C. The Identifying Characteristic. *A mind that wants all sentient beings to be free from suffering and its causes.*

D. Method of Practice. *Compassion is cultivated through four reflections based upon one's own mother: reflect on her suffering in a hell realm, suffering as a craving spirit, suffering as an animal, and the suffering of falling into a lower realm.*

E. Measure of the Practice. *When one has fully purified self-cherishing, is fully released or cut from the chain of self-cherishing, and when, from the depths of the mind, one desires all sentient beings to be free from suffering, then one has perfected the practice of compassion.*

F. The Benefits. *The benefits of this practice are immeasurable. The* Expression of the Realization of Chenrezig *says, "If you had just one quality, it would be as if all the Buddhas' Dharma were in your palm. What quality is that? Great compassion."*

Developing an Attitude Towards Bodhichitta

The Remedy to Not Knowing the Method of Practice for Accomplishing Buddhahood

The development of supreme bodhichitta is covered in twelve points: the foundation, the essence, classification, objectives, the cause and from whom one receives it, the procedure, the benefits, the harm (of violating it), the cause of losing it, the means of regaining it, and the training.

I. The Foundation for Developing an Attitude Towards Bodhichitta. *The foundation for cultivation of the mind of supreme enlightenment is a person who has the Mahayana potential, has taken refuge in the Three Jewels, maintains any one of the seven pratimoksha vows, and has aspiration-bodhichitta.*

A. Having the Mahayana Potential. *Generally, one should have the Mahayana potential, but particularly one should have the awakened potential.*

Chapter 8

Refuge and Precepts

B. Taking Refuge in the Three Jewels. *Nine points summarize the explanation of taking refuge: classification, working basis, the object, the time, the motivation, the procedure, the function, the precepts, and the benefits.*

1. The Classification. *There are two aspects of refuge: the common refuge and the special refuge.*

2. The Working Basis. *There are two different working bases: the common working basis is one who fears the suffering of samsara and holds the Three Jewels as deities and the special working basis is one who possesses the Mahayana potential and who has obtained a human or god birth.*

3. The Object. *There are two objects of refuge, the common and the special.*

The common objects are threefold: 1) the Buddha who possesses the perfection of purification, primordial wisdom and excellent qualities, 2) the Dharma, which has two aspects, the dharma of teachings, comprising the twelve branches, and the dharma of realization, comprising the truth of the path and the truth of cessation, 3) the sangha, which also has two aspects, the sangha of ordinary beings, which is the assembly of four or more fully ordained monks who have properly maintained their vows and the noble sangha, being the eight types of beings belonging to the four stages of result, (stream enterer, once-returner, non-returner, and arhat).

The special objects are also threefold: the first are objects abiding directly in front of us, the second is the object of direct realization, and the third is the ultimate object of refuge, which is Buddha.

***4. The Time.** This also is twofold. In the common way one takes refuge from now until death. In the special way one takes refuge from this time onward until the ultimate enlightenment is accomplished.*

***5. The Motivation.** There are also two types of motivation. The common motivation is to take refuge with the thought of one's own unbearable suffering. The special one is to take refuge with the thought of others' unbearable suffering.*

***6. The Ceremony.** The procedure is again twofold: the common and the special.*

***7. The Function.** The common refuge protects one from all harms, the three lower realms, unskillful means, and belief in an abiding person. The special refuge protects one from the lower vehicles and so forth.*

***8. The Training.** There are three general trainings, three particular trainings, and three common trainings.*

***a) The Three General Trainings.** One should at all times strive to make offerings to the Three Jewels. One should never forsake the Three Jewels even at the risk of one's life or for great reward. One should repeatedly recollect the qualities of the Three Jewels.*

***b) The Three Specific Trainings.** Having taken refuge in the*

Buddha, one should not take refuge in worldly gods. Having taken refuge in the dharma, one should not harm other beings. Having taken refuge in the sangha, one should not follow the direction of heretics.

c) The Three Common Trainings. *One should respect the Buddha in every form, even a small image. One should respect the dharma, the books and texts, even one letter of text. One should show respect for the robes of the Buddha, even a simple yellow patch of cloth.*

9. The Beneficial Effects. *There are eight beneficial effects of taking refuge: we enter the Buddhist path, refuge becomes the foundation for all the other precepts, refuge becomes a cause for purification of all the previous negative actions accumulated, we cannot be affected by obstacles caused by either humans or non-humans, accomplishing all our wishes, we achieve the great cause of merit, not falling into the lower realms,' and we quickly accomplish perfect enlightenment.*

C. The Pratimoksha Precepts. *The third aspect, the pratimoksha precepts, are divided into four groups, but in terms of the individuals who take them, there are eight. Why do you need a pratimoksha precept in order to cultivate action-bodhichitta? It should be understood that they are needed as a foundation for three reasons: analogy, scriptural authority, and reasoning.*

1. Analogy. *We would not invite a great king to reside in a place where there is filth and which is unclean. The place should be clean and decorated with many ornaments. Similarly, the king of bodhichitta cannot be invited to reside while our body, speech and mind are not free from non-virtue and are stained with the dirt of negative karma. Instead, bodhichitta should be invited to abide in our body, speech and mind are which are free of the dirt of defilements and are fully adorned with the moral ethics of abandonment.*

2. Scriptural Authority. *The chapter on cultivating mind in the* Ornament of Mahayana Sutra *says: "Its basis is vast precepts." Thus, the fasting precept, which only lasts twenty-four hours, is not vast." The other seven precepts are not like that, so they are vast vows. Therefore, these seven precepts are explained as the foundation for cultivation of the mind.* The Lamp for the Path to Enlightenment *says. "One who keeps* *one of the seven pratimoksha precepts has the fortune to receive the bodhisattva precepts. Otherwise not." Therefore, any of the seven pratimoksha precepts is said to be the foundation.*

3. Reasoning. *When we take the pratimoksha precepts we abandon harming others and harboring harmful intentions. The bodhisattva's vow causes us to benefit others. Without avoiding harm, there is no method of benefiting others.*

Chapter 9
Cultivation of Bodhichitta

II. The Essence. *The essence of the cultivation of bodhichitta is the desire to accomplish perfect, complete enlightenment in order to benefit others.*

III. The Classification. *There are three classifications within the subject of cultivating supreme enlightenment: by simile, by demarcation of levels, and by characteristics.*

A. Simile. *How bodhichitta can be typified from that of an ordinary being through to a Buddha is shown in twenty-two examples by Arya Maitreya in* The Ornament of Clear Realization. *He expressed them as: earth, gold, moon, fire, treasure, jewel-mine, ocean, vajra, mountain, medicine, spiritual master, wish-fulfilling jewel, sun, melody, king, treasury, highway, conveyance, well, elegant-sound, river, and cloud. These twenty-two examples range from sincere aspiration to realization of the dharmakaya. In addition, they will be related to the five paths.*

B. Different Levels. *There are four levels: the cultivation of bodhichitta with interest, the cultivation of bodhichitta with altruistic thought, the cultivation of bodhichitta in full maturation, and the cultivation of bodhichitta with removed veils.*

C. Characteristics. *The classification is twofold: ultimate bodhichitta and relative bodhichitta. What is ultimate bodhichitta? It is pervading emptiness with compassion as its essence, clear, unmoving, and free from elaboration. What is relative bodhichitta? It is the* *commitment through compassion to liberate all sentient beings from suffering. Ultimate bodhichitta is obtained through realization of dharmata, and relative bodhichitta is obtained through ritual ceremony.*

IV. Objectives. *The objectives of bodhichitta are to accomplish enlightenment and to benefit sentient beings.*

V. The Cause. *The causes for cultivation of bodhichitta are given in* The Ten Dharmas Sutra: *seeing the beneficial effects of bodhichitta, developing devotion for the Tathagata (Buddha), seeing the suffering of all sentient beings, and the inspiration of a spiritual friend.*

VI. From Whom One Receives It. *There are two systems: one with a spiritual friend and one without. If there is no spiritual friend one can receive the vow by, sincerely reciting the liturgy three times in front of an image of the Buddha. If there is no spiritual friend or image, one can receive the vow by, reciting the liturgy three times while visualizing the Buddhas and bodhisattvas in space before one.*

VII. The Method (Ceremony). *There are diverse systems of instruction from the lineages of the great scholars. In Shantideva's tradition, which comes from Nagarjuna and was founded by Arya Manjushri, there are three stages: the preparation, the actual ceremony, and the conclusion. The tradition of Dharmakirti of Acharya Asanga's school, which was founded by Arya Maitreya, has two stages: cultivating aspiration-bodhichitta (has three stages of supplication, actual ceremony, and conclusion), and holding the vow of action-bodhichitta (has three stages of preparation, actual ceremony, and conclusion).*

VIII. The Beneficial Effects. *There are two types: the countable and the uncountable.*

A. The Countable Benefits. *This has two aspects: the beneficial effects of cultivating aspiration-bodhichitta, and the beneficial effects of cultivating action-bodhichitta.*

1. The Beneficial Effects of Cultivating Aspiration-bodhichitta. *This has eight benefits: entering into the Mahayana, it becomes the basis for all the bodhisattva training, all evil deeds will be uprooted, unsurpassable enlightenment becomes rooted, one will obtain* *limitless merits, all the Buddhas will be pleased, one quickly becomes useful to all sentient beings, and one quickly accomplishes perfect enlightenment*

2. Beneficial Effects from Cultivating Action-bodhichitta. *This has two benefits: ones own benefit arises continuously, and benefits for others arise in various ways.*

B. The Uncountable Benefits. *This means that all good qualities arise from this time until we become a Buddha, so they are uncountable.*

IX. The Disadvantages of Losing Bodhichitta. *There are three faults from losing bodhichitta. 1) By not fulfilling the commitment and by abandoning the commitment to the cultivated mind, one deprives all sentient beings; by maturation of that fruit one will be born in the lower realms. 2) One cannot benefit others. 3) It will take a long time to attain the bodhisattvas' levels.*

X. The Cause of Losing Bodhichitta. *There are two ways to lose the mind that has cultivated bodhichitta: the cause of losing aspiration and the cause of losing action.*

The first one consists of forsaking sentient beings, adopting the four unwholesome deeds, and generating the opposite mind, which is disharmonious with virtue. Losing the vow of action is explained in The Bodhisattva Levels, *"If one has committed the four offences through the heavy disturbing emotions it is lost. If committed in a medium or lesser entrapping way it is only an impairment." Furthermore, the* Twenty Precepts *say, "When one loses the aspiration-bodhichitta, it breaks action-bodhichitta."*

Through heavy disturbing emotions means: committing the four root downfalls continuously; without developing the slightest shame or embarrassment; doing it with satisfaction and joy; and considering it a virtue.

The four root downfalls are: out of attachment to gain and honor to praise oneself and speak lowly of others, out of avarice not to give material goods or dharma; out of anger not to forgive others when they apologize; out of deceit to make something artificial as your own teaching.

XI. The Means of Regaining Bodhichitta Once It is Lost. If one has lost aspiration-bodhichitta, taking it again can restore it. If the action vow has been lost by losing the aspiration vow, it is restored automatically by restoring the aspiration vow. If the action vow was broken through other causes, it should be taken again. If through the four offences in a medium or lesser entrapping way, confession is sufficient.

Chapter 10
Training in Aspiration-bodhichitta

XII. The Training. After cultivating bodhichitta, there are two types of training: training in aspiration-bodhichitta, and in action-bodhichitta.

A. Training in Aspiration-bodhichitta. The aspiration instructions are summarized in five points: not forsaking sentient beings from ones heart, recollecting the beneficial effects of bodhichitta, gathering the two accumulations, cultivating the bodhisattva attitude repeatedly, and accepting the four virtues and rejecting the four non-virtues.

Chapter 11
Training in Action-bodhichitta

B. Training in Action-bodhichitta. Action-bodhichitta has three types of trainings: the training in superior morality, the training in superior thought, and the training in superior wisdom.

Generosity, moral ethics, and patience are the training in superior morality. Meditative concentration is the training in superior thought. Wisdom-awareness is the training in superior wisdom. Diligence is the support for all three. These six (paramitas) are the training in action-bodhichitta. They are explained in a concise way and then each in detail. The concise explanation is summarized: definite number, definite order, characteristics, definition, division, and grouping.

1. Definite Number. The six paramitas are explained according to temporary higher rebirth and liberation, with three for higher rebirth and three for liberation. The three for the sake of the higher realms are:

generosity for the sake of riches, ethics for the sake of a good physical body, and patience for the sake of a favorable entourage. The three for the sake of liberation are: diligence for the sake of increasing one's good qualities, meditative concentration for the sake of mental peace, and wisdom for the sake of insight.

2. Definite Order. *They are explained in the order they develop in the mind: generosity without considering the material benefits leads to pure ethics. If one has ethics patience develops. Through having patience one is able to practice diligently. By means of diligence meditative absorption arises. Resting in meditative absorption leads to the full understanding of the true nature of reality.*

The order is also explained from lower to higher practice, or, another way, the order is from the gross to the subtle level.

3. Characteristics. *The characteristics of the paramitas are four: they decrease their opposites, they produce the primordial non-conceptual wisdom, they fulfill all that is desired, and they fully mature sentient beings through the three paths.*

4. Definition. *Generosity dispels suffering, moral ethics achieves coolness, patience endures hatred, diligence is application to that which is sublime, meditative concentration keeps the mind turned inward, and wisdom-awareness realizes the ultimate meaning. They are the cause to cross from samsara to nirvana and are therefore called "paramitas."*

5. Division. *Each of the six paramitas has six subdivisions, the generosity of generosity, moral ethics of generosity etc., totaling thirty-six.*

6. Grouping. *The six paramitas are also grouped into the two accumulations. Generosity and ethics are the accumulation of merit. Wisdom is the accumulation of awareness. Patience, diligence and meditative concentration belong to both kinds of accumulation*

Chapter 12
The Perfection of Generosity

The perfection of generosity is summarized as sevenfold: reflection on the faults and virtues, definition, classification, characteristics of each classification, increase, perfection, and result.

I. Reflection on the Virtues and Faults. *Those who have not practiced generosity will always suffer from poverty and usually will be reborn as a hungry ghost. Even if reborn as a human and so forth, they will suffer from poverty and a lack of necessities. On the other hand, one who practices generosity will have happiness through wealth in all their different lifetimes.*

II. Definition. *The definition of generosity is the practice of giving fully without attachment.*

III. Classification. *Generosity has three classifications: giving wealth, giving fearlessness, and giving dharma. Giving wealth strengthens others' physical lives, giving fearlessness strengthens the quality of their lives, and giving dharma strengthens their mind.*

IV. Characteristics of Each Classification

A. Giving Wealth. *Two topics describe the practice of giving wealth: impure giving and pure giving. The first should be avoided and the second practiced.*

1. Impure Giving. *This is discussed through four aspects: impure motivation, inappropriate gifts, inappropriate recipient, and impure method.*

2. Pure Giving. *There are three subtopics: pure material, pure recipient, and pure method.*

B. Giving Fearlessness. *Giving fearlessness means to give protection from the fear of thieves, wild animals, diseases, rivers, and so forth.*

C. Giving Dharma. *Four topics describe the practice of giving dharma: the recipient, the motivation, the actual dharma, and the method of showing dharma teachings.*

V. Increase. *Even though one's generosity of the above three types may be small, there is a method to increase them. It can increase through the power of primordial wisdom (jnana), it can expand through the power of wisdom-awareness (prajna), and it can become limitless through dedication.*

VI. Perfection. *When generosity practices are supported by emptiness they will not become a cause for samsara. When supported by compassion, they will not become a cause of the lesser vehicles. Thus, generosity is made pure and will become a cause only for the accomplishment of Buddhahood. "Supported by emptiness" means the practice is stamped* *with the four seals of emptiness. "Supported by compassion" means giving because you cannot bear the suffering of sentient beings.*

VII. Result. *The results of generosity are both ultimate and temporary. The ultimate result is unsurpassable enlightenment. The temporary result is that one will gain prosperity through giving wealth, even if one does not wish. By giving fearlessness, one will not be harmed by obstacles and maras. By giving dharma, one will meet the Buddha swiftly, be close to him, and achieve all one desires.*

Chapter 13
The Perfection of Moral Ethics

The perfection of moral ethics is summarized as sevenfold: reflection on the faults and virtues, definition, classification, characteristics of each classification, increase, perfection, and result.

I. Reflection on the Virtues and Faults. *Even though one may have the practice of generosity, without the practice of moral ethics, one will not achieve the very best of existences of gods or humans. Without moral ethics, one will not meet the dharma, one cannot be freed from samsara, and one cannot reach enlightenment. On the other hand, if one has moral ethics, one will attain the very best physical existence, one can establish the foundation of all goodness and happiness, one will find it opens many doors to meditative absorption, all one's aspiration prayers will be accomplished, and it is easy to reach enlightenment.*

II. Definition. *This has four main qualities: taking the vows properly from others, having a pure motivation, renewing the practice if it degenerates, and having respect and mindfulness so that the practice does not degenerate. These four qualities can be categorized under receiving and protecting. The first point being receiving and the other three being protecting.*

III. Classification. *Moral ethics has three classifications: moral ethics of restraint, morality of accumulating virtuous dharma, and morality of benefiting sentient beings. The first means to restrain the mind, the second one means to mature the dharma qualities of our mind, and the third one means to fully mature sentient beings.*

IV. Characteristics of Each

A. Moral Discipline of Restraint. *There is the common and the uncommon. The common one refers to the seven types of pratimoksha vows. The uncommon are the bodhisattva vows.*

B. Morality of Accumulating Dharma Virtue. *After perfectly taking the bodhisattva's vow of moral ethics, accumulate virtues through your body, speech, and mind in order to accomplish enlightenment.*

C. Morality of Benefiting Other Beings. *This can be known as having thirteen main aspects. In the* Bodhisattva Levels*: supporting meaningful activities, to dispel the sufferings of those who are suffering, showing those without skill how to cope intelligently, recollecting others' kindness and repaying it, protecting others' from what frightens them, dispelling the mourning of those who are suffering, giving necessities to the needy, to properly bring together a dharma following, to engage them in that which corresponds to their mentality, creating joy through the perfect qualities, to properly correct someone who is doing wrong, to inspire awe through exceptional abilities, and causing others to be inspired by the teachings. Furthermore, in order to create confidence and faith in others and to prevent oneself from backsliding, one should avoid the impure actions of the three doors and sustain the three purities.*

V. Increase. *Moral ethics will increase through primordial wisdom, wisdom-awareness, and dedication as explained in chapter twelve.*

VI. Perfection. *The perfection of moral ethics is supported by pervading emptiness and compassion, as explained in chapter twelve.*

VII. Result. *The results of moral ethics are both ultimate and temporary. The ultimate result is unsurpassable enlightenment. The temporary result is that one will achieve perfect happiness in samsara, even if one does not wish. A bodhisattva will continue following the path by not being overpowered by the joy and happiness of samsara. And a bodhisattva will receive offerings and be cared for by beings.*

Chapter 14

The Perfection of Patience

The perfection of patience is summarized as sevenfold: reflection on the faults and virtues, definition, classification, characteristics of each classification, increase, perfection, and result.

I. Reflection on the Virtues and Faults. *Even though you may have the practices of generosity and moral ethics, anger will develop if you do not have the practice of patience. If anger arises then all of your previously accumulated virtue will be lost in an instant. On the other hand, if you have patience, it is one of the supreme virtues among all the root virtues.*

II. Definition. *The definition of patience is a feeling of ease.*

III. Classification. *Patience has three classifications: the patience of feeling ease towards someone harmful, the patience of accepting suffering, and patience in understanding the nature of dharma. Of these, the first is patience by investigating the nature of the one who creates harm. The second one is the practice of patience by investigating the nature of suffering. The third one is practicing patience by investigating the unmistakable nature of all phenomena. Put another way, the first two are practiced on the relative level and the third one in terms of the ultimate level.*

IV. Characteristics of Each Classification

A. The Patience of Not Being Disturbed by the Harm Done by Others. *This means practicing patience towards those who either do what one does not want them to do or who prevent one from doing what one wants. What does patience mean in such circumstances? It means to not be disturbed, not retaliate, and not brood on the event.*

B. The Patience of Accepting Suffering. *With a mind of joy and without regret, voluntarily accept all the suffering of the practice leading towards unsurpassable enlightenment.*

C. Patience in Understanding Dharma. *Aspiring to and patiently practicing the realization of inherent emptiness of the two types of self in the ultimate nature.*

V. Increase. *Patience will increase through primordial wisdom, wisdom-awareness and dedication, as explained in chapter twelve.*

VI. Perfection. *The perfection of patience is supported by pervading emptiness and compassion, as explained in chapter twelve.*

VII. Result. *The results of patience are both ultimate and temporary. The ultimate result is unsurpassable enlightenment. The temporary result,* *even if one does not wish, is good health, fame, a long life, and possessing the attributes of a universal monarch.*

Chapter 15
The Perfection of Diligence

The perfection of diligence is summarized as sevenfold: reflection on the faults and virtues, definition, classification, characteristics of each classification, increase, perfection, and result.

I. Reflection on the Virtues and Faults. *Even though you may have all the practices of generosity and so forth, if you do not have diligence you will waste time. When there is time wasting you do not accomplish virtue, you have no ability to benefit others, and you do not accomplish enlightenment. On the other hand, if you have diligence, all your virtuous qualities will increase without being obscured and the accomplishment of enlightenment will be swift.*

II. Definition. *The definition of diligence is a feeling of joy in virtue. Diligence is the antidote to laziness that is detrimental to enlightenment. There are three types of laziness: laziness of apathy and sloth, laziness of discouragement, and laziness as involvement in lower aims.*

III. Classification. *Diligence has three classifications: armour-like diligence, diligence of application, and insatiable diligence. The first is the excellent motivation, the second is excellent applied effort, and the third is what carries the first two through to their conclusion.*

IV. Characteristics of Each Classification.

A. Armour-Like Diligence. *"From now until all sentient beings are established in the unsurpassable enlightenment, I will not give up the diligence of virtue." Such armour should be worn.*

B. Diligence of Application. *This has three types: diligence to eliminate disturbing emotions, diligence to practice virtue, and diligence to benefit other beings*

C. Insatiable Diligence. *You should be diligent without satisfaction until you accomplish enlightenment.*

V. Increase. *Diligence will increase through primordial wisdom, wisdom-awareness, and dedication, as explained in chapter twelve.*

VI. Perfection. *The perfection of diligence is supported by pervading emptiness and compassion, as explained in chapter twelve.*

VII. Result. *The results of diligence are both ultimate and temporary. The ultimate result is unsurpassable enlightenment. The temporary result is that one will have all the supreme joys of existence, even while in samsara.*

Chapter 16
The Perfection of Meditative Concentration

The perfection of meditative concentration is summarized as sevenfold: reflection on the faults and virtues, definition, classification, characteristics of each classification, increase, perfection, and result.

I. Reflection on the Virtues and Faults. *Even though you may have the practices of generosity and so forth, if you are without meditative concentration you can be overpowered by distractions and caught by the fangs of disturbing emotions. Without meditative concentration you cannot achieve clairvoyance and without clairvoyance you cannot benefit others. Further, without meditative concentration you cannot achieve wisdom-awareness and without wisdom-awareness you cannot accomplish enlightenment. On the other hand, when you have meditative concentration you will give up attachment to lesser objects, you will achieve clairvoyance, and many doors of meditative absorption will open for your mind. Further, wisdom-awareness will arise and your disturbing emotions will be abolished, you will have perfect insight into the ultimate meaning and therefore give rise to compassion for all beings, and you can establish all trainees in enlightenment.*

II. Definition. *The definition of meditative concentration is that it has the nature of calm abiding, the mind resting inwardly and one-pointedly on virtue. This kind of meditative concentration is further achieved through complete avoidance of the distractions that are the opposite of concentration.*

A. We Should Avoid Distraction. *The avoidance of distraction is called "solitude," where one is isolated from physical agitation and the mind is isolated from discursive thoughts. This has six topics: the primary characteristic of agitation, the cause of agitation, the faults of agitation,* *the primary characteristic of solitude, the cause of solitude, and the good qualities of solitude.*

B. Isolating the Mind from Discursive Thoughts. *While staying in retreat, contemplate why you went there. Think that you went to that isolated place because of fear of the disturbing influence of the city. Recall why you feared the influence of agitation.*

C. Through the Isolation of Body and Mind, Distraction will not Arise. *Without distraction, you can enter into meditative concentration. You should train your own mind. You should meditate and apply the remedy for whichever afflicting emotions are the strongest: to remedy desire, meditate on the unpleasant; to remedy anger, meditate on loving-kindness; to remedy ignorance, meditate on interdependent origination; to remedy jealousy, meditate on the similarity of self and others, to remedy pride, mediate on exchanging self for others; if the disturbing emotions or discursive thoughts are equally present, then meditate on the breath*

III. Classification. *There are three: meditative concentration which gives one happiness while it is practiced, meditative concentration which produces all good qualities, and meditative concentration that can accomplish the good of beings. The first is the method to make a proper vessel of one's mind, the second is establishing all of the Buddha's qualities on the basis of the proper vessel, and the third is benefiting sentient beings.*

IV. Characteristics of Each Classification.

A. Meditative Concentration which Gives One Happiness while It is Practiced. *The profound absorption of all the bodhisattvas is free from discursive thoughts, perfectly eases the body and mind, is supremely pacified, is free from arrogance, is without involvement with experiencing the "taste" of meditation, and is free from any notion of an object of meditation.*

B. Meditative Concentration which Produces all Good Qualities. *There is the exceptional and the common. The first is a limitless and inconceivable variety of profound absorptions related to the ten strengths. The common ones are liberation, surpassing, increasing exhaustion, discriminating awareness, and so forth.*

C. Meditative Concentration that can Accomplish the Good of

Beings. One can manifest limitless physical emanations depending on any of the profound absorptions and then benefit beings.

V. Increase. *Meditative concentration will increase through primordial wisdom, wisdom-awareness and dedication, as explained in chapter twelve.*

VI. Perfection. *The perfection of meditative concentration is supported by pervading emptiness and compassion, as explained in chapter twelve.*

VII. Result. *The results of meditative concentration are both ultimate and temporary. The ultimate result is unsurpassable enlightenment. The temporary result is that one will attain the body of gods free from the desire realm.*

Chapter 17
The Perfection of Wisdom-awareness

The perfection of wisdom-awareness is summarized as sevenfold: reflection on the faults and virtues, definition, classification, characteristics of each classification, what is to be known, what is to be practiced, and result.

I. Reflection on the Virtues and Faults. *Even though you may have the practices of generosity through meditative concentration, without wisdom-awareness, omniscience will never be achieved. Why is this so? It is like a group of blind people who cannot get to the city of their wishes without a guide. On the other hand, if you possess wisdom-awareness, it is like a guide leading a group of blind people to town. All the wholesome aspects of a bodhisattva's virtue, generosity, etc., are transformed into the path to Buddhahood and omniscience is attained.*

II. Definition. *The definition of wisdom-awareness is the perfect and full discrimination of all phenomena.*

III. Classification. *There are three: wisdom-awareness of the mundane, wisdom-awareness of the lesser supramundane, and wisdom-awareness of the greater supramundane.*

IV. Characteristics of Each Classification.

A. Wisdom-awareness of the Mundane. *This is wisdom that arises from the four aspects of knowledge: the sciences of healing, logic, linguistics, and creative skill.*

*B. **Wisdom-awareness of the Lesser Supramundane.** This is the wisdom that arises through the study, contemplation and meditation of the shravaka and pratyekabuddha.*

*C. **Wisdom-awareness of the Greater Supramundane.** This is the wisdom that arises from the study, contemplation and meditation of the Mahayana.*

*V. **What Needs to be Known: Wisdom-awareness.** From among the three types of wisdom-awareness, the greater supramundane wisdom-awareness must be studied. This has six topics: the refutation of grasping things as being existent, the refutation of grasping things as being non-existent, the fallacy of grasping non-existence, the fallacy of both graspings, the path that leads to liberation, and nirvana, the nature of liberation.*

*VI. **What Needs to be Practiced.** If all phenomena are emptiness, you might ask if it is necessary to practice that which you have understood. Indeed it is. For example, even if silver ore is of the nature of silver, until the ore is refined, the silver does not appear. If one desires silver, one must refine the ore. Likewise, all phenomena are from the very beginning of the nature of emptiness, free from all elaboration. But since there is the appearance of various things to sentient beings and the experience of various sufferings, this wisdom must be understood and practiced.*

To practice, there are four stages: the preliminaries, equipoise, the post-meditative stage, and the signs of practice.

*VII. **Result.** The results of wisdom-awareness are both ultimate and temporary. The ultimate result is unsurpassable enlightenment. The temporary result is that all happiness and fortune will arise.*

CHAPTER 18

The Aspects of the Five Paths

By first cultivating the mind of supreme enlightenment and then persistently training, one will go through all the paths and levels of a bodhisattva. The five paths are: the path of accumulation, the path of junction, the path of insight, the path of cultivation, and the path of accomplishment.

*I. **The Path of Accumulation.** One who has the Mahayana potential cultivates bodhichitta, receives teachings from masters, and makes effort* in the virtues until the heat of wisdom is attained. During this time, progress is classified in four stages: realization, aspiration, greater aspiration, and achievement. Why is this called the path of accumulation? Because on it, one gathers the accumulations of virtue in order to become a vessel for the realization of heat and so forth. Therefore it is called "the path of accumulation." At this stage twelve of the thirty-seven branches of enlightenment are practiced: the four types of mindfulness, the four types of perfect abandonment, and the four feet of miraculous powers.

II. The Path of Junction. The path of junction begins after perfection of the path of accumulation. It has four stages corresponding to the realization of the four noble truths: heat, maximum heat, patience, and realization of the highest worldly dharma. Why is it called "the path of junction?" Because there one makes an effort to directly realize truth. Here there are ten of the thirty-seven branches of enlightenment. During the stages of heat and maximum heat the five powers are practiced. During the stages of patience and highest worldly dharma the five strengths are practiced.

III. The Path of Insight. The path of insight begins after the highest worldly dharma and consists of calm abiding as a basis for special insight focused on the four noble truths. Why is it called "the path of insight?" Because here one realizes the four noble truths that were not seen before. At this stage one is endowed with seven of the thirty-seven branches of enlightenment.

IV. The Path of Cultivation. The path of meditation practice begins after the realization of special insight. It has two stages: the worldly meditation practice, and the meditation practice beyond the world. Through the worldly meditation one destroys the remaining defilements that still remain to be removed, one establishes the special qualities of the four immeasurables, and one creates the foundation for the path beyond the world. The beyond the world meditation consists of Shamatha and Vipashyana focused on the two aspects of primordial wisdom along with their accompanying qualities.

Why is it called "the path of meditation?" Because there one becomes familiar with the realizations that one achieved in the path of insight. During this stage one is endowed with eight (the eight-fold path) of the *thirty-seven branches of enlightenment.*

V. The Path of Accomplishment. *After the vajra-like absorption, one actualizes the nature of awareness, the awareness of exhaustion, and awareness of the unborn. The vajra-like absorption is the state at the edges of the path of meditation and is included in the preparation and unobstructed stages. This absorption is called "vajra-like" because it is unobstructed, hard, stable, of one taste, and all-pervasive. Why is this called "the path of accomplishment?" Because the training is perfected and one enters the city of nirvana. At this stage there are ten attainments.*

Chapter 19
The Levels of the Path

Within the five paths, how many levels are there? Thirteen. Beginner, practice due to aspiration, the ten bodhisattva levels, and the level of Buddhahood. The beginners' level is the path of accumulation because it matures one's previously immature mind. The level of practice due to aspiration is the path of juncture because one is strongly devoted to the meaning of emptiness. The ten bodhisattva levels range from "Overwhelming Joy" to the tenth, "Cloud of Dharma."

TOPIC 5: THE RESULT
The Result is the Body of Perfect Buddhahood

Chapter 20
Perfect Buddhahood

Thus, one attains the perfect Buddhahood of the three kayas by completely passing through all the paths and levels. The summary of Buddhahood is: nature, significance of the nature, classification, definition, reason for the definite number, characteristics, and special traits.

I. Nature. *The nature of a complete, perfect Buddha is perfect purification and perfect primordial wisdom. Perfect purification means that all the defilements and cognitive obscurations have been eliminated. Perfect primordial wisdom is that of sublime awareness of reality as it is, and that of omniscience.*

II. Significance of the Name. *Why is one called "Buddha"? One* *who has fully awakened (Tib. sang) from ignorance, as from sleep, and fully blossomed (Tib. gye) the discriminating wisdom into the two knowledges is called a Buddha (Tib. Sangye).*

III. Classification. *Buddhahood can be divided into three aspects: dharmakaya, sambhogakaya, and nirmanakaya.*

IV. Definition. *Dharmakaya is what the Buddha really is. The two form bodies should be understood to manifest through the combination of the magnificent blessings of the dharmakaya, the subjective experience of beings, and previous aspiration prayers. It should be understood that they appear when these three (conditions) have come together.*

V. Reason for the Definite Number of Three Kayas. *It is out of necessity. Dharmakaya is for one's own benefit and the two form kayas are for others' benefit.*

VI. Characteristics of the Three Kayas. *Dharmakaya is merely labeled as "the exhaustion of all errors and what is delusory through realization of the meaning of the all-pervading emptiness of all phenomena." It can be explained as having eight characteristics: sameness, profundity, permanence, oneness, perfection, purity, radiance, and relationship to enjoyment. Sambhogakaya also has eight characteristics: surroundings, field, form, marks, dharma, activities, spontaneity, and naturally non-existent. Nirmanakaya also has eight qualities: basis, cause, field, time, nature, engaging, maturing, and liberating.*

VII. Special Traits. *There are three special traits of Buddhahood: equality, permanence, and appearance.*

TOPIC 6: THE ACTIVITIES

The Activities are Benefiting Sentient Beings Without Conceptual Thought.

Chapter 21

Activities of the Buddha

First one develops bodhichitta, then the path is practiced and eventually the fruition, Buddhahood, is accomplished. All these are done for the sole purpose of dispelling the suffering and establishing the happiness of all sentient beings. Without conceptual thoughts or efforts, Buddhas manifest benefit for sentient beings spontaneously and unceasingly.

Enlightened activity is summarized in three points: the noble bodies of the Buddhas, without conceptualizing, accomplish the benefits of beings, likewise do their magnificent speech, and noble mind.

I. Spontaneous Activities of the Body to Benefit Beings. *"Appearing as Indra." This is a simile for how the body benefits sentient beings without conceptual thought. For example, Indra, king of the gods, abides in a victorious palace with a retinue of goddesses. That palace has the nature of clear and clean lapis lazuli, and because of that, Indra's image is reflected outside the palace. If from the earth, men and women could see the reflections of Indra with all his enjoyments they would say aspiration prayers that they may also be born there quickly and make effort to develop virtue for that purpose. By that virtue they could be born there after death. The appearance of that reflection has no conceptual thought or movement.*

Similarly, those who enter the highest path, cultivate faith and virtue will see the forms of the perfect Buddhas adorned with the major and minor marks. They will see them manifest various activities: walking, standing, sitting, sleeping, teaching, being absorbed in meditation and so forth. By seeing them, they will develop devotion and motivation to accomplish Buddhahood. They will engage in its cause, the cultivation of bodhichitta and so forth, and eventually achieve it. The appearance of the Buddhas' form kaya manifests with no conceptual thoughts or movement.

II. Spontaneous Activities of Speech to Benefit Beings. *"Like the drum of gods." This is a simile of how the Buddha's speech benefits beings without conceptual thought. For example, above the palace of the gods, there is the sound of a drumbeat. It resounds through the power of the god's former virtuous actions. Without conceptual thought, that drum reminds the heedless gods by sounding the dharma.*

Likewise, even though there is no effort or conceptual thought, the speech of the Buddhas manifests the teachings depending on the dispositions of the fortunate ones.

III. Spontaneous Activities of Mind to Benefit Beings. *"Like a cloud." This is a simile for how the wisdom mind benefits beings without* *conceptual thought. For example, in the summer, clouds gather in the sky without effort, causing crops and so forth to grow perfectly through the rain falling on the ground without conceptual thought.*

Likewise, the activities of the wisdom mind ripen the trainees' crop of virtue through the rainfall of dharma without conceptual thought.

Notes

1. All technical terms are italicized the first time to alert the reader that they may be found in the glossary of terms.

2. There are two truths or levels: the relative level describes the superficial and apparent mode of all things. The ultimate level describes the true and unmistaken mode of all things.

3. Tibetan words are given as they are pronounced, not spelt.

4. There are six realms, or general types of birth one can take. There are three lower realms; hell realms, craving spirit realms, and animal realms. There are three higher realms: the human realm, demigod realm, and god realm. We have for countless lifetimes cycled through these different types of birth and will continue to do so until we achieve liberation. The human realm is the best for dharma practice.

5. This word (Skt. *tathagatagharba*) is called variously Buddha nature, Buddha-essence, or Buddha potential for variety sake and is very close to *sugatagharba*.

6. The Buddha's teachings occurred in three important phases, known as the three *dharmachakras* or three turnings of the wheel of dharma. The first turning includes the teachings common to all traditions, those of the Four Noble Truths, the Eight-fold Path, selflessness and impermanence, which can lead to liberation from suffering. The second turning expanded on the first, the fruition of its teachings on the emptiness of all phenomena and universal compassion is Buddhahood. The teachings of the third turning are those on the Buddha potential and its inherent qualities. For a detailed

account of the three wheels of dharma see Thrangu Rinpoche's *The Three Vehicles of Buddhist Practice* published by Namo Buddha Publications.

7. This sutra has great significance in relation to Gampopa. During the life of the Buddha, Gampopa was a bodhisattva called Candraprabhakumara, and it was in response to his questions that the Buddha taught this sutra. In addition, the Buddha predicted in this sutra the future birth of Gampopa, and that he would keep alive the profound meaning of this teaching.

8. The liberation or nirvana of a shravaka or pratyekabuddha is not the final nirvana. Their nirvana is a state of unafflicted meditative concentration that they believe to be nirvana. One may wonder why the Buddha taught such paths. The answer is that such paths are taught to help beings that would be discouraged and frightened by the path to Buddhahood they believe accomplishing Buddhahood is a great hardship. So, for those not interested in entering this path or who would otherwise turn back, the Buddha taught the shravaka and pratyekabuddha paths as a sort of intermediate step. Once they have reached this stage and are well rested the Buddha encourages them on to the final goal of Buddhahood advising them that their nirvana is not the final one.

9. The word "liberation" is generally used to define the state of being free from the cycle of samsara. This occurs when one has removed the emotional obscurations, such as desire, anger etc, however subtle obscurations still remain. This state is accomplished by arhats and eighth level bodhisattvas (see chapter 19). The term "ultimate liberation" is here used to distinguish what is also called "Buddhahood" or "enlightenment," and is the complete and final realization of a Buddha.

10. The twelve links of interdependent origination are 1. Ignorance. 2. From ignorance we create the mental formations of the karma of virtue and non-virtue, called "mental formation conditioned by ignorance." 3. This seed of karma, which is carried by the mind, is called "consciousness conditioned by mental formation." 4. The power of that karma forces the mind into the mother's womb, called "name and form conditioned by consciousness." 5. This development gives rise to all the senses of the eye, ear, nose etc, known as "six sense fields conditioned by name and form." 6. The interaction of the sense organs such as the eye with their corresponding objects and consciousness is "contact conditioned by the six fields." 7. From contact we experience feelings of happiness, suffering and indifference,

called "feeling conditioned by contact." 8. When there is feeling and happiness there is attachment called "craving conditioned by feeling." 9. From attachment our craving increases due to not wanting to be separated from the object of attachment, which is called "grasping conditioned by craving." 10. From grasping, we create more karma and existence by body, speech and mind, called "existence conditioned by grasping." 11. From that karma come the five aggregates (Skt. *skandhas*), which is called "birth conditioned by existence." 12. After birth the aggregates increase, ripen (aging) and cease (death), which is "aging and death conditioned by birth." Ignorance, craving and grasping are the afflictive mental states, mental formation and existence are karma, and the remaining seven are suffering. For a detailed explanation of this see Thrangu Rinpoche's *The Twelve Links of Interdependent Origination*, available from Zhyisil Chokyi Ghatsal Publications.

11. Due to the failure of the mind to recognize its own nature we develop the cognitive obscuration of dualistic perception, of self and other. This clinging to an "I" and what is "other" is something that we have had since beginningless time and is not removed until enlightenment.

Based on this dualistic clinging arise the three root disturbing emotions of ignorance, desire and aversion. From these arise some 84,000 various disturbing emotions all of which comprise the emotional obscuration.

12. There are two kinds of selflessness – the selflessness of other, that is, the emptiness of external phenomena and the selflessness of a self, that is, the emptiness of a personal self. The selflessness of the person asserts that when we examine or look for the person, we find that it is empty and without self. The person does not possess a self (Skt. *atman*, Tib. *bdag-nyid*) as an independent or substantial self. Most Buddhist schools hold this position.

The selflessness of phenomena doctrine asserts that not only is there the selflessness of the person, but when we examine outer phenomena, we find that external phenomena are also empty, i.e. they do not have an independent or substantial nature. This position is not held by the Hinayana (shravaka and pratyekabuddha) schools, but is put forth by the Mahayana schools.

13. Those born in the realms of gods do so due to the accumulation of virtue and meditative practice in previous lives. While their present state is

one of great happiness it is temporary and dependent on past actions. Being completely absorbed in their present state of bliss they have no time or inclination for dharma. Unlike the human realm where we have moments of satisfaction, in the god realm there is a continual craving and continual gratification of that craving. But once their previous store of virtuous karma is exhausted they fall into lower states of existence. However, there are many beings in the god realms who are not totally bewildered by their experience of pleasure and do practice the dharma

14. From the ultimate view point the Buddha is omniscient and all-pervading. However, from a relative view point it depends upon the karma of individuals and the group karma of those of certain worlds as to whether they can perceive a Buddha or not. Therefore, there are periods and times when beings' karma is so poor that no Buddhas appear.

15. The point is that if a person has a handicap that prevents communication they cannot receive instructions to practice and work towards Buddhahood.

16. While in the human realm we experience some degree of suffering, it is actually beneficial as it helps to generate renunciation for samsara. It also pacifies our arrogance and can become the cause to cultivate compassion and altruism and to engage in virtue and abandon harmful actions.

17. This may be far fetched, but actually tens of thousands of Tibetans were faced with this very choice under the Chinese occupation.

18. A classical example to illustrate this is that of the causes and conditions to produce a flower. The flower seed is like our Buddha potential, the primary cause; the fertile soil is like the human life, the working basis; and the light, heat, water and fertilizer are like the spiritual friend, the condition.

19. To choose a spiritual friend you should look for the qualities that are described and if the spiritual friend has these, then the person is a good spiritual friend. If they don't have them then they aren't the right kind of spiritual friend. Having a karmic link with the spiritual friend as Marpa and Milarepa had is not necessary. A karmic link is not always possible. If you meet a person in this life and there's the right kind of contact, that is all that is needed.

20. More completely a spiritual friend is "ge pe she gnyen" and the shortened "geshe" also has the second meaning of a high religious degree.

21 The term enlightenment and the verb to *accomplish* enlightenment are used in some Buddhist scriptures to describe various states of bodhisattvas on the various levels and paths beyond the path of seeing (see chapters 18 and 19). Therefore the terms perfect or complete enlightenment are used to refer to the enlightenment of a Buddha, the ultimate realization.

22. Fully enlightened beings, Buddhas, and their manifestations are often understood by way of the three kayas: The dharmakaya is enlightenment itself, wisdom beyond any reference point which can only be perceived by other enlightened beings; the sambhogakaya, often called the enjoyment body, manifests in the pure lands which can only be seen by advanced bodhisattvas; and the nirmanakaya which can be seen by ordinary beings as in the case of the historical Buddha, but this can also be any type of being or relative appearance to assist ordinary beings.

23. Although they may appear to us as an ordinary person, which in fact could be the case, they may also be an emanation of a Buddha or bodhisattva.

24. Realization is used to refer to a stable and clear understanding as opposed to experience, which are mere glimpses that can come and go.

25. In *The Jewel Ornament* it says we should think of our lama as the Buddha. When we come to the dharma we are trying to discover the truth and if we think the lama is the Buddha then that can lead to more delusion because he or she is not really the Buddha, and because of this it will not benefit us. However, the lama may not have all the qualities of a Buddha, but from the viewpoint of the instructions of what he can teach us, he is like the Buddha to us. The instructions and teachings we receive from a lama are those of the Buddha. So it is as if the Buddha were here and giving us teachings now. We didn't have the chance to meet the Buddha who lived 2,500 years ago and the Buddha can't help us directly. In fact the only person who can help us is our lama. So for us he's doing what the Buddha would do if we could meet him. He's like the Buddha to us. If we try to think in terms of the spiritual friend's words being like those of the Buddha – since we know if we practice according to the teachings of the Buddha we will accomplish liberation – if we do what our guru tells us to do we will also accomplish liberation. So we should have great respect towards what the lama tells us. We must be very open and appreciative to our teacher and feel great joy in his presence.

In our relationships with ordinary persons there are times when they are good for us and help us and times when they harm us. But our relationship with a lama is different; they will only do what will help us, never what will harm us. This is why when we relate to the lama it should be with great respect.

26. This refers to the twelve ordeals Naropa underwent in his service of his teacher Tilopa. These included getting beaten up, jumping off a high building, drinking polluted water, etc.

27. Direct experience is for example watching the sun set as opposed to knowing how the world looked one million years ago which is an indirect experience known by reason or logic.

28. Unless one purifies one's karma then whatever karmic causes we have will ripen and will be experienced, either in this life or a future one. Therefore, killing oneself is not a shortcut or a release from one's present suffering. On the contrary, one will still experience one's past negative karma and will also be accumulating more negative karma by the act of killing oneself, which is heavier karma than that of killing someone else. In addition, the state of mind at the time of death is like an arrow being shot from a bow in that it is the directing factor leading one to the next rebirth. Thus dying with a tormented mind will lead to a lower rebirth where greater suffering will ensue.

29. This means something that is created and exists dependent on causes and conditions. A perceived object appears to be something that exists external to us and independent of other factors. It is however, in fact, constantly changing and a collection of parts, which appears in dependence on a perceiving subject. Our perception of the world is quite subjective and due to previous karma and habits in our mind. Mental formation is the second of the twelve links of interdependence, because it is based on ignorance of ultimate truth it clings to dualistic delusions, so this composite samsaric perception has the very nature of suffering.

30. This suffering is often compared to a hair in the palm of one's hand which does not bring suffering or discomfort. So for ordinary beings they do not see all-pervasive suffering as suffering. However, if the hair were in one's eye this does bring suffering and discomfort. This is how it is experienced by realized beings.

31. The traditional example is that of a glass of water; for beings in the hell realms it is perceived as molten metal, for craving spirits it is pus and blood, for demi-gods a weapon, and for gods amrita.

32. For example, if we have committed some negative action and we then engage in some practice to purify this, then instead of the result being losing our life or some severe injury the result may only be a headache.

33. Wrong view here refers to three main types: wrong view of cause and result (not believing that happiness comes from virtue and suffering from non-virtue), wrong view of truth (not believing that nirvana is attained even if the truth of the path is practiced), wrong view of the Three Jewels (not believing in them and slandering them).

34. The ten meritorious actions are the opposites of the ten non-meritorious actions. The three of body are, to protect the lives of others, practice generosity, and to maintain moral ethics. The four of speech are, to speak the truth, harmonize those who are unfriendly, speak peacefully and politely, and to speak meaningfully. The three of mind are, to practice the reduction of attachment and the development of contentment, practice loving-kindness, and engage in the perfect meaning.

35. For a detailed explanation of the ten non-meritorious actions the ten meritorious actions see *Buddhist Conduct: The Ten Virtuous Actions* by Thrangu Rinpoche, available from Zhyisil Chokyi Ghatsal.

36. There have to be four factors present to make an action complete. There has to be the object of the action, the intention, the action itself, and that action has to be completed. For example, in order for the act of killing to occur and be a negative act there must first be the object of a living being that will be killed (from an insect to a person). Second, there must be the intention, one must have the intention to kill or harm that being (to be negative the motivation to kill is anger, desire or ignorance). Third, there must be the undertaking of the action; one actually commits the act (either oneself or instructing someone else to commit the act). Fourth, there must be the completion of the act; the being actually dies. If these four aspects of the action are not all present then it isn't the complete negative act of killing

37. An example of a remedy would be saving lives when one has harmed or killed beings or going on pilgrimage. An example of an antidote would

be the practice of the Vajrasattva mantra recitation. Of course the best and ultimate antidote or remedy is meditation on and recognizing the ultimate truth.

38. This is a very important heading. While neither one of the six main topics or the twenty-one chapters, it is as Rinpoche mentions, the subtle subject of the whole book and begins here an extensive commentary from this point.

39. In Sanskrit "bodhi" means "awakened" or "enlightened" and "chitta" means "mind," so bodhichitta means awakened mind. The term is however used for both the mind striving for enlightenment and the mind of enlightenment. Many translators prefer "awakened" over "enlightened" because the word enlightened is a non-Buddhist term that was first used when Buddhism was introduced. In Tibetan this "awakened mind" was translated as "chang chup kyi sem" in which "chang chup" means "awakened" and "kyi" is a conjunction and "sem" is mind. So the Tibetan translators translated the Sanskrit quite literally into Tibetan

The generation of bodhichitta is based on the altruistic wish to bring about the welfare, and ultimately the total liberation, of all sentient beings from all forms of suffering. What distinguishes bodhichitta from the ordinary compassionate aspirations to benefit others shared by all people of good will is the recognition that one cannot ultimately fulfill these aspirations until one has attained the state of mental purification and liberation of Buddhahood, which is the source of all positive qualities, including the omniscience that can see, individual by individual, the causes of suffering and the causes and path of liberation from suffering. This understanding gives rise at some point to the initial generation of the aspiration to attain the state of Buddhahood in order to liberate all sentient beings from suffering and to establish them all in states of happiness. This is called aspiration-bodhichitta, which must be followed by what is called the bodhichitta of entering or action-bodhichitta, which is the training in loving-kindness, compassion, the six paramitas or transcendent perfections, etc., which lead to the attainment of Buddhahood. Aspiration-bodhichitta and action-bodhichitta are both included in the term relative bodhichitta. Ultimate bodhichitta is direct insight into the ultimate nature. This state of primordial awareness *is* compassion and loving-kindness and gives rise spontaneously and without preconception to compassionate activity.

40. "Common" as in the sense of it being shared as opposed to being ordinary.

41. There are actually eight types of pratimoksha precepts. However one of these is the one-day vows for lay persons which involves fasting and while beneficial is not considered vast enough to be a suitable foundation for cultivating bodhichitta. The seven suitable precepts are, laywoman's precepts, layman's precepts, female novice, male novice, and female ordination (there is no male equivalent of this. As the nun's tradition was lost in Tibet this was an alternative ordination held by Tibetan nuns), full female ordination, and full male ordination.

42. The five paths are: the path of accumulation, the path of junction, the path of insight, that of cultivation and the path of accomplishment. These are explained in chapter eighteen.

43. This refers to the Eastern calendar, which is lunar based, and consists of thirty days in each month to match the cycle of the moon. The middle of every month, the fifteenth, is the full moon.

44. It is important to understand that the term prajna includes in one term the notions of knowledge, wisdom, and primordial awareness or transcendental awareness, which is the highest form of prajna. Worldly knowledge – medicine, literature, business management, economics or anthropology – is one form of prajna. Knowledge of the teachings of the Buddha and other enlightened beings is spiritual prajna. Both worldly and spiritual prajna are based on the acquisition of information, and though they may have a great deal of practical benefit, they will not by themselves liberate one from the root causes of suffering. Only the highest form of prajna, jnana – primordial awareness, which is liberated from the superimposition on experience of perceiver and perceived – will free one from the root causes of suffering.

45. When using the word beginning, this doesn't mean it was there a long time ago and is not there now. It means the basic awareness that is present in every moment of cognition, which is there naturally and innately. However, for us this becomes obscured by ignorance and conceptual thought.

46. Explained in the nineteenth chapter.

47. These five also comprise the special path of a bodhisattva, which refers to the eighth, ninth, and tenth bhumis.

48. This means all the obscurations that veil Buddhahood have been eliminated.

49. The Tibetan term for what is relative is "kundzop," which means artificial or fake. So, whereas ultimate bodhichitta is naturally present, relative bodhichitta is adopted. And where ultimate bodhichitta is non-conceptual emptiness full of natural meaning and spontaneous compassion, relative bodhichitta relies upon conceptual conventions as meanings. Ultimate bodhichitta is attained from the realization of dharmata on the first bodhisattva level.

50. The following four causes relate to relative bodhichitta. Ultimate bodhichitta is accomplished through reading scriptures, practice and realization.

51. Bodhichitta is unstable when developed through the power of friends, because it is due to the effort of others. The other causes are however stable because they arise from our own efforts.

52. The "Seven Branch Prayer" consists of: prostrating, offerings, purifying non-virtues, rejoicing in virtues, requesting the wheel of dharma be turned, beseeching the Buddhas not to pass into paranirvana, and dedication of the root of virtue.

53. The tradition of Profound View, is the lineage of the bodhisattva vow, which has come from Arya Nagarjuna, passed to his disciple Aryadeva, and eventually to Master Shantideva, and has reached us from them. The second lineage, the tradition of Vast Conduct, is the lineage of the bodhisattva vow, which comes from the bodhisattva Maitreya to the bodhisattva Asanga and his brother Vasubandhu, and subsequently to Master Chandragomin, and it was introduced into Tibet by Lord Atisha. These are also referred to as the two chariots of the bodhisattva discipline.

Either path is sufficient to take one to Buddhahood and it is considered supreme if one can unify them both and understand the special features of each. There is much to be learned from both traditions.

One can understand the special features of the Profound View lineage by studying the works of Arya Nagarjuna, his texts on the *Middle-way*, and the commentaries such as Acharya Chandrakirti's *An Entrance to the Middle Way*, and so forth. Briefly put Arya Nagarjuna's approach is to first emphasise correct view. In order to reveal correct view Nagarjuna's approach is to use reductive reasoning to refute all incorrect views, thereby eliminating all possible routes except the correct one. The source of his approach is the Prajnaparamita Sutras.

The lineage of Vast Conduct can be understood from the *Five Dharmas of Maitreya* and the commentaries by Asanga. This approach is like pointing to the destination and revealing its qualities and benefits. It is like giving you a very clear picture of the place and the path to get there.

In the Karma Kagyu tradition both of these traditions are equally emphasized.

The lineage of the Profound View is the more common one and most forms of the vow we use come from this lineage. In the case of the lineage of Profound View the aspiration and action-bodhichittas are generated together in the same ceremony, one immediately after the other. In this sense it is an easier and more simple ceremony as opposed to the lineage of Vast Conduct which has two ceremonies over two days; one for the aspiration-bodhichitta and one for the implementation or action-bodhichitta.

54. The antidote to non-virtue is virtue and bodhichitta is the supreme virtue.

55. If the commitments of bodhichitta have deteriorated due to abandoning the aspiration they can be restored through taking again the bodhisattva vow. If the vow of action is broken by some other cause it is necessary to retake it or else purify it through confession. In the tradition of the Profound View to recite within four hours of the downfall or abandonment the Sutra of the Three Heaps (Thirty-five Buddhas). It is said in the text describing the bodhisattva vow that if this is recited within four hours of the violation, the violation is repaired. So for that reason it is always recommended that this be chanted six times a day. One divides the day into six sessions of four hours – three during the day and three during the night – and reviews the vows and chant the Sutra every four hours. If not one can recite it three times a day, or just in the morning and evening.

Generally if one does not amend the downfall within a four-hour period following the transgression then confession is overdue and it becomes an actual downfall. So if the offence is acknowledged within the four hours then a sincere act by the above means restores one's commitments. If more than four hours have passed then it must be repaired through confession, resorting to the four powers: 1: The Power of Reliance. This means to reassert one's commitment of refuge in the Three Jewels and bodhichitta, by reciting the vows. This is the basis that one reaffirms. 2: The Power of Renunciation or Abandonment This is to sincerely regret the downfall or violation one has committed. 3: The Power of Remedial Action. To engage in some specific method in order to repair or counteract the power of the violation. 4: The Power of Restoration. It means the attitude of commitment not to commit that deed again.

There are three manners in which these four powers can be applied. These three ways are essentially three varieties of the third one, the remedial conduct. The best one is meditation on emptiness. The second best is to use such techniques as the Vajrasattva mantra. The third best is to base the confession simply on the recollection of the downfall, and confess it using the four powers.

If more than four hours have passed one must confess using the four powers to oneself. After that, one has to retake the bodhisattva vow. This can be done on one's own by reciting it again yourself.

56. Even an animal will not forsake "all" beings; therefore even if we forsake one being and do not apply the remedy bodhichitta will be lost.

57. The literal meaning of paramita is "gone to the other side" or "reached the other shore," the other side or shore being enlightenment. This covers both that which *will* carry one to the other side (the development of the six paramitas), and that which *has* reached the other side, (the perfection of those qualities).

58. These three result in temporary states of higher rebirth, generosity brings material prosperity, moral ethics brings a good physical existence and patience brings a favorable entourage.

59. Diligence increases virtue, meditative concentration brings calm abiding and prajna brings special insight.

60. They are also in order as to how they develop in one's mind. Through the practice of generosity one can have correct moral ethics without concern for material well-being. Being endowed with moral ethics one can cultivate patience. Having patience one can be diligent. Through diligence meditative concentration will arise. And the mind in calm abiding can realize the true nature of all phenomena.

61. The long term consequence is poverty in a material sense. In addition one can suffer from a poverty-stricken mentality, which is not in terms of what a person has but how satisfied they are with what they have. For example, a wealthy person can feel very dissatisfied with what they have while a poor person can feel very content with their lot.

62. However, before we give something away we should check our attitude because it is better not to give than to give with a stingy mind. If we give with a stingy mind, we will later regret having given the gift and this means that whatever goodness may arise from giving will be totally wasted. Also, we have lost the object, so there is no point; we have gained no virtue and have lost the object. So, it is better to try to check our attitude before we are generous.

63. In addition there is the inferior intention of giving based on a fear of poverty in the next life.

64. When generosity practices are permeated by emptiness they will not become a cause of samsara and when they are permeated by compassion they will not become a cause of the lesser vehicle. They will only be a cause for Buddhahood.

65. This has four qualities; taking the vows properly from others, having a pure motivation, renewing the practice if it degenerates, and having respect and mindfulness so that the practice does not degenerate. These four qualities can be categorized under receiving and protecting. The first point being receiving and the other three being protecting.

66. There is the common and uncommon morality of restraint. The common morality of restraint refers to the pratimoksha vows, which benefit oneself. The uncommon morality of restraint is that of a bodhisattva who does it for the benefit of others.

67. The accumulation of virtues are explained in the *Bodhisattva Levels* as:

maintaining and sustaining the bodhisattva's morality; joyfully making effort in hearing, contemplating and meditating; performing service for and honoring all teachers; helping and nursing sick people; giving properly and proclaiming good qualities; rejoicing in others' merit and patience; having patience when others look down on you; dedicating virtue toward enlightenment and saying aspiration prayers; making offerings to the Three Jewels and making efforts for the virtuous teachings; sustaining introspection; recollecting the bodhisattva's training; protecting the bodhisattva's training with vigilant awareness; protecting all the sense doors and moderately eating food; making effort in meditation practice without sleeping too early in the evening or too late in the morning; attending spiritual masters and authentically holy people; investigating your own mistakes and purifying them – in this way, practicing these good qualities, protecting, and increasing them are called the moral ethics of accumulating virtues..

68. In the *Bodhisattva Levels*, thirteen aspects of moral ethics to benefit others are mentioned: supporting meaningful activities, to dispel the sufferings of those who are suffering, showing those without skill how to cope intelligently, recollecting others' kindness and repaying it, protecting others' from what frightens them, dispel the mourning of those who are suffering, giving necessities to the needy, to properly bring together a dharma following and to engage them in that which corresponds to their mentality, creating joy by reporting the perfect qualities, to properly correct someone who is doing wrong, to inspire awe through exceptional abilities, and causing others to be inspired by the teachings.

69. The Sanskrit for this is "ksanti." We have kept the translation as patience, which is how it is most often translated. However as Rinpoche explains in the following paragraphs it has to do with coping with situations and being able to face up to difficulties and a sense of being able to bear a load. In this sense forbearance seems closer to the meaning.

70. This is why in general it is not very significant to become too involved with our body, since it is devoid of any lasting substance or entity. This body isn't like stone or anything solid; it can break very easily, which is true of the flesh, blood and bones also. It doesn't even take the impact of weapons to destroy the body; even stone or wood can break the bones. In this respect, there is no difference whether one is a man or woman. As soon as you have a body, it is very vulnerable and is subject to being hurt and having pain.

71. Often when examples are given of the accomplishments of great masters it is the case that they are mostly men. If we speak of bodies in terms of the results of previous actions it is indeed true that due to past negative actions we have to experience various kinds of sufferings from time to time. But, it is also true that we now have a very precious human life, either as a man or as a woman it is a very good result and the opportunity is the same; both can practice and achieve results equally. When the Buddha gave teachings he didn't say, "This is only intended for men and women cannot do it." In fact, the Buddha really went against the stream of the times because in India then there were strong discriminations in terms of the caste system and against women. The Buddha, I think, was the very first to speak in terms of self-determination of men and women alike, giving everyone the same rights, the same possibility of choice. In a sense, the Buddha can be called the pioneer of women's liberation. He opened the doors for women.

72. Milarepa was on his own and accomplished the highest results. If someone doesn't have that much diligence it might be quite helpful to practice with others who are doing the same thing. They encourage our own diligence.

73. Here the text mentions five types of diligence: 1. constant effort (without getting tired in body or mind), 2. effort with devotion (persevering quickly with joy and happiness), 3. unshakable effort (with a mind not shaken by conceptual thought, disturbing emotions, or the hardships of suffering), 4. effort without turning back (from seeing harm, wild behavior, disturbances, and wrong views), 5. effort without arrogance.

74. Seeing here does not mean seeing physically, but refers to a lack of awareness of the true nature of things, which leads us to view things dualistically with a self and what is other to it. From this dualistic perception comes the basic feeling towards things as good or bad that then gives rise to the disturbing emotions.

75. Disturbing emotions are kleshas that in Sanskrit means "pain, distress, and torment." This was translated as "afflictions" which is the closest English word to what causes distress. However, the Tibetan word for kleshas is "nyon mong" and these almost always refer to passion, anger, ignorance, jealousy, and pride which are actually negative or disturbing emotions so we prefer the translation negative or disturbing emotion since "afflictions" imply some kind of disability. *The Great Tibetan Dictionary* for example

defines "nyon mong" as, "mental events that incite one to non-virtuous actions and cause one's being to be very unpeaceful."

76. There are several books by Thrangu Rinpoche on meditation practice, including *Pointing Out the Dharmakaya* and *Teachings on the Practice of Meditation*, both available from Zhyisil Chokyi Ghatsal Publications, however it is best to get personal meditation instruction from a qualified teacher.

77. There is, of course, a great incentive for beginners to look at thoughts of anger, because anger is so vexatious and causes so much trouble in one's life. It is much more difficult to remember to look at the mind when it is experiencing feelings of attachment, happiness, love, pleasure, etc., because these emotions are not generally experienced as vexatious. Nevertheless, the attachment associated with these experiences sooner or later, when they change or are disrupted, becomes the basis of suffering. Therefore, it is very important to develop one's mindfulness and train one's mind to look directly and nakedly at thoughts that we experience as happiness as well

78. The first aspect is the method for making the mind a proper vessel. The second aspect establishes all the enlightened qualities of a Buddha in one who is a suitable vessel. The third one is working for the benefit of all sentient beings.

79. The three realms are the desire realm (this includes the six realms of hells, craving spirits, animals, humans, demi-gods and gods), the form realm (gods of subtle form), and the formless realm (beings in high meditative states of absorption).

80. However this shouldn't lead one to think that wisdom-awareness alone is sufficient. The bodhisattva's path requires both method (the first five paramitas) and wisdom (the sixth paramita). If a bodhisattva depends solely on wisdom-awareness without method they will fall into the nirvanic peace of the Hinayana path result. In addition, just as a small amount of wood cannot produce a large, long burning fire, a small accumulation of merit cannot produce great awareness wisdom. So, great wisdom-awareness depends on the accumulation of merit from practicing the first five paramitas.

81. This is the realization that the afflicted aggregates (skandhas) are impure, have the nature of suffering, are impermanent and are without self.

82. There are many explanations of the personal self that we grasp at, but basically a person is the combination of awareness and the continuity of the afflicted aggregates. This continuity is always moving and fluctuating about. Believing this person to be a permanent and unique entity we cling and become attached to it as "I" and "self." This is the personal self or mind. From this comes the disturbing emotions that produce karma (virtuous, non-virtuous and neutral) and the result is suffering. It is however important to understand that what is being negated is a true, permanent and ultimate existence of a self, not the relative self or personality. This is why it is compared to dreams and illusions, because while having no true existence, they do appear on the relative level due to circumstances and certain conditions.

83. Subject and object or perceiver and what is perceived, are interdependent, one cannot exist without the other, they arise simultaneously. Therefore, in order to confirm the existence of the subject or perceiver, we must confirm the existence of an object or what is perceived. Being unable to confirm the existence of any object, the logical result is that there can be no truly existing subject. The fact that the relationship of subject and object is one of dependence, through simultaneous arising, is also proof of their emptiness because something that truly exists would not be dependent on something else for it to arise and abide.

84. What is given here is the definition of the well-known Buddhist path, "Middle-way." It is middle because it avoids all philosophical extremes, in particular those of eternalists (those who believe things truly and permanently exist), and nihilists (those who believe that everything is just voidness and disregard karma and relative appearances). One avoids these extremes and the intellect's grasping at defining that which is beyond or inadequate of being defined. The result is the direct and clear realization of truth.

85. Saying that something does not arise on an ultimate level does not prevent things from arising or appearing on a relative level. Therefore, that fact that an object is empty does not prevent it from appearing, and the appearance of an object does not preclude it from being empty. As Nagarjuna said, "Because of emptiness everything can arise, without emptiness nothing can arise."

86. At this stage twelve of the thirty-seven branches of enlightenment are practiced: the four types of mindfulness (sustaining mindfulness of body, feelings, the mind, and phenomena) which occur during the lesser stage, the four types of perfect abandonment (abandoning non-virtues which have been created, not allowing new non-virtues to be produced, producing the virtuous remedies not yet present, and assuring the increase of those virtues which have already arisen) which occur during the middle stage, and the four feet of miraculous powers (the absorption of strong aspiration, perseverance, through intention, and investigation) which occur during the greater stage of the path of accumulation.

87. All meditation can be divided into the two categories of tranquility meditation (Shamatha) and insight meditation (Vipashyana). Vipashyana in turn can be divided into the Vipashyana of the sutra tradition and the Vipashyana of the Mahamudra tradition. In the sutra tradition there is analytical Vipashyana and placement meditation. In the Mahamudra or tantric tradition, Vipashyana is based on the direct pointing out of the nature of mind and the nature of things by a fully qualified and experienced holder of the Mahamudra lineage.

88. The path of junction follows on from the perfection of the path of accumulation. There are four stages that correspond to the understanding of the Four Noble Truths.

During the first two stages there are five powers (five of the thirty-seven branches of enlightenment) to be practiced: the power of 1) faith, 2) diligence, 3) mindfulness, 4) absorption, and 5) wisdom-awareness.

During the second two stages there are five strengths (five of the thirty-seven branches of enlightenment) to be practiced: the strength of 1) faith, 2) diligence, 3) mindfulness, 4) absorption, and 5) wisdom-awareness.

The end of the fourth stage is the highest point of samara, meaning that after this is the path of insight when one's whole experience changes and there are no more samsaric rebirths.

89. From a basis of calm abiding one gains insight into the Four Noble Truths. There are four insights that correspond to each of the four truths, giving sixteen in total. These sixteen are direct realizations of the truth of the four truths, as opposed to an intellectualized or limited understanding of them that we have prior to this stage. At this stage one is endowed with seven of the thirty-seven branches of enlightenment: the perfect 1)

mindfulness branch, 2) discrimination branch, 3) diligence branch, 4) joy branch, 5) relaxation branch, 6) absorption branch, and 7) equanimity branch.

90. At this path there are two types of meditation, worldly (meaning the result is better worldly rebirth as opposed to liberation) and beyond the world. The worldly consists of meditative concentrations and formless absorptions; these suppress the afflicting emotions, establish the special qualities of the four immeasurables and create the foundation for the meditation beyond the world. The beyond the world meditation consists of furthering tranquility and insight focused on the two aspects of primordial wisdom (jnana). At this stage one is endowed with eight of the thirty-seven branches of enlightenment: 1) perfect view, 2) perfect conception, 3) perfect speech, 4) perfect action, 5) perfect livelihood, 6) perfect effort, 7) perfect mindfulness, and 8) perfect absorption (these are more commonly known as the eight-fold right path).

91. At the end of the path of cultivation is what is called the vajra-like profound absorption. This absorption is completely unshaken by worldly activity, unable to be destroyed by obscurations, unshaken by thoughts or disturbing emotions, has the realization of emptiness and knows the suchness of all knowledge. Following this arises the primordial wisdom-awareness of the Buddha which is focused on the Four Truths and sees the exhaustion of the causes of suffering and thus the non-arising of the result, which is suffering, which are the two kinds of awareness'.

Having perfected the cultivation stage one enters Buddhahood. There are ten attainments: the perfection of each of the eight-fold right path, plus the full liberation of no-more-training, and the perfect primordial wisdom of no-more-training.

92. This level can apply to quite advanced practitioners. The reason it is considered practiced out of aspiration is because there is not yet any direct realization of emptiness. One is strongly devoted to the meaning of emptiness and has many experiences and a clear conceptual appreciation but the direct experience, which constitutes release from samsara, has not yet occurred.

93. This level is mastered by training in ten subjects: pure motivation, purely practicing, an attitude of equanimity, generosity, properly attending spiritual masters, seeking the fruition of the pure dharma of the three

vehicles, disliking or renouncing worldly life, wishing to accomplish the dharmakaya, always teaching pure dharma, and protecting others.

Bodhisattvas on this level generally practice all of the ten paramitas but in particular they emphasis the paramita of generosity. While in meditative absorption bodhisattvas on the ten levels have the same realization. If explained individually, differences occur during post-meditation. A bodhisattva on this level is also free of five fears; fear of not making a living, fear of not being praised, fear of death, fear of rebirth in a lower realm, and stage fright in large gatherings. A bodhisattva on this level usually becomes a universal ruler and dispels miserliness in all beings. A bodhisattva on this level can enter one hundred absorptions, see one hundred Buddhas, go to one hundred *Buddhafields*, abide for one hundred kalpas, see one hundred previous and future kalpas, and manifest one hundred bodies with an entourage of one hundred bodhisattvas.

94. This level is mastered by eight trainings in moral ethics: purity in moral ethics, repaying the kindness of others, benefiting others, rejoicing in virtue, love and compassion to all beings, honoring and respecting one's spiritual masters, properly keeping the training received, and always training in the six paramitas. As on the other levels, a bodhisattva generally practices all the ten paramitas but here particular emphasis is on moral ethics. Rebirth is usually as a *Chakravartin* establishing beings in the ten virtues by dispelling the ten non-virtues. Whereas the bodhisattva on the first level can achieve things by one hundred times, on the second level it is one thousand times. For each level this is multiplied ten-fold.

95. The third level is mastered by training in five topics: insatiable hearing of dharma, teaching dharma without concern for material reward or honor, purifying the Buddhafield where one is to accomplish enlightenment, never being discouraged by others' ungratefulness to your kindness and, being without arrogance. The particular emphasis of practice is the paramita of patience. Rebirth is usually as a great king of the gods with the skill to dispel the desires of beings.

The fourth level is mastered through ten trainings: abiding in solitude, having no desire for wealth obtained, being content with obtaining basic wealth, maintaining ascetic training, not forsaking training received, being disgusted by seeing the faults of sensual objects, establishing students in nirvana, completely giving up all possessions, never being discouraged by doing virtue and, not being concerned with one's own benefit. Particular emphasis is on the paramita of perseverance. Rebirth is usually as a great king of gods and can destroy the false view of a self.

96. This level is mastered by avoiding ten faults: associating with relatives (who are the basis of attachment), attachment to the homes of benefactors, abiding in agitated places, praising oneself with attachment, deprecation of others, the ten non-virtues, conceit and arrogance, wrong perceptions (of purity, happiness, permanence and self), unwholesome knowledge of wrong views and, patience with disturbing emotions. Particular emphasis is on meditative concentration. Rebirth is usually a king of gods with skill in dispelling the wrong views of non-Buddhists.

97. This level is mastered through twelve trainings: accomplishing the six paramitas and, avoiding attachment to the accomplishments of hearers, avoiding attachment to pratyekabuddhas, avoiding fear of emptiness, not being discouraged to give when asked, not being unhappy if you have given all your possessions and, even if you have given everything, not abandoning beggars. Particular emphasis is on practicing the prajnaparamita. Rebirth is usually as a king of gods with skill in dispelling the arrogance of beings.

98. This level is mastered by renouncing twenty subjects of: self, perception of beings, one's life force, persons that perform real actions, the discontinuation of beings, the permanence of beings, signs of duality of phenomena, various causes, the five aggregates, the eighteen elements (dhatus), the twelve sense sources (*ayatanas*), the three realms, afflicting emotions, being discouraged in the path, Buddha as the fruition, dharma as its cause, sangha as its base, the view of moral ethics, profound emptiness and, relative emptiness as contradictory. These are renounced by practicing their twenty opposites. Particular emphasis is on the paramita of skilful means. Rebirth is usually as a king of gods with skill in establishing the direct realizations of shravakas and pratyekabuddhas.

99. This level is mastered by eight trainings: directly understanding the actions of all beings' mind, compassion through clairvoyance of miracle powers, establishing Buddhafields, gathering great merit by attending Buddha, maturing beings by understanding their different capacities, purifying the Buddhafield by mastering the pure realms, seeing all phenomena as illusory by mastering nonconceptual thought and, willingly taking rebirth in samsara by mastering birth. Particular emphasis is on

practicing the paramita of aspiration. On this level a bodhisattva has ten powers: power over life span, mind, necessary provisions, karma, birth, wishes, aspiration, prayers, miracles, wisdom-awareness, and dharma. Rebirth is usually as a king of the gods with great skill in establishing the teachings of arhats and pratyekabuddhas.

100. This level is mastered through twelve trainings: infinite aspirations to benefit beings, understanding languages of gods and others, mastery over dharma, rebirth (only entering a suitable womb), choosing an excellent family, choosing an excellent caste, choosing excellent relatives, choosing excellent surroundings, choosing an exceptional birth, renouncing the house by the inspiration of the Buddha, accomplishing enlightenment under the bodhi tree and, perfecting all Buddha qualities. Particular emphasis is on practicing the paramita of strength. Rebirth is usually as a king of gods with great skill in answering whatever is asked.

101. The trainings on this level are ten: fully discriminating phenomena, perfecting all qualities, completely gather all accumulations of merit and wisdom, vast achievement of great compassion, becoming expert in all the various types of worlds, engaging in actions to benefit confused beings, bringing attention to mind in order to enter into the action of Buddha, entering the supreme projection of strength, entering the supreme projection of fearlessness and, entering the supreme projection of unequaled qualities. Particular emphasis is on the practice of the paramita of primordial wisdom. Rebirth is usually as a king of gods with great skill in giving teachings on the paramitas to all beings.

102. When explained in terms of taking three limitless kalpas to achieve, the first level is attained during the first limitless kalpa, the eighth level during the second limitless kalpa and the tenth during the third.

103. There is however difficulty in translating the meaning of this term. Often this is translated as "body" or "embodiment" of Buddhahood. However, as this chapter explains, of the three bodies of a Buddha, the dharmakaya is formless and the other two manifest in and to the minds of beings like rainbows in terms of their own subjective realities.

104. What are removed are the two obscurations of the disturbing emotions and the obscurations to knowledge (the cognitive obscuration that obscures the true nature of the mind). What is realized is the primordial awareness

of reality (dharmakaya), as it is, and omniscience (seeing all the knowledge of the three times).

105. It may be helpful here to understand the term for "consciousness," which in Sanskrit is "vijnana," which is a specific type of cognition. It is the term for "cognition," "jnana," with the prefix "vi," which means complete or fully developed. This is a more specific term than cognition and although it may sound like a positive thing to say "fully-developed cognition," in this context it is actually somewhat pejorative because it refers to cognition that has become developed in the sense of becoming coarsened. This is the type of cognition, or consciousness, what we as ordinary individuals have and is what is divided into the eight or six types of consciousnesses. All of these consciousnesses are considered manifestations of the mind's impurity. They are things that arise when a mind does not recognize its own nature. The basic idea of the development of consciousness is that when a mind does not recognize its own nature, its inherent lucidity, which is just a mere cognition, it runs wild. And running wild it becomes coarse or develops into deluded cognition or consciousness, which is characteristic of samsara. Nevertheless, in the midst of all of this confusion, the nature of these consciousnesses, the nature of this deluded mind is unchanged. This unchanging nature of the mind is called "the pure all-basis" as opposed to the "all-basis consciousness," one of the *eight consciousnesses*. That pure all-basis is mere cognition, fundamental jnana itself. Also, if you wish to make a distinction between the mind in its impure manifestations and the nature of the mind, mind itself, then mind (impure) will be called "sem," and the mind itself, that mere cognition itself, will be called "sem nyi," mind in itself.

106. The twelve deeds are: 1) He descends from Tushita to take birth, 2) he entered his mother's womb, 3) his birth in Lumbini, 4) he attained knowledge and skilful in all arts and crafts, 5) he married, had a child and enjoyed his royal pleasures, 6) he renounced his worldly life, 7) he practiced austerities, 8) he gave up practicing austerity, 9) he subdued all maras (disturbing emotions), 10) he accomplished enlightenment under the bodhi tree, 11) he taught the three cycles of teachings, 12) his paranirvana at Kushinagar. For a detailed explanation of these see The Life of the Buddha and The Four Noble Truths by Thrangu Rinpoche, available from Zhyisil Chokyi Ghatsal Publications.

107. Meaning that the Buddha should not be seen as the form bodies, which manifest through the combination of the blessings of the dharmakaya, the projection of disciples, and previously devoted aspiration prayers.

108. Some texts mention two, four or five kayas, however, they are all included in the three mentioned.

109. The three kayas are also explained as each having eight characteristics, the eight of the dharmakaya are: 1) there is no difference between the dharmakaya of all Buddhas, 2) it is free from elaboration and difficult to realize, 3) it is not compounded, 4) it is indivisible, 5) it is unmistaken, 6) it is free from all obscurations, 7) there are no discursive thoughts, 8) embodying the nature of vast good qualities it is the foundation of the sambhogakaya. The eight of the sambhogakaya are: 1) its surrounding retinue are all bodhisattvas abiding on the levels, 2) its field of enjoyment is a Buddhafield, 3) the way it is experienced is in the form of Buddha Vairochana, etc, 4) it possesses the thirty-two major and eighty minor marks of physical perfection, 5) the full enjoyment of dharma is the Mahayana in contrast to the nirmanakaya which due to its disciples has to use various other means and expedient truths), 6) its activities are prophesizing bodhisattvas' enlightenment etc, 7) all its activities are spontaneous and free from effort, 8) although it manifests in various forms, they are not its true nature, they are but like colors of a crystal. The eight of the nirmanakaya are: 1) its basis is the dharmakaya, 2) its cause is great compassion to benefit all beings, 3) its fields are usually both pure and impure fields, 4) it is unceasing for as long as the world exists, 5) it manifests in three forms, a) creative emanations endowed with skill and mastery of arts such as lute-playing etc, b) birth emanations of various inferior bodies such as an animal and so on, c) supreme emanations that manifest the twelve deeds. 6) he encourages beings to enter the dharma according to the different capacities, 7) he brings to full maturity those who have already entered the path, 8) he liberates from existence those who are fully matured.

110. Dharmadhatu and dharmakaya are essentially the same; they are two indivisible aspects of the same thing. The dharmakaya emphasizes the wisdom aspect while dharmadhatu emphasizes the emptiness aspect.

111. 1) The palms of his hands and soles of his feet bear the signs of a wheel, 2) His feet are well set upon the ground like a tortoise, 3) His fingers and toes are webbed, 4) The palms of his hands and soles of his feet

are smooth and tender, 5) His body has seven prominent features: broad heels, broad hands, broad shoulders blades, and broad neck, 6) His fingers are long, 7) His heels are soft, 8) He is tall and straight, 9) His ankle-bones do not protrude, 10) The hairs on his body point upward, 11) His ankles are like an antelope's, 12) His hands are long and beautiful, 13) His male organ is withdrawn, 14) His body is the color of gold, 15) His skin is thin and smooth, 16) Each hair curls to the right, 17) His face is adorned by a coil hair between his eyebrows, 18) The upper part of his body is like that of a lion, 19) His head and shoulders are perfectly round, 20) His shoulders are broad, 21) He has an excellent sense of taste, even of the worst tastes, 22) His body has the proportions of a banyan tree, 23) He has a protrusion on the crown of his head, 24) His tongue is long and thin, 25) His voice is mellifluent, 26) His cheeks are like those of a lion, 27) His teeth are white, 28) There are no gaps between his teeth, 29) His teeth are evenly set, 30) He has a total of forty teeth, 31) His eyes are the color of sapphire, 32) His eyelashes are like those of a magnificent heifer.

112. Just as the moon is reflected in as many water bowls as are present without any effort or thought, so too the Buddha appears and helps beings without thought and effort and while never moving from the dharmakaya.

Glossary of Terms

84,000 teachings. (Tib. *cho kyi phung po gyad khri bzhi stong*) 21,000 teachings on each of the Vinaya, Sutra, Abhidharma, and their combination. Their purpose is to eliminate the 84,000 different types of disturbing emotions latent in one's mind.

Abhidharma. (Tib. *chö ngön pa*) The Buddhist teachings are often divided into the Tripitaka: the sutras (teachings of the Buddha), the Vinaya (teachings on conduct,) and the Abhidharma which are the analyses of phenomena that exist primarily as a commentarial tradition to the Buddhist teachings.

Acharya. (Tib. *lo pon*) A spiritual master. (Similar to a geshe scholar)

Arhat. "Free from four maras." The mara of conflicting emotions, the mara of the deva, the mara of death and the mara of the skandhas. The highest level of the Hinayana path. Arhat is male and arhati is female.

Asanga. (Tib. *thok may)* A fourth century Indian philosopher who founded the Cittamatra or Yogacara school and wrote the five works of Maitreya which are important Mahayana works. Also brother of Vasubandhu.

Atisha. (982-1055 C.E.) A Buddhist scholar at the Nalanda University in India who came to Tibet at the invitation of the King to overcome the damage done by Langdarma. He helped found the Kadampa tradition.

Ayatanas. These are the six sensory objects of sight, sound, smell, taste, and body sensation; the six sense faculties, the visual sensory faculty, the auditory sensory faculty, etc., and the six sensory consciousnesses, the visual consciousness, the auditory consciousness, etc. They make up the eighteen constituents for perception.

Bhumi. Level or stage. There are ten bodhisattva levels that begin with the path of seeing in the sutra tradition. The tantric tradition has thirteen levels.

Bodhichitta. (Tib. *chang chup chi sem*) Literally, the mind of enlightenment. There are two kinds of bodhichitta: ultimate bodhichitta, which is completely awakened mind that sees the emptiness of phenomena, and relative bodhichitta which is the aspiration to practice the six paramitas and free all beings from the suffering of samsara. In regard to relative bodhichitta there is also two kinds: aspiration-bodhichitta and action-bodhichitta.

Bodhisattva. (Tib. *chang chup sem pa*) "Heroic mind." *Bodhi* means blossomed or enlightened, and *sattva* means heroic mind. Literally, one who exhibits the mind of enlightenment. Also an individual who has committed him or herself to the Mahayana path of compassion and the practice of the six paramitas to achieve Buddhahood to free all beings from samsara. These are the heart or mind disciples of the Buddha.

Bodhisattva vow. The vow to attain Buddhahood for the sake of all beings.

Buddha. (Tib. *sang gye*) An individual who attains, or the attainment of, complete enlightenment, such as the historical Shakyamuni Buddha.

Buddha Shakyamuni. (Tib. *shakya tubpa*) The Shakyamuni Buddha, often called the Gautama Buddha, refers to the fourth Buddha of this age, who lived between 563 and 483 BCE.

Buddhafield. (Tib. *sang gye kyi zhing*) 1) One of the realms of the five Buddha families, either as sambhogakaya or nirmanakaya. 2) Pure personal experience.

Buddhahood. (Tib. *sang gyas*) The perfect and complete enlightenment of dwelling in neither samsara nor nirvana. Expression of the realization of perfect enlightenment, which characterizes a Buddha. The attainment of Buddhahood is the birthright of all beings. According to the teachings of Buddha, every sentient being has, or better is already, Buddha nature; thus Buddhahood cannot be "attained." It is much more a matter of experiencing the primordial perfection and realizing it in everyday life.

Buddha nature. (Tib. *de shegs nying po*) The essential nature of all sentient beings. The potential for enlightenment.

Chakravartin. (Tib. *koro gyur wa*) Literally, the turner of the wheel and also called a universal monarch. This is a king who propagates the dharma and starts a new era.

Chenrezig. The bodhisattva embodying the compassion of all the Buddhas. Depicted holding the wish-fulfilling gem between folded hands. One of the eight main bodhisattvas. The mantra associated with this bodhisattva is known as the king of mantras, OM MANI PEME HUNG.

Clarity. (Tib. *salwa*) Also translated as luminosity. The nature of mind is that it is empty of inherent existence, but the mind is not just voidness or completely empty because it has this clarity which is awareness or the knowing of mind. So clarity is a characteristic of emptiness (*shunyata*) of mind.

Cognitive obscurations. There are two types of obscurations that cover one's Buddha nature. The obscuration of the afflictive or disturbing emotions and the obscuration of dualistic perception, or sometimes called the intellectual obscurations or cognitive obscurations. The cognitive obscuration is the subtle obscuration of holding onto the concepts of subject, object and action.

Cognizance. (Tib. *sal wa*) The mind's inherent capacity for knowing.

Commentary. (Skt. *shastra*, Tib. *tan chö*) The Buddhist teachings are divided into the words of the Buddha (*sutras*) and the commentaries of others on his works (*shastras*).

Common tradition. A way of referring to those teachings held in common by all traditions of Buddhism, which are the teachings on personal liberation of the Hinayana or lesser vehicle.

Common vehicle. The Hinayana.

Conditioned (cyclic) existence. (Skt. *samsara*, Tib. *khor wa*) Ordinary existence which contains suffering because one still possesses attachment, aggression, and ignorance. It is contrasted to liberation or nirvana.

Craving Spirits. (Tib. *yid dvags*) One of the six classes of sentient beings. Such beings are tormented by their own impure karmic perception causing them to suffer tremendously from craving, hunger and thirst. It is said that even if they came upon a lake of pure fresh water, due to their heavy karmic obscurations, they would see it as an undrinkable pool of pus. They are depicted with very large bodies and very thin necks.

Definitive meaning. The Buddha's teachings that state the direct meaning of dharma. They are not changed or simplified for the capacity of the listener, in contrast to the provisional meaning.

Desire realm. Comprises the six realms of gods, demi-gods, humans, animals, hungry spirits and hell-beings.

Dharma. (Tib. *chö*) This has two main meanings: first, any truth, such as that the sky is blue; and secondly, the teachings of the Buddha (also called "Buddha-dharma").

Dharma protector. (Skt. *dharmapala*, Tib. *cho kyong)* A Buddha, bodhisattva or powerful but ordinary being whose job is to remove all interferences and bestow all necessary conditions for the practice of pure dharma.

Dharmadhatu. (Tib. *chö ying*) The all-encompassing space, unoriginated and without beginning, out of which all phenomena arises. The Sanskrit means "the essence of phenomena" and the Tibetan means "the expanse of phenomena," but it usually refers to the emptiness that is the essence of phenomena.

Dharmakaya. (Tib. *chö ku*) One of the three bodies of Buddhahood. It is enlightenment itself, that is, wisdom beyond any point of reference. (see *kayas, three.)*

Dharmata. (Tib. *chö nyi*) Dharmata is often translated as "suchness" or "the true nature of things" or "things as they are." It is phenomena as it really is or as seen by a completely enlightened being without any distortion or obscuration, so one can say it is "reality." The nature of phenomena and mind.

Disturbing emotions. (Skt. *klesha*, Tib. *nyön mong*) Also called the "afflictive emotions," these are the emotional afflictions or obscurations (in contrast to intellectual obscurations) that disturb the clarity of perception. These are also translated as "poisons." They include any emotion that disturbs or distorts consciousness. The main kleshas are desire, anger and ignorance.

Eight consciousnesses. (Skt. *vijñana*, Tib. *nam she tsog gye*) These are the five sensory consciousnesses of sight, hearing, smell, taste, touch, and body sensation. Sixth is mental consciousness, seventh is afflicted consciousness, and eighth is ground consciousness.

Eight fold noble path. Right view, right thought, right speech, right action, right livelihood, right effort, right mindfulness and right concentration.

Eight freedoms & ten endowments. (*Tal jor*) *Tal* is often translated as "freedom" and *jor* as "qualities," "resources," and "opportunities" which constitute a precious human birth to practice dharma. The eight freedoms are traditionally enumerated as freedom from birth as a hell being, a hungry ghost, an animal, a barbarian, a long-lived god, a heretic, a mentally handicapped person, or living in a dark age (here meaning when no Buddha has come, in other contexts, according to the teachings on five degenerations we are living in a dark age). Of the ten conjunctions or resources, the five personal conjunctions are having a human body, being born in a land to which the dharma has spread, having all of one's senses intact, not reverting to evil ways, and having confidence in the three jewels. (Having one's senses impaired to the extent that one's mind could not function properly in the study and practice of dharma would constitute the loss of one's precious human birth.) The five conjunctions that come by way of others are that a Buddha has been born in this age, that the Buddha taught the dharma, that the dharma still exists, that there are still followers who have realized the meaning and essence of the teachings of the dharma, and there are benevolent sponsors.

Eight worldly concerns. (Tib. *jik ten chö gysh*) These keep one from the path; they are attachment to gain, attachment to pleasure, attachment to praise, attachment to fame, aversion to loss, aversion to pain, aversion to blame and aversion to a bad reputation.

Emotional obscurations. There are two types of obscurations that cover one's Buddha nature. The obscuration of the afflictive or disturbing emotions and the obscuration of dualistic perception, or sometimes called the intellectual obscurations or cognitive obscurations. The emotional obscurations prevent liberation and consist of the kleshas. (see *klesha*)

Emptiness. (Skt. *shunyata*, Tib. *tong pa nyi*) Also translated as voidness. The Buddha taught in the second turning of the wheel of dharma that external phenomena and the internal phenomena or concept of self or "I" have no real existence and therefore are "empty."

Enlightenment. (Tib. *jang chub*) The definition varies according to the Buddhist tradition; usually the same as Buddhahood. The Hinayana tradition defines liberation as the freedom from rebirth in samsara, with mind free of ignorance and emotional conflict. The Mahayana tradition holds that enlightenment is not complete without development of compassion and commitment to use skilful means to liberate all sentient beings. In the Vajrayana teachings, the foregoing stages of enlightenment are necessary, but ultimate enlightenment is a thorough purification of ego and concepts. The final fruition of complete liberation transcends all duality and conceptualization.

Eternalism. (Tib. *rtag lta*) The belief that there is a permanent and causeless creator of everything; in particular, that one's identity or consciousness has a concrete essence which is independent, everlasting and singular.

Experience and realization. (Tib. *nyam togs*) An expression used for insight and progress on the path. "Experience" refers to temporary meditation experiences and "realization" to unchanging understanding of the nature of things.

Five actions of immediate consequence. Killing one's father, killing one's mother, killing an arhat, intentionally wounding a Buddha and causing them to bleed, and creating a schism in the sangha. They are called actions which have an immediate result in that they are the cause for one's very next rebirth to be in a lower realm.

Five aggregates. (Skt. *skandha*, Tib. *phung po nga*) Literally, "heaps." These are the five basic transformations that perceptions undergo when an object is perceived. First is form, which includes all sounds, smells, etc., everything that is not thought. The second and third are sensations (pleasant and unpleasant, etc.) and their identification. Fourth are mental events, which actually include the second and third aggregates. The fifth is ordinary consciousness, such as the sensory and mental consciousnesses.

Five degenerations. 1) the times, meaning the outer events of the world such as wars and social unrest are becoming worse, 2) of beings, meaning their mindstreams are becoming coarser, 3) length of life is becoming shorter, 4) increase in the emotional afflictions of beings, causing instability in their minds, 5) and degeneration of view, meaning people's understanding of reality is growing further from the truth. Based on these five degenerations we are now living in a dark age.

Five paths. (Tib. *lam nga*) According to the sutras there are five paths; the path of accumulation, the path of junction, the path of insight, (attainment of the first bodhisattva level), the path of cultivation, and the path of accomplishment (Buddhahood). The five paths cover the entire process from beginning dharma practice to complete enlightenment.

Five poisons. (Tib. *ldug nga*) Temporary mental states that inhibit understanding: ignorance, pride, anger, desire, and jealousy. The three root poisons are ignorance, desire and anger.

Five wisdoms. The dharmadhatu wisdom, mirror-like wisdom, wisdom of equality, discriminating wisdom and all-accomplishing wisdom. They should not be understood as separate entities but rather as different functions of one's enlightened essence.

Fixation. (Tib. *dzin pa*) The mental act of holding on to a material object, experience, concept or set of philosophical ideas.

Form realm. God realms of subtle form.

Formless realm. (Tib. *zug med kyi kham*) The abode of an unenlightened being who has practiced the four absorptions of: infinite space, infinite consciousness, nothing whatsoever, and neither presence nor absence (of conception).

Four extremes. (Tib. *tha shi*) Existence, non-existence, both and neither.

Four foundations of meditation. (Tib. *tun mong gi ngon dro shi*) These are the four thoughts that turn the mind toward dharma. They are reflection on precious human birth, impermanence and the inevitability of death, karma and its effects, and the pervasiveness of suffering in samsara.

Four immeasurables. Love, compassion, emphatic joy, and impartiality.

Four noble truths. (Tib. *pak pay den pa shi*) The Buddha began teaching with a talk in India at Saranath on the four noble truths. These are the truth of suffering, the truth of the cause of suffering, the cessation of suffering, and the path. These truths are the foundation of Buddhism, particularly the Theravadin path.

Four seals. The four main principles of Buddhism: all compounded phenomena are impermanent, everything defiled (with ego-clinging) is suffering, all phenomena are empty and devoid of a self-entity, and nirvana is perfect peace.

Four truths. The Buddha's first teachings. 1) All conditioned life is suffering. 2) All suffering is caused by ignorance. 3) Suffering can cease. 4) The eight-fold path leads to the end of suffering: right understanding, thought, speech, action, livelihood, effort, mindfulness and meditation.

Gampopa. (1079-1153 C.E.) One of the main lineage holders of the Kagyu lineage in Tibet. A student of Milarepa, he established the first Kagyu monastic monastery and is known also for writing the *Jewel Ornament of Liberation.*

Graded path. This refers to being guided through the path to enlightenment through the three principle paths, 1) renunciation, 2) enlightened motive of bodhicitta, 3) and a correct understanding of emptiness (wisdom).

Great Perfection. (Skt. *Mahasandhi,* Tib. *Dzogchen*) The teachings beyond the vehicles of causation, first taught in the human world by the great vidyadhara Garab Dorje.

Guru. (Tib. *lama*) A teacher in the Tibetan tradition who has reached realization.

Habitual patterns. (Skt. *vasana.* Tib. *bakchak*) Patterns of conditional response that exist as traces or tendencies stored in the alaya-vijnana, the eighth consciousness sometimes called the store-house or all-base consciousness. So called because it is a repository of all karmically conditioned patterns. All dualistic or ego-oriented experiences leave a residue, which is stored in the alaya-vijnana until a later time when some conscious occurrence activates the habitual pattern. The pattern then generates a response in the form of a perception or an action. This response leaves its own karmic residue, stored again in the unconscious repository, and the cycle continues. The explanation of this system is a central teaching of the Cittamatrin tradition of Mahayana Buddhism.

Heart sutra. (Skt. *Mahaprajnaparamita-hridaya-sutra*) One of the shorter sutras on emptiness.

Higher realms. The three higher realms are birth as a human, demi-god and god.

Hinayana. (Tib. *tek pa chung wa*) Literally, the "lesser vehicle." The first of the three *yanas*, or vehicles. The term refers to the first teachings of the Buddha, which emphasized the careful examination of mind and its confusion. It is the foundation of Buddha's teachings focusing mainly on the four truths and the twelve interdependent links. The fruit is liberation for oneself.

Idiot compassion. This is the desire to help others but it is not accompanied by sufficient wisdom, so that what one does may not really be beneficial. An example is teaching someone who is hungry to fish, yet the person receives negative karma for killing the fish.

Interdependent origination. The twelve links of causal connections which binds beings to samsaric existence and thus perpetuate suffering: ignorance, mental formation, consciousness, name and form, the six sense bases, contact, feeling, craving, grasping, becoming, rebirth, old age, and death. These twelve links are like an uninterrupted vicious circle, a wheel that spins all sentient beings around and around through the realms of samsara.

Insight meditation. (Skt. *Vipashyana*, Tib. *lhak tong*) This meditation develops insight into the nature of reality (Skt. *dharmata*). One of the two main aspects of meditation practice, the other being Shamatha.

Jnana. (Tib. *yeshe*) Enlightened wisdom that is beyond dualistic thought.

Kadampa. (Tib.) One of the major schools in Tibet, it was founded by Atisha (993-1054 C.E.).

Kagyu. (Tib.) *Ka* means oral and *gyu* means lineage; The lineage of oral transmission. One of the four major schools of Buddhism in Tibet. It was founded in Tibet by Marpa and is headed by His Holiness Karmapa. The other three are the Nyingma, the Sakya and the Gelugpa schools.

Kalpa. (Tib. *kal pa,* Skt. *yuga*) An eon that lasts in the order of millions of years.

Karma. (Tib. *lay*) Literally "action." The unerring law of cause and effect, e.g, positive actions bring happiness and negative actions bring suffering. The actions of each sentient being are the causes that create the conditions for rebirth and the circumstances in that lifetime.

Karmic latencies or imprints. (Skt. *vasana*, Tib. *bakchak*) Every action and that a person does has an imprint which is stored in the eighth consciousness. These latencies express themselves later by leaving the eighth consciousness and entering the sixth consciousness upon being stimulated by external experience.

Kayas, three. (Tib. *ku sum*) There are three bodies of the Buddha: the nirmanakaya, sambhogakaya and dharmakaya. The dharmakaya, also called the "truth body," is the complete enlightenment or the complete wisdom of the Buddha that is unoriginated wisdom beyond form and manifests in the sambhogakaya and the nirmanakaya. The sambhogakaya, also called the "enjoyment body," manifests only to bodhisattvas. The nirmanakaya, also called the "emanation body," manifests in the world and in this context manifests as the Shakyamuni Buddha. The fourth kaya is the svabhavakakaya, which is the "essence body," the unity of the other three.

King Trisong Deutsen. He was a dharma king of Tibet (790 - 858 CE) who invited Guru Rinpoche and Padmasambhava to Tibet to establish the dharma there.

Klesha. (Tib. *nyön mong*) Also called the "disturbing emotions," these are the emotional afflictions or obscurations (in contrast to intellectual obscurations) that disturb the clarity of perception. These are also translated as "poisons." They include any emotion that disturbs or distorts consciousness. The three main kleshas are desire, anger and ignorance. The five kleshas are the three above plus pride and envy/jealousy. (see reference note 75)

Lama. (Skt. *guru*) *La* means nobody above himself or herself in spiritual experience and *ma* means expressing compassion like a mother. Thus the union of wisdom and compassion, feminine and masculine qualities. Lama is also a title given to a practitioner who has completed some extended training.

Liberation. (see *enlightenment*)

Lojong. Mind Training. The Mahayana meditation system of the early Kadampa school, brought to Tibet by Atisha.

Lotsawa. Sanskrit for "translator."

Lower realm. The three lower realms are birth as a hell being, hungry ghost and animal.

Luminosity. (Tib. *salwa*) In the third turning of the wheel of dharma, the Buddha taught that everything is void, but this voidness is not completely empty because it has luminosity. Luminosity or clarity allows all phenomena to appear and is a characteristic of and inseparable from emptiness (Skt. *shunyata*).

Luminosity. (Tib. *osel*) Literally, "free from the darkness of unknowing and endowed with the ability to cognize." The two aspects are "empty luminosity," like a clear open sky; and "manifest luminosity," such as colored light images, and so forth. Luminosity is the uncompounded nature present throughout all of samsara and nirvana.

Mahamudra. (Tib. *cha ja chen po*) Literally means "great seal" or "great symbol" meaning that all phenomena are sealed by the primordially perfect true nature. This form of meditation is traced back to Saraha (10th century) and was passed down in the Kagyu school through Marpa. This meditative transmission emphasizes perceiving mind directly rather than through rational analysis. It also refers to the experience of the practitioner where one attains the union of emptiness and luminosity and also perceives the non-duality of the phenomenal world and emptiness; also the name of Kagyupa lineage.

Mahapandita. (Tib. *pan di ta chen po*) *Maha* means great and *pandita* Buddhist scholar.

Mahasiddha. (Tib. *drup thop chen po)* A practitioner who has a great deal of realization. *Maha* means great and *siddha* refers to an accomplished practitioner. These were particularly Vajrayana practitioners who lived in India between the eight and twelfth century and practiced tantra. The biography of some of the most famous is found in *The Eighty-four Mahasiddhas.*

Mahayana. (Tib. *tek pa chen po*) Literally, the "Great Vehicle." These are the teachings of the second turning of the wheel of dharma, which emphasize shunyata (see *shunyata*), compassion and universal Buddha nature. The purpose of enlightenment is to liberate all sentient beings from suffering as well as oneself. Mahayana schools of philosophy appeared several hundred years after the Buddha's death, although the tradition is traced to a teaching he is said to have given at Rajgriha, or Vulture Peak Mountain.

Manjushri. One of the eight bodhisattvas. He is the personification of transcendent knowledge.

Mantra. (Tib. *ngags*) 1) A synonym for Vajrayana. 2) A particular combination of sounds symbolizing the nature of a deity, for example OM MANI PEME HUNG. These are invocations to various meditation deities which are recited in Sanskrit. These Sanskrit syllables, representing various energies, are repeated in different Vajrayana practices.

Mara. (Tib. *du*) Difficulties encountered by the practitioner. The Tibetan word means heavy or thick. In Buddhism mara symbolizes the passions that overwhelm human beings as well as everything that hinders the arising of wholesome roots and progress on the path to enlightenment. There are four kinds: *skandha-mara*, which is incorrect view of self; *klesha-mara*, which is being overpowered by negative emotions; *matyu-mara*, which is death and interrupts spiritual practice; and *devaputra-mara*, which is becoming stuck in the bliss that comes from meditation.

Marpa. (1012-1097 C.E.) Marpa was known for being a Tibetan who made three trips to India and brought back many tantric texts, including the Six Yogas of Naropa, the Guhyasamaja, and the Chakrasamvara practices. His root teacher was Tilopa, the founder of the Kagyu lineage and the teacher of Naropa. Marpa initiated and founded the Kagyu lineage in Tibet.

Mental consciousness. (Tib. *yid kyi namshe*) The sixth consciousness is the faculty of thinking which produces thoughts based upon the experiences of the five sense consciousnesses or its own previous content. (see *eight consciousnesses*).

Mental factors. (Tib. *sem yung*) Mental factors are contrasted to mind in that they are more long term propensities of mind including eleven virtuous factors such as faith, detachment, and equanimity, and the six root defilements such as desire, anger, and pride, and the twenty secondary defilements such as resentment, dishonesty, harmfulness.

Middle-way. (Tib. *u ma*) or Madhyamaka school. A philosophical school founded by Nagarjuna and based on the Prajnaparamita sutras of emptiness. The most influential of the four schools of Indian Buddhism. The name meaning it is the middle way between eternalism and nihilism. The main postulate of this school is that all phenomena – both internal mental events and external physical objects – are empty of any true nature. The school uses extensive rational reasoning to establish the emptiness of phenomena. This school does, however, hold that phenomena do exist on the conventional or relative level of reality.

Milarepa. (1040-1123 C.E.) Milarepa was a student of Marpa who attained enlightenment in one lifetime. *Mila,* named by the deities and *repa* means white cotton. His student Gampopa established the (*Dagpo*) Kagyu lineage in Tibet.

Nalanda. The greatest Buddhist University from the fifth to the tenth century located near modern Rajgir which was the seat of the Mahayana teachings and had many great Buddhist scholars who studied there.

Naropa. (956-1040 C.E.) An Indian master best known for transmitting many Vajrayana teachings to Marpa who took these back to Tibet before the Moslem invasion of India.

Nihilism. (Tib. *chad lta*) Literally, "the view of discontinuance." The extreme view of nothingness: no rebirth or karmic effects, and the non-existence of a mind after death.

Nirmanakaya. (Tib. *tulku*) There are three bodies of the Buddha and the nirmanakaya or "emanation body" manifests in the world and in this context manifests as the Shakyamuni Buddha. (see *kayas, three.)*

Nirvana. (Tib. *nyangde)* Literally, "extinguished." The term nirvana can have the utmost positive sense when referring to enlightenment or it can have a limiting or pejorative sense when referring to a limited goal of cessation. Individuals live in samsara and with spiritual practice can attain a state of enlightenment in which all false ideas and conflicting emotions have been extinguished. This is called nirvana. The nirvana of a Hinayana practitioner is freedom from cyclic existence, an arhat. The nirvana of a Mahayana practitioner is Buddhahood, free from extremes of dwelling in either samsara or the perfect peace of an arhat.

Obscurations. There are two categories of obscurations or defilements that cover one's Buddha nature: the defilement of conflicting emotions (see *five poisons* and *emotional obscurations*) and the defilement of latent tendencies or sometimes called the obscuration of dualistic perception, or the intellectual/cognitive obscurations (see *cognitive obscurations*).

The first category prevents sentient beings from freeing themselves from samsara, while the second prevents them from gaining accurate knowledge and realising truth.

Pandita. A great scholar.

Paramita. "Transcendental" or "Perfection." Pure actions free from dualistic concepts that liberate sentient beings from samsara. The six paramitas are: generosity, diligence, patience, morality, contemplation, and transcendental knowledge or insight.

Partial compassion. The desire to feel sorry for and want to help others, but only if they are of a certain gender, race, ethnic group, social status, etc.

Paranirvana. After the Buddha Shakyamuni passed from this realm: Buddhas are not said to have died, since they have reached the stage of deathlessness, or deathless awareness.

Prajna. (Tib. *she rab*) In Sanskrit it means "perfect knowledge" and can mean wisdom, understanding or discrimination. Usually it means the wisdom of seeing things from a high (e.g. non-dualistic) point of view.

Prajnaparamita. (Tib. *she rab chi parol tu chinpa)* Transcendent perfect knowledge. The Tibetan literally means, "gone to the other side" or "gone beyond" as expressed in the prajnaparamita mantra, "Om gate gate paragate parasamgate bodhi svaha." The realization of emptiness in the Prajnaparamita Hridaya or Heart Sutra made possible by the extraordinarily profound dharma of the birth of Shakyamuni Buddha in the world and the practices that came from it, such as the Vajrayana tantras, which make use of visualization and the control of subtle physical energies.

Prajnaparamita sutras. Used to refer to a collection of about 40 Mahayana sutras that all deal with the realization of prajna.

Pratimoksha vows. "Individual liberation." The seven sets of precepts for ordained and lay people according to the Vinaya.

Pratyekabuddha. "Solitary Awakened One." These are the body disciples of the Buddha. One who has attained awakening for himself, and on his own, with no teacher in that life. Generally placed on a level between arhat and Buddha. It is the fruition of the second level of the Hinayana path through contemplation on the twelve interdependent links in reverse order.

Provisional meaning. The teachings of the Buddha which have been simplified or modified to the capabilities of the audience. This contrasts with the definitive meaning.

Sakya Pandita. A hereditary head of the Sakya lineage. A great scholar (1181-1251 C.E.)

Samadhi. (Tib. *tin ne zin*) A state of meditation that is non-dualistic. There is an absence of discrimination between self and other. Also called meditative absorption or one-pointed meditation; this is the highest form of meditation.

Sambhogakaya. (Tib. *long chö dzok ku*) There are three bodies of the Buddha and the sambhogakaya, also called the "enjoyment body," is a realm of the dharmakaya that only manifests to bodhisattvas (see *kayas, three*).

Samsara. (Tib. *kor wa*) "Cyclic existence." The conditioned existence of ordinary life in which suffering occurs because one still possesses attachment, aggression and ignorance. It is contrasted to nirvana. Through the force of karma motivated by ignorance, desire and anger one is forced to take on the impure aggregates and circle the wheel of existence until liberation.

Sangha. (Tib. *gen dun*) "Virtuous One." *Sang* means intention or motivation and *gha* means virtuous. One with virtuous motivation. One of the three jewels. Generally refers to the followers of Buddhism, and more specifically to the community of monks and nuns. The exalted sangha is those who have attained a certain level of realization of the Buddha's teachings.

Selfessness. (Tib. *dag me*) Also called selflessness. There are two kinds of selfessness — the selfessness of other, that is, the emptiness of external phenomena and the selfessness of self, that is, the emptiness of a personal self.

Selflessness of person. (Skt. *pudgalanairatmya*) This doctrine asserts that when one examines or looks for the person, one finds that it is empty and without self. The person does not possess a self (Skt. *atman*, Tib. *bdag-nyid*) as an independent or substantial self. This position is held by most Buddhist schools.

Selflessness of phenomena. (Skt. *dharma-nairatmya*) This doctrine asserts than not only is there selflessness of the person, but when one examines outer phenomena, one finds that external phenomena are also empty, i.e. they do not have an independent or substantial nature. This position is not held by the Hinayana schools, but is put forth by the Mahayana schools, particularly the Cittamatra school.

Sentient beings. With consciousness; an animated being as opposed to an inanimate object. All beings with consciousness or mind who have not attained the liberation of Buddhahood. This includes those individuals caught in the sufferings of samsara as well as those who have attained the levels of a bodhisattva.

Shamatha. (Tib.) See tranquillity meditation.

Shamatha with support. (Tib. *shinay ten cas*) The practice of calming the mind while using an object of concentration, material or mental, or simply the breath.

Shamatha without support. (Tib. *shinay ten med*) The act of calming the mind without any particular object, resting undistractedly. This practice serves as a prelude for Mahamudra and should not be mistaken for the ultimate result.

Shantideva. A great bodhisattva of classical India, author of the *Bodhicharyavatara: The Guide to the Bodhisattva's Way of Life.* - (late 7th century - mid 8th century CE.)

Shastra. (Tib. *tan chö*) The Buddhist teachings are divided into words of the Buddha (the *sutras*) and the commentaries of others on his works the (*shastras*).

Shravaka. "Hearer" corresponds to the level of arhat, those that seek and attain liberation for oneself through listening to the Buddhas teaching and gaining insight into selflessness and the four truths. These are the Buddha's speech disciples.

Siddha. (Tib. *drup top)* An accomplished Buddhist practitioner.

Siddhi. (Tib. *ngodrup*) "Accomplishment." The spiritual accomplishments of accomplished practitioners. Usually refers to the "supreme siddhi" of complete enlightenment, but can also mean the "common siddhis," eight mundane accomplishments.

Six consciousnesses. The five sensory consciousnesses and the mental consciousness

Six realms. The realms of the six classes of beings: gods, demigods, humans, animals, hungry ghosts and hell beings.

Skandha. See five aggregates.

Skilful means. Ingenuity in application.

Sugata. An epithet for the Buddha.

Sugatagarbha. The Buddha nature.

Supreme siddhi. Another word for enlightenment.

Sutra. (Tib. *do*) Literally "Junction." The combination of the Hinayana and Mahayana, or the combination of wisdom and compassion. Texts in the Buddhist cannon attributed to the Buddha. They are viewed as his recorded words, although they were not actually written down until many years after his *paranirvana.* They are usually in the form of dialogues between the Buddha and his disciples. These are often contrasted with the tantras which are the Buddha's Vajrayana teachings and the shastras which are commentaries on the words of the Buddha.

Sutra Mahamudra. (Tib. *mdo'i phyag chen*) The Mahamudra system based on the Prajnaparamita scriptures and emphasizing Shamatha and Vipashyana and the progressive journey through the five paths and ten bhumis.

Svabhavakąkaya. (Tib. *ngo bo nyid kyi sku*) The "essence body." Sometimes counted as the fourth kaya, the unity of the first three.

Tantra. (Tib. *gyu.*) Literally, tantra means "continuity," and in Buddhism it refers to two specific things: the texts (resultant texts, or those that take the result as the path) that describe the practices leading from ignorance to enlightenment, including commentaries by tantric masters; and the way to enlightenment itself, encompassing the ground, path, and fruition. One can divide Buddhism into the sutra tradition and the tantra tradition. The sutra tradition primarily involves the academic study of the Mahayana sutras and the tantric path primarily involves practicing the Vajrayana practices. The tantras are primarily the texts of the Vajrayana practices.

Tantra Mahamudra. (Tib. *sngags kyi phyag chen*) The same as mantra Mahamudra. The Mahamudra practice connected to the six dharmas of Naropa.

Tathagatagarbha. The same as Buddha nature. The inherently present potential for enlightenment in all sentient beings.

Ten non-virtuous actions. Killing, stealing, sexual misconduct, lying, slander, abusive words, idle gossip, covetousness, ill-will, and wrong views. Acts are non-virtuous or unwholesome when they result in undesirable karmic effects. Thus, this list of ten unwholesome acts occurs generally in discussions of the functioning of karma. The first three are actions of body, the next four of speech, and the last three of mind. The ten virtuous actions are the opposites of the above ten non-virtuous actions.

Ten levels. The stages or bodhisattva levels in the Mahayana path which are: 1) Overwhelming Joy, with an emphasis on generosity, 2) Stainless, with an emphasis on discipline, 3) Radiant, with an emphasis on patience, 4) Luminous, with an emphasis on exertion, 5) Difficult to Practice, with an emphasis on samadhi, 6) Obviously Transcendent, with an emphasis on wisdom, 7) Far Gone, with an emphasis on skilful activity, 8) Unshakeable, with an emphasis on future, 9) Excellent Discriminating Wisdom, with an emphasis on efficacy, 10) Cloud of Dharma, with an emphasis on accomplishing enlightenment. In the tantric (Vajrayana) literature there are three more stages of manifesting enlightenment, making thirteen in total.

Three jewels. (Tib. *kön chok sum*) Literally "three precious ones." The three essential components of Buddhism: Buddha, dharma, sangha, i.e., the Awakened One, the truth expounded by him, and the followers living in accordance with this truth. Firm faith in the three precious ones is the stage of "stream entry." The three precious ones are objects of veneration and are considered "places of refuge." The Buddhist takes refuge by pronouncing the threefold refuge formula, thus acknowledging formally to be a Buddhist.

Three realms. These are three categories of samsara. The desire realm includes existences where beings are reborn with solid bodies due to their karma ranging from the deva paradises to the hell realms. The form realm is where beings are reborn due to the power of meditation; and their bodies are of subtle form in this realm. These are the meditation paradises. The formless realm is where beings due to their meditation (samadhi), have entered a state of meditation after death and the processes of thought and perception have ceased.

Three roots. Guru, yidam and dakini. Guru is the root of blessings, yidam of accomplishment and dakini of activity.

Three sufferings. These are the suffering of suffering, the suffering of change, and pervasive suffering (meaning the inherent suffering in all of samsara).

Three vehicles. Hinayana, Mahayana and Vajrayana.

Tilopa. (928-1009 C.E.) One of the eighty-four mahasiddhas who became the guru of Naropa who transmitted his teachings to the Kagyu lineage in Tibet.

Tranquillity meditation. (Tib. *shinay*, Skt. *Shamatha*) One of the two main types of meditation, calm abiding, the meditative practice of calming the mind in order to rest free from the disturbance of thought activity; the other is insight.

Two accumulations. (Tib. *shogs nyis*) The accumulation of merit with concepts and the accumulation of wisdom beyond concepts.

Two truths. Relative truth and ultimate truth. Relative truth describes the superficial and apparent mode of all things. Ultimate truth describes the true and unmistaken mode of all things. These two are described differently in the different schools, each progressively deeper leading closer to the way things are.

Vajradhara. (Tib. *Dorje Chang*) "Holder of the vajra." *Vajra* means indestructible and *dhara* means holding, embracing or inseparable. The central figure in the Kagyu refuge tree, and indicating the transmission of the close lineage of the Mahamudra teachings to Tilopa. Vajradhara symbolizes the primordial wisdom of the dharmakaya and wears the ornaments of the sambhogakaya Buddha, symbolizing its richness.

Vajrasattva. (Tib. *Dorje Sempa*) The Buddha of purification. Vajrasattva practice is part of the four preliminary practices. A sambhogakaya Buddha who embodies all the five families. He is also a major source of purification practices.

Vajrayana. (Tib. *dorje tek pa*) Literally, "diamond-like" or "indestructible capacity." *Vajra* here refers to method, so you can say the method yana. There are three major traditions of Buddhism (Hinayana, Mahayana, Vajrayana) The Vajrayana is based on the tantras and emphasizes the clarity aspect of phenomena. A practitioner of the method of taking the result as the path.

View, meditation, and action. (Tib. *ta ba gom pa yodpa*) The philosophical orientation, the act of growing accustomed to that – usually in sitting practice, and the implementation of that insight during the activities of daily life. Each of the three vehicles has its particular definition of view, meditation and action.

Vinaya. One of the three major sections of the Buddha's teachings showing ethics, what to avoid and what to adopt. The other two sections are the sutras and the abhidharma.

Vipashyana meditation. See insight meditation.

Wheel of dharma. (Skt. *dharmachakra*) The Buddha's teachings correspond to three levels which very briefly are: the first turning was the teachings on the four noble truths and the teaching of the egolessness of person; the second turning was the teachings on emptiness and the emptiness of phenomena; the third turning was the teachings on luminosity and Buddha nature.

Yana. Means capacity. There are three yanas, narrow, (Hinayana) great (Mahayana) and indestructible (Vajrayana).

Index

O

P

O

P